The Rising Moon

POLITICAL CHANGE IN SARAWAK

The Rising Moon

POLITICAL CHANGE IN SARAWAK

Michael B. Leigh

Foreword by
Datuk Haji Abdul Rahman Ya'kub
CHIEF MINISTER OF SARAWAK

SYDNEY UNIVERSITY PRESS

SYDNEY UNIVERSITY PRESS
Press Building, University of Sydney

UNITED KINGDOM, EUROPE, MIDDLE EAST, AFRICA, CARIBBEAN
Prentice/Hall International, International Book Distributors Ltd
Hemel Hempstead, England

NORTH AND SOUTH AMERICA
International Scholarly Book Services Inc., Portland, Oregon

SINGAPORE, MALAYSIA, THAILAND, HONG KONG, PHILIPPINES, INDONESIA
Angus & Robertson (S.E. Asia) Pty Ltd, Singapore

First published 1974
Copyright © Michael Beckett Leigh 1974

Library of Congress Catalog Card Number 72-76423
National Library of Australia registry card number and
ISBN 0 424 06580 0 cloth bound edition
ISBN 0 424 06590 8 paper bound edition

This book is supported by money from
THE ELEANOR SOPHIA WOOD BEQUEST

Printed and bound in New Zealand by Wright & Carman Limited, Trentham

CONTENTS

ILLUSTRATIONS

PLATES

between pages 104 and 105

A supp speaker expressing opposition to Malaysia at a meeting in 1962

The late Datu Bandar and Abang Ikwan Zainie wait to present their views to the United Nations Mission of enquiry, Kuching 1963

Abdul Raman Ya'kub addressing an election rally in a Kuching Malay Kampong, 1968

A Malay fisherman at Santubong

Malay Kampong at Mukah

Longhouses at Baram

The Sarawak Coalition Cabinet, 1970

MAPS

FIGURES

TABLES

FOREWORD

There are not many good books written on post-war Sarawak and a good book on politics in Sarawak is a very rare commodity. Those interested in developments in Malaysia, and Sarawak in particular, will find *The Rising Moon* a useful source of information.

Michael Leigh has recorded, in minute to minute manner, the origins and developments of politics in Sarawak. His research provides a comprehensive coverage of political events in the State at the crucial stages of its independence within the Federation. It is a commendable attempt to understand the complex nature of political growth and political changes in the State, which by no means are peculiar to Sarawak. Politics and political systems grow and develop with time and experiences; so too must the politicians. In this respect I am proud to say that the direction of growth in Sarawak is healthy and full of promises.

For those who wish to be familiar with the political problems in Sarawak, I would recommend this book. In doing so I am not in any way endorsing the interpretations on events, judgments or conclusions in the book which are the full responsibility of the writer.

Pejabat Ketua Menteri   **DATUK HAJI ABDUL RAHMAN YA'KUB**
Kuching   Chief Minister of Sarawak
December 1972

PREFACE

The rising moon is both a symbol and a reality. Though a symbol of Islam, its appeal and significance goes beyond a single faith. The reality of the rising moon lies in its constancy. Politics involves the constancy of land and people in the same way as it involves the progression of time signified by the moon's place in the eternal cycle of life.

This interpretation of political change in Sarawak is of necessity quite personal. It is through the constant exercise of many interpretations that we gain knowledge and approach the elusive truth. It is to this end that I dedicate my initial efforts to the people of Sarawak.

The research for this study was undertaken over a period of ten years, the latter five of which were given vibrancy and depth by sharing them with Barbara. The author is deeply indebted to numerous friends who willingly gave of their understanding and insights. The Curator of the Sarawak Museum, Benedict Sandin, the Assistant Curator, Lucas Chin and staff generously assisted my research with their special knowledge of the various peoples of Sarawak.

Barbara and I have fond memories of the friendships shared whilst in Malaysia. Selecting people to whom to offer explicit thanks is a difficult task, for to just so many we owe a debt both personal and professional. Among these people are Hj. Abdul Rahman Ya'kub, Hj. Abdul Taib Mahmud, Stan Bain, Fred and Salli Black, Barbro Body, Don Brown, William Chew, Che Lily Eberwein, Jerome Goh, Tom Harrison, Adrian Johnson, Peter and Paula Ling, Nelson Liap Kudu, Elaine McKay, Abang Muas dan Che Hafsah Harun, Sidi and Heidi Munan, Ong Kee Hui, John Pike, Safri Awang, Tony Shaw and Stephen Yong.

My work was greatly facilitated by the skills of Lindi Benson, Cheng Thiam Yong, Anne Christie, Dayang Halimah, Kuan Wei Seng, Lim Lian Hiok, Raymond Lim and Tay Siew Sim.

The study of politics at the local level necessitated working in each of the twenty districts of the state. I should like to acknowledge the helpfulness of people at every level, particularly the District Officers and Secretaries of District Councils. Thanks are due to all those officials in Malaysia and in the United Kingdom who gave of their time and experience.

At Cornell University I appreciated the support of the 102 West Avenue 'family', especially Milly Wagemann and Elizabeth Graves for their editorial assistance and John Mapes and Ron Witton for their tireless wrestling with the computer.

The advice and encouragement of Professor George McT. Kahin has been of inestimable value. Professors Ben Anderson, John Lewis and

Stephen Morris provided constant guidance and support to the endeavour. Professors Spann and Mayer, my present colleagues, helped greatly with their incisive comments upon the manuscript.

Appreciation is also due to the following organizations whose financial support made possible my research in Sarawak: Australian National University Hunter Douglas Fund (1962-3), Australian Institute of International Affairs (1964), London-Cornell Project (1967-8), Cornell University China Program (1970) and the Australian Research Grants Committee (1971-2).

University of Sydney   M.B.L.
1973

The sky is dark and red like the
tail of the perching hornbill
Slowly it wraps its silken sarong
around the soft outline of
the new moon.

Richness
Beauty
Blackness . . .

The pale crescent turns
to a golden arc
rising into the deepening
azure sky.

BARBARA LEIGH

INTRODUCTION

The politics of Sarawak have maintained a complexity unique to that state and not shared by the other component states of Malaysia. Ever since the introduction of political parties, each major ethnic community has been internally divided, a fact that has undermined racial solidarity and so promoted a fluidity in the political process within which the political groupings have manoeuvred in shifting patterns. This in turn has led to the formation of viable political parties whose support spans ethnic divisions. Though race and ethnic group determine the predominant lines of cleavage, the politics of Sarawak display a more variegated and flexible pattern than is the case elsewhere in Malaysia where the influence of all-pervasive ethnic identities is only too apparent.

This study focuses upon the incorporation of Sarawak into the Malaysian political system, one that was designed to mediate the more rigid ethnic divisions apparent in West Malaysia. The process of integrating Sarawak into a wider pan-Malaysian political system involves the accentuation of local ethnic cleavages. This entails a focus upon ethnicity to the exclusion of other cross-cutting divisions. The more pluralistic Sarawak system has been under pressure to change in that direction since the beginning of the era of party politics. The pressure came first from the British and latterly from the way in which federation politics have structured divisions inside Sarawak itself. In both cases pressure has been exerted to limit recruitment by multi-racial parties to those of one race.

The dynamism and fluidity of the state's politics can be attributed in part to the specific nature of the ethnic complex. Sarawak has three major groups, not one of which approaches a majority of the population. This tripartite division stands in marked contrast to the predominance of a Malay versus non-Malay dichotomy in West Malaysia, and has produced a situation in which each group has found it necessary to manoeuvre to gain the support of elements outside its own community.

The population of one million can be arbitrarily divided into the following major ethnic groups.[1]

The native peoples	%	
Malay	18.7	
Melanau	5.4	'Malay' 24.9%
Kedayan	0.8	

[1] The proportions are calculated from the total population (975,918) of Sarawak by ethnic group at August 1970. The percentages have been rounded.

1

Iban	31.0	
Land Dayak	8.5	'Dayak' 44.2%
Other indigenous	4.7	

Non-natives
Chinese	30.1
Indians	0.3
European/Eurasian	0.1
Others	0.2

Adherance to the Muslim religion and associated culture is the defining characteristic of a Malay. The principal Malay settlements are all quite close to the coast, a reflection of the process of Islamization and of their having historically earned a living from sedentary agriculture and fishing. More than half the Malays reside in the western-most first division of the state. The early coastal traders were Malays and they represented the maritime-based authority of the Sultanate of Brunei. This association of Malays with government continued until after the World War II, for the Brooke government relied upon Malays to provide almost all locally recruited officers.

The Melanau have been grouped together with the Malay for they are coastal peoples who are steadily adopting Islam. By 1960 three-quarters of all Melanaus had become Muslim, many then describing themselves as Malay, thus demonstrating the importance of Islam in defining a person as 'Malay'. Historically the Melanaus are sago producers living in the coastal Mukah district of the third division. The continual falling world price of sago flour has left them in an unenviable economic plight. The other Islamic group, the Kedayans, are a type of Malay found in the north-eastern fourth and fifth divisions of the state.

The Dayak peoples can best be defined as indigenous non-Muslims, in accord with Dutch usage. The live in the *ulu* (up-river) areas of the state and have always practised shifting rice cultivation supplemented by hunting and gathering. They customarily live in longhouse settlements, normally located adjacent to rivers. Since the 1920s their cash income has been largely derived from growing rubber, an activity that is a 'half-way house' between shifting and settled agriculture. In the past growing rubber has been analagous to putting money in the bank— making withdrawals by tapping the trees, smoking and selling the sheets of rubber whenever cash was needed. However, the dramatic decline in world rubber prices, combined with rising expectations that required cash income, has led to a great deal of Dayak dissatisfaction. In many areas where all virgin land has been burned, population pressures have compelled them to shorten drastically the time allowed for rice fields to regenerate, thus further reducing the per capita yield.

The Iban (Sea Dayak) are a migratory people who have dispersed widely throughout the second, third and fourth divisions of the state. By contrast the Land Dayak have adopted a more settled pattern of existence. They are found almost exclusively in the first division and many have forsaken longhouse living. Unlike the Iban they are divided linguistically into four main groups, the largest being the Bidayuh. Their past political allegiances have been equally fragmented.

Most of the other indigenous groups are found in the fourth division of Sarawak and are listed here according to their numerical strength at August 1970.

Kayan	11,347
Kenyah	9,932
Murut	7,368
Punan	3,924
Bisayah[2]	3,253
Kelabit	2,541
Other	4,099

The first Chinese were of Hakka dialect. They migrated overland from Sambas district of what is now the north-west of Indonesian Borneo (Kalimantan), in order to develop gold mines at Bau, south-west of Kuching. They wished to be left to run their own affairs and clashed with the early colonial settlement in what could perhaps be called the first independence struggle against Europeans, a battle that involved their capture and sacking of the capital in 1857. The luckless Land Dayaks of the first division were caught between maritime Brunei Malay impingement and interior Chinese invasion.

The advent of a relatively stable Brooke rule coupled with the general breakdown of order in China led to a stream of Chinese migration to Sarawak, particularly round the turn of the century. Map 1 shows the principal areas of origin of each of the dialect groups.

The numerical composition of the Sarawak Chinese community (in 1970) was as follows:

Hakka (Kheh)	91,610	Cantonese	20,694
Foochow	90,704	Henghua	10,642
Hokkien	36,518	Hainanese (Hailam)	7,033
Teochew	27,262	Other Chinese	9,557

Upon arrival in Sarawak the Chinese community first organized their schools and community associations on the basis of dialect groups. Even though the Hakka were the most numerous in the first and second divisions, the Hokkien and Teochew dominated commerce and industry. The Foochow and Henghua settlements began early this century, those migrants arriving to set up a Christian (Methodist) colony. The Foochow concentrated in the third division where they account for two-thirds of all the Chinese. Though they arrived as farmers they have become notorious, even amongst other Chinese, for their business acumen and sheer endurance. The Foochow initiated rapid exploitation of the state's timber resources and by the 1970s had become economically the most powerful dialect group in the state.

Though most of those engaged in commerce are Chinese, the converse is not true and many more Chinese are employed in agricultural

---

[2] Except for the small Bisayah group, very few of the peoples we have described as Dayak have yet adopted Islam. There is certainly no movement amongst the Iban and Land Dayak comparable to that amongst the Kadazan of Sabah.

pursuits than in any other sphere. The Chinese traditionally have produced for the market, concentrating on the production of rubber, pepper and latterly entering the timber trade in a grand manner. The age structure of the Chinese is skewed heavily in favour of the young, with more than half being aged less than fifteen. Such a high proportion of youth has created severe problems of under-employment. The ensuing frustration has increased support for the radical political solutions of the communist organization.

The total population of one million is widely dispersed throughout the state. Rivers remain the principal thoroughfares and only in the

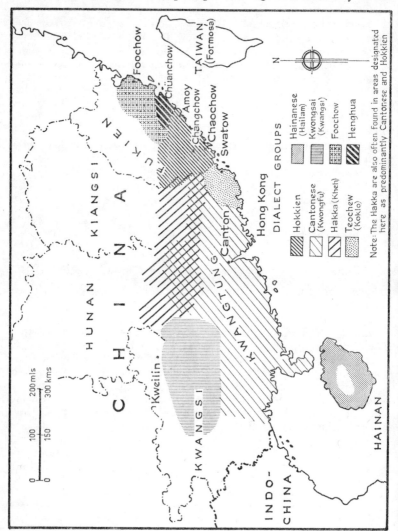

Map 1

mid-1960s did a road even link the two principal towns of the state—Kuching the centre of government, and Sibu the centre of commerce. Sarawak is located to the north-west of the island of Borneo and the European impact had been mediated through three successive white Rajahs: James, Charles and Vyner Brooke.

Table 1

Occupation of Economically Active Males:
Malay, Iban and Chinese in 1960

	Malay	Iban	Chinese	All groups
		(percentages)		
Agriculture, forestry, workers fishermen	65	96	43	74
Production workers, labourers	17	1	19	10
Sales workers	2	—	19	6
Service workers	4	1	5	3
Technical, etc., workers	3	1	4	3
Transport and communications	5	—	4	2
Clerical workers	3	—	5	2
Others	1	—	1	1
All occupations	100	100	100	100

Source: Sarawak, *Report on the Census of Population Taken on 15th June 1960 by L. W. Jones,* Government Printing Office, Kuching 1962, p. 109. Figures have been rounded to the nearest whole number.

James Brooke, an English naval adventurer, first settled in Borneo in 1841 and after interfering in a dispute between Brunei and dissident Dayaks, he became Rajah. Gradually by treaty and conquest he increased his area of control from the immediate surrounds of Kuching to the north-east of Borneo. This process was continued by Charles Brooke (from 1868 to 1917) who chose to rely heavily upon the Iban. The Brookes attracted a series of colourful adventurers and the state was administered as a private colony. Very little was done to promote education or to improve transport and communications and the Brookes did not permit the development of a European plantation economy. The result was a lack of economic development and an absence of the social problems accompanying foreign-sponsored growth. The last of the Rajahs, Vyner Brooke, was the least committed of the three to Sarawak, spending most of his time in England. Not long after the brief Japanese occupation (1941-5) he formally ceded Sarawak to the British Crown (1946), despite strong opposition from local Malays.

The era as a Crown Colony lasted until 1963 when Sarawak and Sabah were joined together with Malaya (and temporarily Singapore) to form the new nation: Malaysia. Sarawak is the largest state in Malaysia, a federation that spans an arc from the north-western tip of Kedah, down through the states of Malaya, across 500 miles of South China sea to Sarawak and then along the northern third of Borneo to the north-eastern state of Sabah. Prior to 1963 politics in East and West Malaysia had broadly followed their own distinct courses, the only common ingredient having been a British colonial heritage.

1

PARTY FORMATION IN SARAWAK
1959-63

Relative to West Malaysia the formation of political parties was a particularly late development in Sarawak, and the process did not start until 1959. Before that, local political activity was channelled through various community organizations, and was confined almost exclusively to Islamic and Chinese groups.

For Muslims, the central question at issue was the Cession of Sarawak from the Brooke Rajahs to the British Crown in 1946. A vigorous series of mass protests took place from 1946 to 1949, after which the British government firmly closed all legitimate means of reversing this alteration in constitutional status.

For the Chinese, the struggle on the mainland of China was the object of considerable attention and helped stimulate analogous conflicts within the leadership of Sarawak Chinese. The result of that conflict was a decided shift in the distribution of power within the Chinese community away from the conservative and wealthy toward those of a more left-wing disposition. By contrast with Malaya, the Left in Sarawak was not emasculated by an abortive insurrection.

For almost all who can be called Dayak, political activity was a completely new sphere and even in the early 1960s it can be characterized as essentially a reaction to the activities of the other communities.

The stimuli for forming political parties varied a good deal. The first party was an outgrowth of those pressure groups which had resisted government policy in education and trade licensing; it also expressed an inchoate desire for a measure of self-determination. The process that set the party in motion included a good deal of official British encouragement. The second party was concerned less with grievances than with protecting communal interests, in the light of the successes achieved by its predecessor. The last four parties were all formed after it had become clear that the state was shortly to gain independence within the Federation of Malaysia.

Articulation of grievances became progressively less important as first inter-communal and then intra-communal rivalries became the dominant motivation. In order to highlight this shift of emphasis we shall examine in turn the political activity of each of the three major racial groups: Chinese, Malay, and Dayak.

Sarawak United People's Party (SUPP)

The Brookes used, but did not really attempt to understand, the Chinese community. They respected the industry of that race but harboured a suspicion of Chinese activities and intentions, a suspicion firmly based upon mutual ignorance and common disdain. Ever since the 1857 revolt —in which Bau Chinese *kongsi* members sacked Kuching—the Brookes had rigidly enforced the law that membership in a secret society was a capital offence. Thus that organizational form of the overseas Chinese was ended. The resulting functional void was in due course filled by a variety of Chinese commercial, dialect and religious organizations.

The Sarawak government officially sponsored Chinese immigration, and until 1931, a Chinese could legally be regarded as a native, a term then of nationality rather than ethnic status. Since that year 'native' has been defined to mean, in effect, non-Chinese.[1] The classification 'native' denoted a privileged status, not carrying any of the pejorative connotations only too evident elsewhere in Asia and Africa.

A coincidence of interest existed between China and Britain throughout World War II, and the Chinese in Sarawak, with but a few individual exceptions, proved to be generally anti-Japanese. They had much to gain from the new, more equal, post-war colonial order which resulted from the Cession to Britain in 1946; their educated manpower was immediately placed at a high premium because 335 Malay civil servants had resigned in protest. Due to their private school system, the Chinese was the only community able to provide the requisite skilled personnel.[2]

Chinese political interest throughout the turbulent 1940s was focused upon the momentous struggle taking place on the Chinese Mainland, not on what were regarded as the relatively insignificant changes in Borneo. The British colonial government, moreover, was slow to define, much less to reform, its policies toward the local Chinese. The only apparent early change in policy was the institution of tight immigration control when the Communist regime took over in China.

A central question for the community in Sarawak was to determine who would represent the Chinese—what mechanisms would be used to select leaders who could deal with the government on behalf of the whole community. Prior to World War II, the Chamber of Commerce had been recognized as the official organ and mouthpiece of the Chinese community, and thus had served as primary political link between the government and the Chinese.[3] Kapitans China and Area Headmen had

---

[1] See Robert M. Pringle, *The Ibans of Sarawak under Brooke Rule, 1841-1941*, unpublished Ph.D. dissertation, Cornell University, 1967, p. 523. Exclusion of Chinese and non-Islamic Indians from the status of native was underlined in the *Land Rules, 1933*, Government Printer, Kuching 1933.

[2] Elementary literacy by race in 1947 was: Chinese 34%; Malay 15%; Melanau 9%; Land Dayak 7%; Iban and 'other indigenous' 2%. Sarawak, *Colonial Development and Welfare Plan 1947/8-1955/6*, mimeo., Kuching 1950, Appendix B (2). A total of 338 civil servants resigned because of the Cession, 335 were Malay and 3 Dayak.

[3] *Sarawak Tribune*, 2 August 1946. The Chinese Chamber of Commerce was also registered with the Central government of China at that time.

been officially appointed for each dialect group, the chief criterion for their selection being economic power—sheer wealth.[4] The Chamber of Commerce thus formed the apex of the Chinese community, granting representation and leadership roles in accordance with relative wealth.

Four months after the Japanese capitulated, a general assembly attended by representatives of twenty-two Sarawak Chinese associations was called in order to form, in Kuching, one central Chinese organization with which the military administration could deal directly,[5] thus avoiding the pitfalls inherent in dealing with a multitude of dialect associations. The resulting Chung Hua Association directed immediate concern toward clarifying the Chinese position on the question of Cession, and forming a 'Chinese Democratic Political Society'. No less pressing was the problem of resuscitating the Chinese school system. The Chung Hua Association had a short life. Its political functions were assumed by the Chinese Advisory Board, established in 1947 by the new colonial government,[6] and by the new Chinese Consul installed in Kuching in 1948.[7] Both the Chung Hua Association and the Chinese Chamber of Commerce issued statements welcoming the new Consul, adding that he would now become the representative of Sarawak Chinese to the Chinese government and to the local Sarawak government.[8] The Colonial government took immediate exception to such a suggestion, for Sarawak-born Chinese were regarded as British subjects, and not the responsibility of a foreign Consul.[9]

By this time, the administration was seeking to expand the role of its urban Chinese advisory boards and planning Chinese participation in its new structure of local government.[10] At any rate, the change of regime in China ended official Chinese representation in Sarawak.[11] It also brought a new government emphasis upon the necessity for local Chinese to choose whether their future allegiance would be directed toward China or toward Sarawak. The Sarawak government emphasized that British recognition of Communist China 'does not mean that the determination of the British government to oppose the extension of com-

---

[4] Tien Ju-k'ang, *The Chinese of Sarawak: A Study of Social Structure*, London School of Economics, London 1953, especially Chapter 9.

[5] *Sarawak Tribune,* 29 January 1946.

[6] Ibid., 8 March 1947.

[7] Early in 1947 the British government accepted an official Chinese proposal to establish a consulate, and Dr Chan Ying-ming, former Consul in San Francisco, arrived in Kuching in January 1948. The local business community immediately began raising funds to build a permanent consulate in Kuching. See *Sarawak Tribune,* 28 April, 9 and 28 August 1947; 20 January 1948. In the interim a Kuomintang official had toured Sarawak, concluding his trip with an address delivered to the Kuching branch of that party.

[8] Ibid., 9 March 1948. The Chinese Chamber of Commerce decided to divest itself of any representative functions, issuing a statement that: 'The Consulate now becomes the authorized and recognized official body representing the Chinese community as a whole'. Ibid., 7 January 1949.

[9] Ibid., 8 January 1949.

[10] Ibid., 5 February 1949.

[11] The consulate was formally closed on 7 January 1950. Ibid., 9 January 1950.

munism into British Territories is in any way weakening'.[12] Flying of any foreign flag was restricted, a measure that sought both to avoid demonstration of divisions within the Chinese community, as well as to prevent the old Sarawak flag being flown as a symbol of the struggle against Cession. The government did permit the community to celebrate the new Chinese National Day with mass meetings, and the government's Secretary for Chinese Affairs even addressed at least one of these rallies. The 'double tenth' anniversary of the Nationalist Chinese was also celebrated, but it was sponsored by a dwindling number of community associations, and by October 1952, received public support from only two local bodies.[13]

Education has always been a matter of pivotal concern for the whole of the Chinese community. Chinese settlers, wherever they have located themselves in Sarawak, have invariably established their own schools, which in due course became the focal meeting points for each local community. Prior to World War II, community leadership was held by the wealthy, who were usually government-supported (holding the position of Kapitan or Area Headman) and who had the 'correct' Kuomintang connections. These men usually underwrote the schools, and, as a result, their views regarding selection of teachers and management of schools were dominant.

Before the war, the Chinese community in Kuching ran the schools on a dialect group basis. Thus the Hokkien School was meant to serve the Hokkien community only, the Min Teck School to serve children of the Teochew community, and so on. Shortly after the war, a single board was formed to manage all Chinese secondary schools in Kuching, and the various associations lent their school properties to that board.[14]

No Chinese schools were included among the responsibilities of the Education Department until 1946. Any liaison on matters pertaining to these schools was directed through the Government Secretary for Chinese Affairs. Addressing the Council Negri in 1924, Rajah Vyner Brooke had said: 'He was sorry to find in certain Chinese schools the opportunity had been taken by unscrupulous teachers to preach revolution propaganda [sic]'.[15] Nonetheless, his government actually did little more than issue regulations. For instance, the 1924 General Regulations enjoined teachers and pupils to be clean and tidy and not to spit upon the floor.[16] They also forbade the smoking of opium or the cooking of food in the classroom.

A dramatic change occurred after the war, when young militants began to challenge effectively the conservatives' control of the Chinese schools.

---

[12] Ibid., 7 January 1950.
[13] The Secretary spoke at length on 'liberty' under the new Chinese regime, contrasting the restrictions there with the freedoms prevailing in Sarawak. Ibid., 2 October 1951. For a list of the associations sponsoring the yearly 'double tenth' celebrations, see ibid., 12 September 1950; 27 September 1951; 23 September 1952.
[14] Ibid., 10 May 1951.
[15] Ibid., 17 May 1957.
[16] Chief Secretary of Sarawak, *General Regulations for Schools, Order No. LX, 1924*, Government Printing Office, Kuching 1930, p. 2.

As a result of a series of incidents in the early 1950s, most boards of management were 'taken over' by the Left, and the Chinese school system as a whole became the focus of a new Chinese leadership, opposed to the older and wealthier government-recognized leaders. Chinese schools thus became the scene of sporadic conflict as the government extended its control over activities formerly within the confines of the Chinese education system and sought to bolster the authority of all who could hinder the leftward trend.

For a time the scene was quite lively. In 1951, 200 Kuching students went on strike. The government reacted by bringing criminal charges against the leaders and proscribing two youth organizations as subversive. The government itself precipitated a confrontation in early 1954 by dropping the 17th Mile (Kuching-Serian Rd) Chinese school from its register of accredited schools because of alleged pro-Communist activity by its teaching staff and Board of Management. The following year, a two-month student strike occurred in Kuching, ending only after direct government intervention. In the course of the strike, Stephen Yong and Ong Kee Hui, two leaders who subsequently gained political prominence, played a key role in a special committee established to resolve the strike. Other incidents occurred in Kuching, Sibu and Miri which the government believed were exacerbated by the refusal, or at least inability, of school management committees to take a firm stand against dissenters.

Meanwhile the Left was making considerable inroads, in a manner that the government could not readily confront. Disparaging comments and rumours which called into question the morality of certain teachers were circulated and proved difficult to rebut directly. As a result, many teachers requested transfer to other districts, or simply did not have their local contracts renewed. The precarious economic position of Chinese school teachers made them especially vulnerable to any concerted pressure from those opposed to their political views.[17]

After completing an official study on financing education and conditions of service in the teaching profession, the government published a White Paper and new Grant Code regulations to take effect from 1956. These recommendations, though hardly radical, represented the first real attempt by the government substantially to assist and redirect the system of Chinese education. In his report, Woodhead had noted the reliance of Chinese schools upon donations (some in the form of a levy upon merchants) and had suggested a 'bargain', with the government offering substantial financial assistance in return for a measure of government control over the content of the curriculum.[18]

---

[17] Report of the District Officer, Lubok Antu, for the second half of 1956, and Tien, *The Chinese of Sarawak*, p. 8.

[18] 'The recommendations are based on two assumptions; first, that aid of a sufficient size is necessary to make a reasonable bargain; second, that Chinese understand a bargain and, if the parties enter into it in the right spirit, will keep it. It is natural that they should wish to maintain their heritage of Chinese language and culture. It is clear also that, being intelligent people, they must appreciate the necessity for a loyalty to and a knowledge of the country in which they live.' E. W. Woodhead, *The*

The instinctive Chinese reaction was to reject the proposals out of hand, and a Preserve Chinese Education Committee swung into action; telegrams of support came from all over Sarawak. A Sarawak Chinese Education Council was formed, in line with a suggestion from Sarikei, where local Chinese representatives had not rejected outright the government proposals. After long and rather more sober discussion this council resolved, by thirteen votes to twelve, to accept the Grants under the new regulations.[19] The government had indeed struck a bargain, though this bargain was of a transient character. By the start of the new decade, a major new controversy had surfaced as the government sought to determine the future of Chinese education.

In December 1954, Council Negri approved a revised scale of trade licensing fees, designed to yield a further M$3.5 million per annum in revenue to the government in order to maintain social services and meet the increased demands for educational expansion outlined in the Woodhead Report.[20] The new rates, in some cases amounting to increases of 1,000 per cent, were to take effect from 1 January 1955. On Christmas Day, a protest committee met at the Sarikei Chinese Chamber of Commerce and resolved to close all shops for the first ten days of the new year. Binatang shopkeepers met the next day and decided to follow suit. Sibu traders 'warmly aired their viewpoints in an electrifying atmosphere', and decided to close shop, as did the Kuching traders, following the example set by Sarikei traders. The *hartal* (closure) spread to Bintulu, Miri and throughout the colony.[21]

Representatives of all major trading centres converged on Kuching to make their feelings known to the government. As a result of this unprecedented pressure, the government postponed application of the new fees, formed a Committee of Enquiry with significant local participation, and presented a substantially modified Bill to the Council Negri two months later.[22]

These debates concerning education and commerce were political in character and brought to the fore certain leaders of *ad hoc* bodies in Kuching, Sarikei and elsewhere. Shortly thereafter, they coalesced to explore the depth of support for a more enduring organization—a political party. Those Chinese who had led the opposition to government policy in the areas of education and trade licensing were among the prime movers in forming the first political party of Sarawak. Their experiences were coupled with a heightening of political activity in

---

Financing of Education and Conditions of Service in the Teaching Profession in Sarawak, Government Printing Office, Kuching 1955, p. 32.

[19] *Sarawak Tribune,* 30 September and 22 November 1955. The twelve votes were cast in favour of postponing acceptance of the grants, no votes were cast for outright rejection of government assistance.

[20] Ibid., 30 December 1954.

[21] On the *hartal,* see: for Sarikei, ibid., 29 December 1954; for Binatang, 30 December 1954; for Sibu, 31 December 1954 and 4 January 1955. There the chairman left during the meeting presumably in a 'state of shock'.

[22] Sarawak, Council Negri, *Debates: Official Report,* Government Printing Office, Kuching 1955, 29-30 March, pp. 5-6, 11-23.

neighbouring Singapore, and they were encouraged by the then Chief Secretary of Sarawak, J. H. Ellis, who circulated an internal government memorandum on the need for a political party under leaders such as Ong Kee Hui.

The question of launching a multi-racial party was first raised in 1956 by Ong Kee Hui, Stephen Yong and S. K. Reddi with the encouragement of T. G. Dunbar.[23] But the Malay National Union and the Sarawak Dayak Association activists responded, in essence: 'We have our organizations already, you form a Chinese one and then we can talk together.'[24] Thus the efforts came to naught, and the idea was abandoned. The Governor, Sir Anthony Abell, privately encouraged Ong Kee Hui to form a broadly representative party, but the principal difficulty was the absence of significant native interest in and support for the idea.

Spurred by a local newspaper article[25] written by an influential young Malay, Safri Awang, which introduced the possibility of real native participation, Ong Kee Hui, Stephen Yong and Song Thian Cheok earnestly set about founding a party that was to be 'non-communal in

[23] Ong Kee Hui comes from a prominent and wealthy Hokkien family and is the grandson of Ong Tiang Swee, the most important Chinese leader during the Third Rajah's rule (1917-41). Educated first in Kuching, then in Singapore, Ong Kee Hui next attended the Serdang College of Agriculture in Malaya. From 1936 to 1946 he worked with the Department of Agriculture—an experience that gave him a familiarity with the Dayak people that is normally missing among urban Chinese. He was stationed for a long time at Kapit. Beginning as English Secretary to the Kuching Chinese Chamber of Commerce, he helped organize the petition against increased trade license fees; he also acted as an investigator and consultant for the community committees investigating school disturbances and the Woodhead Report. A member of the Kuching Municipal Council since 1953 (President from 1960 to 1965), he represented that Council in the Council Negri from 1956 to 1963 and served concurrently as a member of the Cabinet, the Supreme Council. He had a close rapport with Sir Anthony Abell, Governor of Sarawak in the 1950s, but as he persisted in his intent to lead SUPP in opposition to British policy, colonial officials began to lose faith in him as their chosen leader for the state.

Stephen Yong, by contrast, came from quite humble origins, his father being a Hakka small trader in the outlying town of Simunjan. After his father's death, Yong left school and worked for a time as a messenger before receiving a scholarship to further his education. Immediately after the war he was a merchant and in 1950 went to England, becoming a barrister-at-law. Upon his return, he worked closely with Ong Kee Hui on the various aspects of Chinese education. His background is much more Chinese and rather more proletarian than that of Ong Kee Hui, though he is linked by marriage to a Kuching Hokkien of the Ong clan.

Both Reddi and Dunbar had practiced law in Singapore. In 1956, Dunbar and Stephen Yong had a common legal practice. S. K. Reddi, finding himself in an awkward position after representing workers at the British base in Singapore, established his permanent residence in Sarawak. T. G. Dunbar was more closely associated with the Singapore Left, and in due course he returned there.

[24] Interview, Ong Kee Hui, November 1967. The Kuching Municipal elections of 1956 were then the focus that stimulated political organization. Behind the scene activities directed toward the organization of a party, or parties, were strongly rumoured at the time. *Sarawak Tribune*, 24 May 1956, editorial.

[25] *Sarawak Tribune*, 4 March 1959.

character, with emphasis on loyalty to Sarawak and unity of all races'.[26] They were aided in their efforts by discreet government encouragement and a letter from the Tuan Muda, Anthony Brooke, to the Malay National Union encouraging the latter to support the formation of a party.

Native reaction was generally non-committal. Mohd bin Haji Bakri, president of the Malay National Union, said, 'He fully and sincerely supported the suggestion and emphasized that if necessary his Union would join the party as one unit'. The General Secretary of the Malay National Union, Ikhwan Haji Zainie, thought, however, 'It would be much better for each community to form a National Union, such as the Chinese, Malay, Dayak and Indian National Unions, and eventually merge to form an Alliance like that in the Federation of Malaya.' In the opinion of the Sarawak Dayak National Union President, Edward Brandah, 'It was still too premature for the whole of Sarawak to form any political parties. At this stage, we should concentrate on the education for our younger generation and the raising of the standard of living for all communities'.[27] Safri himself withheld personal commitment to the party, and shortly thereafter he was sent overseas for further education. No other important Malays were willing to participate in the party, but after talking with the Governor and gaining his approval, various Dayak leaders, including Temenggong Jugah and Pengarah Montegrai, did agree to support it.[28]

However, a few weeks before the party was formally inaugurated the Governor cautioned that:

> It is . . . essential that party politics should not cause further divisions in our community but should have a unifying and binding effect. If a party tends to be dominated by one race or class . . . it may have a disintegrating effect on our community. . . . I frankly doubt if political parties at the present stage of development will spell faster progress in this small country. . . .[29]

Government ambivalence on the issue worried Dayaks who hitherto were accustomed to clear directives. The Governor's declaration had the immediate effect of persuading various important Dayaks not to join. To be successful, the party desperately needed a solid native component. The process of party formation had gained too much momentum to be halted readily, and on 12 June 1959, the Sarawak United People's Party (SUPP) was formally inaugurated, ushering in the new era of party politics.

Why had the government appeared to lose its enthusiasm for this

---

26 Ibid., 5 March 1959.
27 Ibid.
28 Subsequently each side interpreted 'support' differently. The Temenggong and Pengarah claimed that they had simply agreed not to oppose formation of the party; the SUPP leadership felt that a commitment to lead the party had been made and were bitterly disappointed by the failure of these two important Dayaks to join SUPP.
29 Sarawak Information Service, Sarawak By the Week, Week No. 21, 1959, (24-30 May), p. 3.

party, even before it had been formed? The government had been aware of communist activities within the Chinese community, but it had not anticipated the enthusiasm with which the 'angry young Chinese' would cluster behind SUPP. In early 1959, the underground communist organization distributed a treatise entitled 'On the Formation of an Open Political Party and the Struggle for Independence'. It was intercepted by the government. Among other things, the pamphlet stated:

> The revolution is now at a low-ebb, a passive atmosphere exists not only in the masses but even in our organization. What can be done about it? According to the analysis above, the only way open to us is to form an open political party. If we persist in secret work and fail boldly to organize a political party, we shall crawl along as before. We must readjust our ranks, propagate amongst the masses and create favorable conditions for the formation of a political party.[30]

The militant left-wing Chinese did wholeheartedly support SUPP, somewhat too eagerly in fact, and their enthusiasm aroused native suspicion. As time passed, the government became progressively more worried by the militant character of SUPP branch leaderhip.

Recruitment and control

There is no simple way to assess recruitment to each of the political parties as they developed—particularly in the absence of access to membership lists. Even if reliable lists were available, a good deal of biographical data would still be necessary in order to interpret them. Indeed the very definition of a party member is open to question, considering that each political party received less votes in the 1963 elections than the total number of members it claimed.[31]

The characteristics of those recruited by each party can be assessed in three ways. First, one may study official party documents that describe the party membership, divided according to locality and ethnic group. But these sources are easily manipulated and must be treated with great reservations as they probably represent the most optimistic estimate within the realm of credibility. Second, one may examine the composition of the branch executives of each party, that is the leaders chosen to head each party at the local level. This approach is much less susceptible to distortion. From this information one can ascertain both the areas where the party estimated that it had enough support to form a branch and, given the salient characteristics of branch

---

[30] Sarawak Information Service, *The Danger Within: A History of the Clandestine Communist Organisation in Sarawak,* Government Printing Office, Kuching 1963, pp. 25-9.

[31] SUPP was the closest to its claim; PANAS claimed 72,249 members and received 28,242 votes, and SNAP scored about the same proportion. The total number of members claimed by SUPP was 44,767 in June 1962, 50,219 in January 1963, 51,901 in November 1965 and 49,042 in June 1967. This reduction was attributed to the legal requirement that, as from January 1966, only Malaysian citizens could be members of political parties, thus excluding various Chinese born outside Malaysia until they had been naturalized. SUPP secured 45,493 votes in the 1963 District Council elections.

executive members, the predominant ethnic group among which the party had gained support in any particular district. Third, one may identify and analyse the type of candidate nominated and/or elected by each party.

Each of these three approaches has been employed wherever data were available. The third approach is the most informative and reliable and the results of this detailed analysis are to be found in Appendix I.

A study of official party releases shows that SUPP branches and sub-branches spread slowly throughout Sarawak. Initial efforts were concentrated in the first and third divisions, but during the latter half of 1960, branches were established in all other divisions. By the end of 1961, half the branches were located in the first division, almost a third in the third division, and the remainder elsewhere. By mid-1962, SUPP appeared to have spread its influence fairly pervasively throughout the state, for its overall geographic distribution of members accorded well with a breakdown of total population by division.

Table 2

SUPP Membership by Division: June 1962

	Division of Sarawak				
	First	Second	Third	Fourth	Fifth
			(percentages)		
SUPP members	34.5	13.5	41.0	9.0	2.0
Total population	35.0	14.0	34.0	13.0	4.0

Source: Report of the Secretary-General, S. K. T. Yong, given at the SUPP Third Delegates' Conference, *Sarawak by the Week,* Week No. 23, 1962.

But its racial balance was skewed in favour of Chinese and against Malays, Melanaus and the 'other indigenous' peoples.

Table 3

SUPP Membership by Ethnic Group: January 1963

	Ethnic Group			
	Chinese	Iban	Land Dayak	Malay, Melanau, other indigenous
			(percentages)	
SUPP members	54.0	32.0	6.5	7.5
Total population	31.5	31.0	8.0	29.5

Source: SUPP records.

The composition of SUPP branch executives, though tending to over-represent natives as against Chinese, gives an accurate indication of the party's success at recruiting new members. During the period 1959 to 1962, six of the thirteen SUPP branches for which information is available did have a majority of non-Chinese executive members, and by the 1965 to 1968 period, this was true for six of the nineteen branches. The membership of branch executives by ethnic group is recorded in Table 4. The proportion of natives in each of the branch executives has been summarised by a simple 1 through 5 ranking.

1 = 1-24% of the branch executive members are native
2 = 25-49% of the branch executive members are native
3 = 50-74% of the branch executive members are native
4 = 75-99% of the branch executive members are native
5 = a totally native executive.

For actual control however, the position of the branch secretary is crucial. If the branch secretary is Chinese an asterisk (*) has been placed alongside the number indicating the proportion of natives on the executive committee. Were this scale to be employed as an index of control only those branches with a score of four or five could be said with certainty to be native controlled. Number 3 may represent native hegemony but not necessarily, particularly if the branch secretary is Chinese. SUPP practice has been to appoint a native to the prestigious position of chairman, while using Chinese as secretaries. From 1959 to 1962, five of the six native-majority branches had Chinese secretaries, and counting the nineteen branches legally registered at October 1967, fifteen had Chinese secretaries and fifteen had native chairmen—fourteen Dayaks and one Malay.[32] By employing the requirement of both a clear native majority and a non-Chinese branch secretary, one finds that only the Kapit, Simanggang and Lower Sadong branches were under native control. Even that control is doubtful in the latter two, for some forty per cent of the executive members were Chinese in both these branches.

Of all the sub-branches existing at the end of 1967, only four could have been controlled by other than Chinese—Bekenu, Song, Pangkalan Ampat and Bengoh. The Bengoh sub-branch and the Kapit branch were the only all-native SUPP organizations. This was a new phenomenon and designed to ensure real native control over the branches. Recourse to such a radically-exclusive organizational form had been necessitated by the SUPP's conspicuous success at recruiting Chinese and its concomitant failure to attract solid native support. It also represented an effort by the 'moderate' top leadership of SUPP to develop a measure of real support on the branch level, hitherto the province of the militant Left.

Control of SUPP is ultimately vested in its Central Committee, whose sixty-three members are elected by the Delegates' Conference. Day-to-day management of the party is handled by the fifteen-member Central

---

[32] This has been a consistent policy; in May 1962 thirteen of the sixteen SUPP branches had native chairmen. Sarawak Information Service, *Extracts from the Chinese and Malay Press*, Kuching, 26 May 1962.

Table 4

Membership of supp Branch Executive Committees:
1959-62 and 1965-8

Location	Established	1959-1962	1965-1968
First Division			
Kuching	June 1959	1*	1
Bau	Nov. 1960	3*	1*
Lundu	Nov. 1960	2*	(proscribed May 1964)
Batang Kayan	1967	(to replace Lundu but refused registration)	3*
Upper Sadong	Nov. 1961		
Lower Sadong			3
Second Division			
Simanggang	Sept. 1960	3*	3
Engkilili	Dec. 1960	3*	3*
			(proscribed Dec. 1967)
Pantu-Lingga	May 1961	4*	3*
Saratok			2*
Saribas			2*
Third Division			
Sibu	June 1959	1*	2*
Sarikei	June 1960	2*	(proscribed Sept. 1965)
Lower Rejang	Dec. 1965	(to replace Sarikei branch)	3*
Binatang	Oct. 1960	2*	2
Kanowit	April 1961	3*	2*
Mukah	Sept. 1961	3	2*
Belaga			2*
Kapit	Oct. 1966		5
Fourth Division			
Miri	Oct. 1960	2*	1*
			(proscribed Jan. 1968)
Bintulu			2*
Baram			2*
Fifth Division			
Limbang	Dec. 1960	2	(no longer legally registered)

Source: The information on which this table is based has been taken from a large number of lists of supp branch executive committees. The ethnic group of members has been determined with the assistance of knowledgeable local leaders.

Working Committee. Half of the first, comparatively small, Central Committee were educated at St Thomas' Anglican Mission School in Kuching,[33] and the majority came from Kuching. The ethnic breakdown was: 13 Chinese; 3 Ibans; 2 Malays; 1 Land Dayak; and 1 Christian Melanau, but one of the two Malays resigned within three weeks of his selection.

The character of the Central Committee changed markedly as the party developed its mass base. Within a year, it certainly could not be caricatured as an 'Old Thomians' Association'. From 1960 onward, half of the Central Committee members have been natives, though natives have formed only one-third to one-quarter of the Central Working Committee each year.[34] The racial composition of the Central Committee in the period 1960 to 1962 was: 20 Chinese; 10 Ibans; 5 Malays; 3 Melanaus; and 2 Land Dayaks. A lower proportion (less than half) were from Kuching.

The characteristics of Central Committee members did not change drastically in the ensuing years, with the exception of 1962, when ten Chinese members departed for China, the Centre for Protective Custody, or the jungle—most in the wake of the abortive Brunei revolt. Five natives also resigned at that time from the Central Committee. The Central Committee elected in June 1966 included: 17 Ibans; 9 Malays; 2 Land Dayaks; 1 Kenyah; and 28 Chinese.[35] The twenty-eight Chinese were: 13 Hakka/Kheh; 9 Hokkien; 3 Foochow; 2 Hailam; and 1 Cantonese. When compared with the breakdown of the Chinese population given in the 1970 Census, one notes a significant over-representation of Hakka and Hokkien within SUPP, and an under-representation of Foochow, Teochew and Cantonese.[36]

The party claims to receive most of its financial support from membership fees and donations. SUPP nominees are expected to donate to the party their salaries as members of the Council Negri or the Federal Parliament. This major source of support totalled M$41,000 in the financial year 1966-7. Large creditors to the party in that year included the Kwong Lee Bank, the Sarawak Transport Company and Ho Ho Lim, the party Treasurer. Funds were borrowed from the Bian Chiang Bank in order to assist in meeting campaign expenses for the 1963 elections.[37]

---

[33] Of the twenty members, I have positive information that nine were students and one a teacher at St Thomas'; others may also have been educated there.

[34] The proportion of natives on the Central Committee has been as follows: 1960, 50%; 1962, 49%; 1966, 47%. The proportion of natives on the Central Working Committee has been: 1962-4, 33%; 1964-6, 13%; 1968-70, 23%.

[35] Another five Chinese under detention were symbolically elected, but, for official purposes, the party did not consider them on the Committee, and they will not be counted in this analysis.

[36] The Chinese dialect groups in order of numerical importance are Foochow (92,000), Hakka (91,000), Hokkien (37,000), Teochew (27,000), Cantonese (21,000), Henghua (11,000) and Hailam (8,000). The rounded figures are taken from the 1970 Census of population.

[37] Wee Kheng Chiang, the founder of the bank, married the daughter of Ong Tiang Swee, thus consolidating his position as a rising power in the

An important source of funds for SUPP was the revenue from its periodic 'fun fairs', usually held in connection with anniversary celebrations for each of the branches and for the party as a whole. These were an important means of profitably directing the energies and enthusiasm of young supporters. The government has steadily restricted these fairs by withholding or withdrawing police permission for such gatherings. Other important sources of organized support were the Chinese trade unions; their political activities have been heavily circumscribed because the government has sought to encourage the development of a multiplicity of smaller 'peanut' unions.

The Sarawak Transport Company has played a very important role both as a source of funds and as a conduit for channelling SUPP influence throughout the first and second divisions. The company's buses ply almost every passable through road in those divisions, and extend as far as Sarikei in the third division. A labour-intensive business, the company employs a large number of drivers, conductors and ticket sellers, many of whom are party members. The company is also able to transport party workers throughout its network and carry propaganda materials and newspapers. The managing-director of the company, Chan Siaw Hee,[38] is publicity officer of SUPP and a prominent militant member of the party's Central Working Committee. Because its continued prosperity is dependent upon official licenses, the company is vulnerable to government pressure, especially at a time when, in other divisions, natives are accorded clear preference in the field of transportation. Thus twin arguments—both political and native advancement—could readily be employed to re-allocate licenses from the Sarawak Transport Company, thus removing an important financial and organizational prop from SUPP.

Based upon a check of overlapping membership, SUPP members and sympathizers over the past decade have controlled the Kuching Chinese Chamber of Commerce, the leading commercial body in Sarawak since 1930. This was true for each year except 1964 and 1965, the same two years in which there was a dramatic increase in the proportion of the

---

Hokkien business community. Wee appointed his nephew, Ong Kee Hui, as manager of the bank, a position he held whilst chairman of SUPP. Ong was later replaced as managing-director by Wee Hood Teck, son of Wee Kheng Chiang. In 1966 Wee Hood Teck joined SNAP and was elected a vice-chairman of the party.

In 1967, this same bank, under the management of Ong Kee Hui's brother-in-law, Dato Wee Hood Teck, made political donations totalling M$55,478 to the rival party SNAP. Bian Chiang Bank Berhad, *Director's Report for the Financial Year Ending December 31, 1967*, Kuching, 29 July 1968, p. 4.

[38] Chan, a Chao Ann of respectable means, has long been an enigmatic figure within the party. He could deal authoritatively with the government on behalf of the militant left wing of the party and regularly issued strident denunciations of government policy, yet he remained free from political detention, unlike many who were more cautious. He was finally detained in August 1968 (for fourteen months). Upon release he issued a quite conditional confession, phrased to allow him to continue an active role within the party.

party executive who were Teochew and Cantonese and a decrease in the number of Hokkien and Hakka. Almost to a man, the new Teochew and Cantonese committee members were supporters of the conservative Sarawak Chinese Association. Those who favoured SCA were defeated when control was regained by the Hokkien and Hakka, who supported SUPP.

Communist penetration of SUPP is the subject of many government statements and documents. The other side of the issue, apart from strident denials, has not been adequately aired, and it is difficult to evaluate how much weight and reliability to place upon official statements released to serve as political polemic. The moderate leaders of SUPP faced a dilemma about how to treat those party members detained by the government but not tried and convicted by a court. Party leaders could not justify expulsion without any substantive evidence being proffered by the government, evidence which would satisfy a court of law.[39] On the other hand, the government became annoyed, then somewhat suspicious, at the failure of the leaders to act against men it considered to be dedicated communists.

SUPP, though recruiting many Dayaks throughout the state, is Chinese controlled. The Hokkien and Hakka Chinese are consistently over-represented within its ranks and the Teochew, Cantonese and Foochow are under-represented. SUPP members lead such disparate organizations as the Kuching Chinese Chamber of Commerce and the Sarawak Communist Organization. The latter influences the party at the branch level whilst the former has made its impact at the top echelons of SUPP. There was only one openly publicized crisis between the moderate and militant members of the party's Central Committee. That dispute occurred in 1965 and concerned participation of SUPP in the Malaysia Solidarity Convention, a front of pro-Malaysia opposition parties headed by Lee Kuan Yew. On this issue, the Central Committee divided, with twenty-four 'moderates' favouring and twenty-nine 'militants' against SUPP participation; at this juncture, the chairman and secretary-general, Ong Kee Hui and Stephen Yong, resigned temporarily.[40] But since the return of those two top leaders ultimate control of the party has remained with the 'moderates', who were aided by the fact that since the government has severely limited the scope for branch-level fund raising activities the SUPP organizational machinery has come to rely

---

[39] Interviews with Ong Kee Hui, 21 January 1963, and 3 September 1964. The Central Working Committee did decide to expel all members convicted of subversive activities by the Court—a substantial concession since the law interpreted 'subversion' quite broadly. The party also 'relieved of their duties' members held under the Restricted Residence Ordinance. The left-wing members clearly feared that the government, working together with the 'moderate' SUPP leaders, would follow the example of Singapore, where a cleverly timed wave of detentions tipped the balance of control within the People's Action Party, enabling Lee Kuan Yew and his colleagues to maintain control at a critical period. Some SUPP members feared that their leadership had access to security records.

[40] *Sarawak Tribune*, 28 June 1965.

even more upon the salaries and allowances of the party's Council Negri and Dewan Ra'ayat members.[41] Those members, who are expected to give all such remuneration to SUPP, are moderates almost to a man.

Sarawak Chinese Association (SCA)

With the imminent approach of independence in 1963, various wealthy Chinese had perceived their need for an alternative political organization to SUPP. Though SUPP had gained very substantial support from Sarawak Chinese, it was committed to remain socialist in outlook and might well be left completely outside the government. By mid-1962, moves were afoot, with the Malayan government's encouragement, to form an alliance of Sarawak right-wing parties—similar to that which had success-fully governed the Malayan Federation for the past five years. With the urging of the Malayan Chinese Association, the uniracial Sarawak Chinese Association (SCA) was inaugurated in July 1962. The party pledged to work toward communal unity as a preliminary to broader national unity, based upon an alliance of racial parties, and also con-sidered the possibility of affiliation with the Malayan Chinese Associa-tion.[42] The chronological connection between the visits of Malayan Chinese Association delegates, the founding of the Sarawak Chinese Association and the formation of a Sarawak Alliance was rather too close to be coincidental.

The founders of the SCA were drawn from two business groups con-spicuously absent from SUPP Central Committees—the Kuching Teo-chews and the Sibu Foochows. William Tan, the first president of the party and a former civil servant, was a 'Queen's Chinese' in every way.[43] In addition to wealthy businessmen, the founders included some younger English-educated Chinese and others who were simply dissatisfied with SUPP. SCA also attracted the older, more conservative Chinese-educated who considered SUPP a youngsters' party and resented its activities, but SCA was marked by its nearly complete failure to engender enthusiasm among the young. This is explained by its image as just another Chinese Association, a group of wealthy businessmen of the past era seeking to perpetuate their influence by participation in the new Malaysian ruling

---

[41] See pages 47-9 (a) for an account of the structure of government at the end of the colonial period.

[42] *Sarawak Tribune*, 3 August 1962. The original constitution included the sentence: 'The Association may be affiliated to the MCA whose headquarters are in Kuala Lumpur'. This line was typed, but then struck out from the final draft. The SCA constitution was almost an exact copy of the MCA constitution, with only minor amendments. See also ibid., 27 June 1962.

[43] William Tan is a Teochew, Roman Catholic and was educated at St Joseph's School, Kuching. In these three respects, he differs from Ong Kee Hui and the other wealthy founders of SUPP. Important commercial rivalries between those two men were transferred into the political arena when he became a founder Vice-President of PANAS, and later president of SCA. Before that time, he had been president of the first fully-elected Kuching Municipal Council (1956-9) and a member of the State Cabinet (Supreme Council) from 1957 to 1959. He is presently Speaker of the Council Negri and a Federal senator.

élite.[44] SCA has claimed between 2,000 and 3,000 members throughout Sarawak, a figure considered fairly accurate in contrast to the inflated claims of most other parties.

The Kuching group formed a majority of members of the first Central Committee of SCA. But with the approach of general elections, feelings of dissatisfaction arose within the party regarding alleged inadequate preparation and funding for the SCA campaign, and as a result, the composition of the Central Committee was changed. In the process, William Tan was appointed to the newly-created position of Patron, and a wealthy Sibu timber merchant, Ling Beng Siew, became president.[45]

The representatives from the first division (principally Teochew) held a majority on the first Central Committee, but with the passage of time, the party came under control of third division members (principally Foochow). By 1967, well over, half of the Committee members lived in the third division and just over half of the twenty-three Central Committee members were Foochow. It seems that SCA is in fact striving to stimulate support based upon dialect group, and to establish itself as the party for the rich young aspiring Chinese executive.

Party Negara Sarawak (PANAS)

The relationship between the Brooke Rajahs and their indigenous subjects had acquired a distinctly sentimental character, and there remained strong native support for continuation of the Raj. The Brookes had accorded privileged status to the Malay[46] community in the realm of administration and government and had provided educational facilities principally for that ethnic group. At the end of Brooke rule, the permanent civil service consisted of: 1,371 Malays; 456 Dayaks; 426 Chinese; and 49 Europeans. The ethnic breakdown of the last Brooke-appointed Council Negri was: 19 Malays; 12 Europeans; 4 Dayaks; 3 Chinese; and 1 Indian.[47] Malays, however, accounted for less than one-quarter of the state's population.

---

[44] There were even some 'old school' differences between SUPP and SCA. The top English-educated SCA leaders were from St Joseph's School (Catholic) in contrast to the majority of the SUPP leaders who were educated at St Thomas' School (Anglican, SPG).

[45] Ling Beng Siew is an extraordinarily astute Foochow businessman, who has by his own acumen built from nothing a business empire that rivals any existing in Sarawak. He has been most conspicuously successful in the timber trade, where his enterprises predominate. His sheer drive secured for him the presidency of SCA, at the expense of the more conservative William Tan.

[46] Though described here as an ethnic group it is important to reiterate that the principal criterion defining a Malay is his adherence to the Islamic religion.

[47] Higher ranking Malay civil servants were essentially drawn from a limited number of families with 'aristocratic' connections. Not until September 1940, was the first Malay officer who was not from this 'charmed circle' appointed (Mohd Aton bin Saji). For the ethnic composition of the civil service see Max Seitleman, 'The Cession of Sarawak', *Far Eastern Economic Review*, 11 February 1948, p. 36; and of the Council Negri see *Sarawak Gazette*, 31 July 1964.

Wartime acquiescence in Japanese rule on the part of the Malay leadership only served to confirm Colonial Office opinions that preferential treatment for the Malays should be discontinued. This basic policy change set the British directly at odds with the Malay community, but London successfully effected the policy shift in Sarawak, in contrast to the unsuccessful Malayan Union plan in Malaya. Sarawak was ceded to Britain and formally became a British colony on 1 July 1946. British success in Sarawak resulted largely from the much smaller proportion of Malays in the population—18 per cent, compared with nearly 50 per cent in Malaya. The British expeditiously divided the local Malay aristocracy, obtaining the support of important leaders for the British position as 'the only realistic stance'. At the same time, a British political quarantine of Sarawak during this period assisted efforts to achieve compliance with their plans.

A major cleavage appeared within the Malay community as a result of the bitter dispute over Cession. An analysis of that controversy is beyond the limits of this study, but a few of its enduring consequences should be mentioned. During the late 1940s, a proliferation of essentially nationalist organizations had formed to oppose Cession. Some seventeen associations declared their support for independence under the Rajah, the most important of which was the Malay National Union and its affiliates the Pergerakkan Pemuda Melayu (Malay Youth Movement) and the Barisan Pemuda Sarawak (Sarawak Youth Front). The Malay National Union had been formed in 1939, all the other associations were post-war phenomena. By contrast, the only Malay organization supporting Cession was the Young Malay Association, under the leadership of the Assistant Commissioner of Police, Abang Othman. This latter organization, though avowedly non-political, enjoyed the imprimatur of the colonial authorities, and it fervently celebrated British Royal weddings and births.

The struggle against Cession caused great personal hardship to certain Malay families. The new government insisted that all civil servants in its establishment sign a circular expressing their loyalty to the British Crown. A total of 338 officers (335 of them Malays) in higher government positions refused to comply and resigned (effective from 1 April 1947).[48] For more than two years thereafter, feelings and frustrations simmered throughout the Malay kampongs. Recriminations were rife, directed more against those Malays who had benefited from Cession than against the colonial authorities themselves. The heir apparent to the Raj, Anthony Brooke, was himself prohibited from re-entering Sarawak under a provision of the Undesirable Persons Ordinance.[49]

[48] A breakdown of the government departments from which they resigned indicates the following as the most important: Education, 76 resignations; Posts and Telegraphs, 43; Marine, 40; Customs, 26; Medical and Health, 18; Printing, 18; Land and Survey, 18. Most also lived in the vicinity of Kuching. The government admitted that more than half of its Malay teachers had resigned also because of Cession, causing the closure of one-third of all government Malay schools. Sarawak, *Annual Report, 1947*, Government Printing Office, Kuching 1948, p. 47.
[49] *Sarawak Tribune*, 11 March 1947.

The Chinese community tended to benefit from the withdrawal of the privileged status hitherto accorded to the Malays, as did the Dayaks. Individual Malays were seen to 'adjust' unobtrusively to the new order. The passage of time was against those determined to restore the Brooke Raj. The situation was one of frustration, perhaps desperation, for there appeared to be no legitimate means of restoring Brooke rule. By early 1949, a Sibu-based clandestine association, The Thirteen Essential Ingredients, was formed by members of the Pergerakkan Pemuda Melayu. The thirteen members were sworn to achieve two objects. First, 'To sacrifice themselves if the necessity arose, because they had been resisting in vain for three years. It was essential to get liberation restored as soon as possible. They must take action because the justice they had awaited from the British Government had not materialized'. Second, 'To wait for the opportunity to take precise action and assassinate the Governor and other British officials'.[50]

Concealed among a group of Sibu school children, lined up in honour of the Governor's first visit, two members fatally stabbed Duncan Stewart, the Second Governor. This outrage galvanized opinion against the anti-Cessionists and terminated the effective political influence of all Malay organizations opposed to the Colonial régime. Four conspirators were hanged and another seven given long prison sentences; the Pergerakkan Pemuda Melayu was declared an illegal society.[51] One indication of the chilling and longlasting effect of this political violence is shown by the suspension of all meetings by the Barisan Pemuda Sarawak until 1958.

Two later external developments helped consolidate the position of the colonial government. First, the rapid rise in commodity prices as a result of the Korean War greatly increased the general level of prosperity throughout Sarawak. Second, there was a general decline in the security of the Western position throughout Asia, as evidenced by the Korean War, the Malayan Emergency, and the gravity of the fighting in Indo-China. In view of the international situation, Anthony Brooke, the Rajah Muda, resolved to cease his activities against Cession and urged all in Sarawak to do likewise.[52] From that time onward, the organizations working against Cession lay dormant, never to regain effective popular support.

The formation of SUPP brought to a head Malay apprehension of the growing wealth and power of the Chinese community. The Brooke régime had never quite forgotten the Chinese rebellion of 1857, and consequently had been reluctant to use Chinese industry and talent to its full capacity. Thus they had chosen to rely heavily upon the Malays who were particularly well represented throughout the administrative machine, especially in the police force. Some Malays had come to regard themselves as a privileged class, with a few aristocrats acting as the conduits and dispensers of political power.

[50] Ibid., 7 January 1950.
[51] Ibid., 5, 6 and 7 December 1949.
[52] Ibid., 5 February 1951. For the response of the Anti-Cession Movement and of the Sarawak government, see ibid., 8 February 1951.

With the colonial régime came the spread of education[53] to other native races and the growing economic predominance of the Chinese. The widespread involvement of the other races in government and then politics served to underline the lowered status and importance of the Malay community. The leaders of the Malay community lived close enough to the urban Chinese to observe their growing wealth and power. They were sophisticated enough to grasp the implication of the formation of a party that commanded the active support of the Chinese community. The Malays were also more familiar with the tactics of political manoeuvre than were other natives, for though the campaign against Cession had been unsuccessful, much experience had been accumulated in the process.

The 1959 general elections spurred Malay leaders to action. In that contest, SUPP had achieved notable success not only in the Kuching Municipal area, but also in the predominantly native Kuching rural districts. During that campaign, the Datu Bandar and a handful of colleagues carried out an improvised campaign in the coastal areas, endeavouring to convince over-eager prospective candidates that plural nominations for a single seat would only serve to ensure SUPP victories. On 7 December 1959, the Datu Bandar called all members of Council Negri who had not joined SUPP to a meeting at his residence. There he emphasized the urgency of forming a party 'with an entirely different outlook than the SUPP'. A majority of the Councillors present assured their support, and the Datu Bandar[54] was then given three months leave from his post as Government Advisor for Native Affairs to organize the party.

Party Negara Sarawak (PANAS) was duly registered on 9 April 1960, only ten months after the formation of SUPP. The first Central Executive of the party had a fairly balanced representation of Malays, Chinese and Dayaks, with the Datu Bandar as chairman and his brother, Abang Othman,[55] secretary-general. The party was, in effect, the semi-official

---

[53] Sarawak Information Service, *A Guide to Education in Sarawak,* Brunei Press, Kuala Belait 1961, see especially pp. 6-9.

[54] *Report of the Secretary-General, Abang Othman, to the PANAS General Meeting for 1960 and 1961,* mimeo., Kuching, May 1962. The Datu Bandar, Abang Haji Mustapha, was the grandson of the original Datu Hakim under the first Rajah of Sarawak. In 1941, the Rajah appointed him Datu Pahlawan and promoted him to Datu Bandar in 1946. As the highest ranking Malay, one who had been in government service all his life, he was continually chosen to advise the new government on matters pertaining to his community. He was a member of the Supreme Council from 1960 to 1963. According to one source, the Datu Bandar mortgaged his personal resources to support PANAS; at his death a large part of the receipts from the sale of his house were needed to liquidate his debt to the Bian Chiang Bank—the same bank which played a significant role as financier of SUPP and later SNAP.

[55] Abang Othman retired from his post as Deputy Superintendent of the Sarawak Constabulary to become a founding member of PANAS. While in government service, he had served as secretary of the Young Malay Association, formed to support the Cession.

answer to SUPP.[56] The very name of PANAS, literally translated as 'the party of the state of Sarawak', had an official ring—in contrast to SUPP, which had placed its stress upon being the united peoples' party. PANAS included within its ranks a number of Dayaks, some wealthier Chinese and many Malays—especially those who had not strenuously opposed Cession. The party included a broad group of established leaders, 'established' in the sense that they were government recognized, of reasonable means, and frequently appointed by the government to representative institutions.

Despite initial significant representation of each major race, the party came increasingly under Malay control, with other communities having only token representation. The racial composition of the PANAS Central Executive Committee of 1963, compared with that for 1960 (given in parentheses), serves to underline this change in ethnic support: Malays, 20 (5); Chinese, 6 (7); Ibans, 4 (3); Land Dayaks, 1 (2); Kayans, 1 (0); Indians, 1 (0); uncertain, 2 (2); total, 35 (19).

PANAS rapidly expanded its support throughout the first division, particularly in the Malay kampongs and adjacent Land Dayak districts. The secretary-general of the party reported that, by May 1962, the racial composition of PANAS was:

Table 5

PANAS Membership by Ethnic Group: May 1962

	Ethnic Group						
	Malay	Iban	Land Dayak	Melanau (percentages)	Chinese	Java-nese & Bugis	Other
PANAS members	38.0	37.0	19.5	3.0	1.0	1.0	0.5
Total population	17.5	31.0	8.0	6.0	31.5	6.0	

Source: Report of the Secretary General to the PANAS General Meeting, Kuching, May 1962 (typescript).

The object of the party was primarily, 'To protect, safeguard, support, foster and promote the political, educational, religious, economic, social and cultural interests of the indigenous people of Sarawak particularly and of the Ra'ayat of Sarawak generally'.[57] Though the initial policy of

[56] The Datu Bandar confirmed this by stating in his election policy speech, 'I say outright that PANAS was formed to oppose the SUPP'. *Sarawak by the Week*, Week No. 17, 1963, p. 34.
[57] Object No. 1 of the PANAS constitution; the constitution specifies that the expression 'Ra'ayat of Sarawak' means: 'All persons of whatever race who were born and have their true homes in Sarawak'.

PANAS was to 'provide equality of opportunity for all communities', it became increasingly evident to the leaders that this approach could not solve the problem of uplifting the indigenous races to a level comparable with the Chinese: 'We the indigenous people are backward in almost every sphere of political enterprise such as in education, economy, etc. There is no doubt about it and this is evident in the villages, longhouses and kampongs throughout the country.'[58]

This pro-native emphasis was both cause and consequence of decreased Chinese support for PANAS, and the party soon changed from its broadly non-communal stance. Despite ideological differences, a process only too familiar to the SUPP leadership was occurring also in PANAS. The over-representation of one ethnic group led to emphasis on the issues of most interest to that section, and that led to loss of interest in the party by other races. One further imperative spurred PANAS, and to a lesser degree SUPP, to more strident explication of communal concerns—the formation of more parties with narrower racial bases of support.

Barisan Ra'ayat Jati Sarawak (BARJASA)

Those Malays opposed to Cession had remained politically dormant for a full nine years after the assassination of the Second Governor, Duncan Stewart. In August 1958, supporters of the defunct Barisan Pemuda Sarawak (BPS) met in Kuching and resolved to revive the organization. The former president of Barisan Pemuda Sarawak observed, 'You can see by yourselves how very far our people are being left behind now'. The new president, Ahmad Zaidie bin Adruce, said:

> I am sick at heart to see the present conditions of our people. . . . We are not contented with our present situation and that is why we make various movements to fight for our rights in our own land. I am sad because we are still asleep. I call you all to wake up. . . . If you are afraid that your rice pot be inverted, one day you will find yourselves imprisoned under a big cauldron.[59]

The organization as reconstituted was racial and political; its re-vitalization was in response to growing Chinese preponderance in the economy, the administration and political life. Its leader was clearly Ahmad Zaidie, a passionate Malay revolutionary, and he gathered around himself many young admirers.

Ahmad Zaidie captured, better than any other Sarawak Malay, the feelings of frustrated Malay nationalism. The Malays, who had lost their former privileges, could only look with envy to Indonesia and Sukarno—the great Malay liberator! Ahmad Zaidie focused intellectual Malay discontent upon his vision of a Borneo federation, 'Bornesia', under the Sultan of Brunei, side-by-side with Indonesia. Before the war he had attended the Sultan Idris Training College in Malaya, and then during the Japanese occupation, he had been sent to the Bogor Veterinary College in Java where he became a close friend

---

[58] Report of the Secretary-General to the PANAS General Meeting, May 1962.
[59] Barisan Pemuda Sarawak, General Meeting, 16 August 1958.

of A. M. Azahari. He took part in the struggle against the Dutch, being promoted to a staff officer in the Kalimantan Marine Division.[60] Upon return to Sarawak at the end of 1947, he joined the Education Department, which sent him to Scotland for further training. He studied there until 1955, returning with an MA degree—a much higher educational level than any other Sarawak Malay. He inspired his youthful followers with oratory that glorified the past greatness of the Malays—their Majapahit, their Malacca, their Brunei. He emphasized how the natives must unite and rise. He was bitterly anti-Chinese and believed in bloodshed if they did not submit. In 1956, he was elected Vice-Chairman of the Kuching Municipal Council. The following year he became president of the Barisan Pemuda Sarawak and was appointed a government education officer, the highest ranking Malay officer in that department, and stationed in Sibu. He exerted his greatest influence (from 1957 until late 1961) through his presidency of the BPS and his close relationship with Malay teachers. Primary school teachers can be very influential in the small kampong communities.

The uprising against the British 'colonialists' was to be modelled on the Indonesian experience. But the concept of Malaysia threw Zaidie off balance—it jeopardized his plans, his dream, and was the turning point in his leadership. His followers split. Ahmad Zaidie came to believe that Malaysia was a trick, whereas many of his followers saw it as a sure way to *merdeka* (independence). The 'year of decision' was 1962 and the verdict was against Zaidie's brand of militancy, although the Indonesian appeal to one people, one language, one country still struck a ready chord, and the struggle of the Sarawak Malays retained an affinity with the Indonesian struggle. But Malaysia was to be a reality within two years; Zaidie still offered only a vision. The new party, BARJASA, drew the moderates from his BPS and directed their energies toward the fight for Malaysia. BPS itself declared for Malaysia, and Zaidie lost the chance to lead the mainstream of Malay action. A confidant says he withdrew from the crowds, grew downhearted, and lost his grip on reality. Yet his cause was not without significant pockets of support.

The Sundar branch of BPS (in the fifth division) told the Cobbold Commission, 'The Malaysia Plan was just a ruse used on the Borneo people to make them give up their fight for self-determination. It was a trick by which Malaya hoped to colonise the Borneo territories. . . . The three Borneo territories should be given independence first'.[61] The District Officer reported that 'Barisan Pemuda had a strong following in the Malay/Kedayan parts of the [Fifth] Division. . . . Some of its leaders had strong pro-Indonesian leanings'.[62]

[60] He held the rank of first lieutenant and the position of Kepala Staf I in the Angkatan Laut Republik Indonesia, Divisi IV. H. Hassan Basry, *Kisah Gerila Kalimantan (Dalam Revolusi Indonesia) 1945-1949*, Lambung Mangkurat, Bandjarmasin 1961, p. 92. The occupant of this position usually performs intelligence functions.

[61] *Sarawak Tribune*, 21 March 1962.

[62] Annual Report of the Resident, Fifth Division for 1963, *Sarawak Gazette*, 30 June 1964.

The Brunei revolt came a year too late for any real possibility of 'liberating' more than Brunei and its immediate environs. When it did take place, it was triggered prematurely by the arrest of a number of rebels on the Sarawak side of the border. The outcome was not what Ahmad Zaidie had promised. There was no simultaneous uprising. The only apparent result was the complete discrediting of the Limbang BPS branch for its complicity and the arrest of many associates for their support of the Tentera Nasional Kalimantan Utara (TNKU). Zaidie himself was imprisoned and later placed under house arrest. On Malaysia Day 1963, he slipped away to Indonesia. It is ironic that had he remained in Sarawak, he would probably have been appointed Director of Education by 1967 or 1968. Instead he was on the list of the men most 'wanted' by the Malaysian government during the period of Indonesian Confrontation.

The membership of BPS was limited exclusively to natives. Its stated political objectives were: to unite and prepare the natives of Sarawak for self-determination; to protect the rights of the natives and promote their interests; and to combat any element from inside or outside Sarawak which was deemed detrimental to the interests of the natives and the country.[63] BPS branches were systematically established in Malay kampongs in every Sarawak division in the period from July 1959 to February 1963.

Because of common religion most Malays might have been expected to identify with PANAS. But a great many were not willing to do so, for two main reasons. First, the chairman of PANAS, the Datu Bandar, had strongly supported Cession and the British. He was awarded a CBE, appointed to numerous government boards as the highest-ranking leader of the Malay community, and he tended to be somewhat dictatorial in his dealings with subordinates. His approach particularly alienated the young intelligentsia. Second, PANAS was led by the Kuching Malay 'Abangs', the aristocrats of their community, and thus there was a difference of class, age and outlook between the leaders of PANAS and those who met together to form the state's second Islamic-centred political party.

At the end of 1961, Sarawak's fourth political party was officially registered. The party, Barisan Ra'ayat Jati Sarawak (BARJASA), served to underline and help perpetuate the most basic cleavage within the Malay community, one which had disrupted personal relationships from the time of Cession. The chairman of the party was Datu Tuanku Bujang,[64] the highest ranking Sibu Malay; he had clashed bitterly with the Datu Bandar at the time of Cession. The party set out to include

---

[63] Barisan Pemuda Sarawak, Revised Draft By-Laws, September 1958 (typescript).

[64] Tuanku Bujang was born in Sibu just before the turn of the century and educated there at a Malay school. He was a native officer in the Rajah's service and latterly an administrative officer under the British. He was nominated a Senator from 1963 and elected deputy president of Parti Bumiputera at its inception (1967). In 1969 the Prime Minister appointed Tuanku Bujang Governor of Sarawak to fill the vacancy resulting from the death of Tun Haji Openg.

all natives, but the four Dayaks on the first Central Executive had all been associated with the anti-Cession Sarawak Dayak Association. The party did allow a few Chinese to join (one appeared on the Central Executive in 1962), but they were never in a position to influence policy. BARJASA leaders openly argued in favour of special privileges for the indigenous peoples and omitted Chinese from their list of 'Sarawak races'.[65]

The intellectual drive behind the party came from three men—Abdul Rahman bin Ya'kub, Abdul Taib bin Mahmud and Abang Han bin Abang Ahmad. The first two were public servants and their names could not therefore appear on party executive lists until after they were committed to politics on a full-time basis.

Abang Han was made publicity chief of the party upon formation, and became its executive secretary in 1963. He had an early initiation to politics in Sibu, where he was at one time librarian to the Pergerakkan Pemuda Melayu. He had been sentenced to death in connection with the murder of Duncan Stewart, but the sentence was later commuted, and he served a ten-year term in prison. Abdul Rahman bin Ya'kub, a Muslim Melanau and son of a Mukah fisherman, had surmounted many difficulties in his quest for education and promotion. Through part-time work and study, he finally earned his Senior Cambridge Certificate, and later graduated in law from the University of Southampton. Upon his return to Sarawak, he was appointed a Deputy Public Prosecutor, but his promotion was impeded by unsympathetic expatriate officers. Abdul Taib bin Mahmud, nephew of Abdul Rahman bin Ya'kub, encountered few of the difficulties that hindered Abdul Rahman's progress, mainly due to the changes that had taken place in the eight years that separated the two men. The war was well over when Taib needed his secondary education; qualified natives were promised accelerated promotion, when the time came for Taib to return from his legal training at the University of Adelaide. Though Taib did not stand for election in 1963, he was nominated to the first State Cabinet, and thus became the only well-educated native member.

Other prominent leaders of BARJASA included: Haji Su'ut bin Tahir and Che Ajibah binte Abol, both of whom had been prominent anti-Cessionists; Ainnie bin Dhobi, whose brother had been hanged for the assassination of Duncan Stewart; Ustaz Mohd Mortadza bin Haji Daud; Ustaz Abdul Kadir bin Hassan; and Haji Busrah bin Osman, Imam of the Indian Mosque. Ustaz Mortadza was chosen by BARJASA to broadcast its election policy speech. He and Ustaz Abdul Kadir were at that time lecturers attached to the Majlis Islam of Sarawak, the chief authority for Islamic religion and Malay customary law. Ustaz Mortadza has subsequently been appointed President of the Majlis Islam, and Ustaz Abdul Kadir has been appointed to be the new Mufti. The latter was the Parti BUMIPUTERA candidate who was defeated in 1970 by Wan Alwi of PESAKA. Though both lecturers formally resigned

[65] BARJASA election talk, Sarawak Information Service, *Sarawak by the Week*, Week No. 17, 1963, p. 32.

from BARJASA in December 1963 they continued to be closely associated with the party leadership.

Thus the party had a core of younger activist Muslims, conscious of their religion and tending to be much less friendly to the colonial government than the 'Abangs' of PANAS. Because their appeal to Malays was at the expense of the aristocratic 'recognized' leaders of the first division, their immediate recruitment potential was limited. More than half of the Malays live in the first division, and the old-established ties of respect for the 'Abangs' militated against BARJASA's efforts to win the support of these Malays. In fact, the conspicuous successes were registered among Muslim Melanaus, some Land Dayaks, and Malays resident in the other divisions of Sarawak.

A social profile of the type of candidate successfully elected by BARJASA (in 1963) exhibited the following characteristics, in comparison with the PANAS councillor. The BARJASA councillor was five years younger, had double the chance of being a professional, and was more likely to have been a government employee at some time during his life. He was less well educated, though more likely to have received that education in the English medium than in Malay. Whereas more than one in four of all PANAS Councillors were government-paid Tua Kampongs, only one in nine of the BARJASA Councillors could claim the same distinction. These two Islamic parties were subsequently merged (in 1967), but prior to that time they highlighted the central cleavage within the Malay community. The cleavage between BARJASA and PANAS derived from the Cession dispute and was further reinforced by differences of age, education, occupational experience and relationship with the colonial government between those recruited to PANAS and those who joined BARJASA.

Sarawak National Party (SNAP)

The British colonial administration believed that the Malays and the Dayaks had shown markedly different attitudes toward the Japanese invaders. They instinctively felt that whereas the Malays 'treated the Japanese with respect', the Dayaks had 'fiercely resented their presence and did their best to make things difficult for them'. Moreover, when re-occupation began, 'The Dayaks rose in their thousands and took a heavy toll of the Japanese'.[66]

The Japanese occupation authorities did not impinge upon the local populace as deeply as in neighbouring states of Southeast Asia. In contrast even to Sabah, there were no rebellions as such and only limited Japanese repression. Among the positive features of that period was the initial promotion of Malays and Dayaks to replace lower echelon European administrative officers. A Dayak was even appointed Resident of the second division, one of the top six posts in the Rajah's Government. There were scattered incidents during 1945, mostly attacks against the Japanese, and an ugly situation did develop in the

---

[66] C. W. Dawson, Chief Secretary of Sarawak, private papers, 25 November 1947 (typescript).

Kanowit district of the third division, where some twenty-three Chinese were killed by Dayak irregular forces.[67] This affair soured local race relations, and memory of it was kept alive by persistent Chinese efforts to re-open the case, consequent upon the acquittal of those responsible. Still this one incident was an isolated exception, not the rule.

Because many Malays remained hostile to the Colonial régime, the latter's officers identified emotionally with the Dayaks, whom the Rajah had left as 'happy savages in happy, savage surroundings'.[68] The ideal of the simple and trustworthy Dayaks was juxtaposed against a caricature of scheming Malays and greedy Chinese, both participating in political movements at variance with British colonial desires. There were important historical precedents for reliance upon the Dayaks, for, as Pringle has shown, the very continuance of the Brooke Raj, for a time, was utterly dependent upon the backing of Dayak warriors.[69] But the Brooke régime did little to support their education. Shortly after the war, the British began a major thrust to propel into modernity the hitherto neglected Dayaks. After only a year and a half of colonial rule, the number of non-Malay natives attending school was already almost four times the figure for 1940,[70] such was the higher priority accorded to the Dayaks under the new government.

Early Dayak political aspirations were of a fragmentary character. From the small educated group in Kuching, a Sarawak Dayak Association was formed which supported the Malay National Union in the fight against Cession. At its inception, the Sarawak Dayak Association included representatives of various families whose members have since achieved considerable prominence in the political arena, but as it committed itself more exclusively to the fight against Cession, and then, in December 1947, added 'politics' as one of its aims and objects, the SDA rapidly lost its character as a representative of the educated urban Dayak. Throughout the 1950s, two men controlled the Association, Eliab Bayang and Robert Jitam. Eliab Bayang had been Resident of the second division under the Japanese and became embittered after the British dismissed him from the administration. Robert Jitam, also from a traditionally prominent Sebuyau Dayak family, was detained for a month at the end of 1962 for alleged complicity in the abortive Brunei revolt. Both men identified themselves closely with the Brooke Malay leadership—a new, exclusively-Dayak, leadership passed them by.

Outside the capital, there were few expression of Dayak feeling for or against Cession. The only outbursts were from those who employed the issue as a way of articulating their generalized hostility toward government authority.[71] The third Rajah had maintained a certain

---

[67] Annual Report of the District Officer, Kanowit, for the year 1946 (typescript).

[68] C. W. Dawson, private papers, 7 November 1950 (typescript).

[69] Robert Maxwell Pringle, *The Ibans of Sarawak under Brooke Rule, 1841-1941*, unpublished PhD dissertation, Cornell University, 1967.

[70] Sarawak, Colonial Development and Welfare Plan (typescript) 1950, p. 14.

[71] Some Dayaks took an opposite line to the Malays by espousing a pro-British cause, objecting to claims that 'the natives of Sarawak are against Cession. . . . [On the other hand] a few ex-Penghulus and other trouble

degree of sentimental attachment to the Dayaks, although he did not have as close a personal relationship with them as did his predecessor. This meant that the Dayaks were not basically hostile to Cession, and objectively they had little to lose from the change.

The inclusion by SUPP of a number of Dayaks in its Central Committee indicated its intention to gain maximum native support. The party did in fact successfully gain a good deal of Dayak support in its early years, more than is generally recognized. To the Ibans, particularly of the Saribas areas, PANAS was not a viable alternative, for they believed that party to be Malay controlled. The formation of the third party—the Sarawak National Party (SNAP)—took the government by surprise, for none of the founders were government recognized leaders (Kapitans, Penghulus or Tua Kampongs) or members of the Council Negri.[72] This was in distinct contrast to SUPP and particularly PANAS. The first SNAP Executive Committee was composed exclusively of Ibans originating from the Saribas district of Sarawak's second division. Half of the Executive members had been employed by Shell Oilfields Ltd—in Brunei or in adjacent areas of Sarawak. Shell had provided a somewhat different political tutelage to that of the government in Kuching.

The founders were a particularly mobile self-made group of Ibans. The chairman of SNAP, J. S. Tinker, was born in Padeh (Betong), educated in Sabu, and worked with Shell through the 1920s before joining the government service in Kuching. He worked as a district officer during the Japanese occupation. Both vice-chairmen had spent considerable time in Singapore. Edward Howell was educated there at St Andrew's School and then Raffles Institution. He later worked for Shell in Brunei. Lionell Bediman anak Ketit had visited Singapore and Malaya a number of times before the war. During the Japanese occupation he worked in the Food Control Department at Betong, and then for Brunei Shell from 1949 to 1961. His family is prominent in the Saribas district. Bediman was vice-president of the Dayak Association, Brunei, from its inception in 1958. The secretary-general of SNAP was Stephen Kalong Ningkan, who had worked as a hospital assistant for Brunei Shell from 1950 to 1960. While there he had formed the Dayak Association (1958), in competition with the company-sponsored Dayak Club, and was elected its president. Ningkan had worked earlier with the police in the third division, stationed at Kapit during the Japanese occupation.

---

makers also belong to the Pergerakkan Pemuda Melayu . . . merely because it is "agin the Government".' Annual Report of the District Officer, Kanowit (typescript), 1947.

[72] Not only was SNAP dominated by Ibans, but there has been a conspicuous absence of government-appointed Dayaks at all levels of the party. For instance, the proportion of Penghulus, Pengarahs, Tua Kampongs, Tuai Rumahs and Orang Kaya Pemanchas to Dayak members of the Central Executive Committee rose from 6% in 1964 to only 14% in 1966-7 and dropped to 12% in 1967-8.

These four men—Tinker, Howell, Bediman and Ningkan—were the prime movers behind the formation of SNAP. Other members of the first Central Committee were Edwin Howell, who had served as an engineer with Sarawak Public Works Department; David Lawrence Usit, who had moved to Sabah and spent the years prior to the war working there; Matthew Danna Ujai, who had also spent a short time in Singapore and Malaya; Andrew Bunga, who worked for Brunei Shell most of his life; and Azarias Malong.

The actual decision to form the party was taken in Brunei; the prime movers then resigned from their Shell positions and proceeded to Kuching to effect registration. The party was formally inaugurated on 10 April 1961. It appears to have existed on meagre resources, principally the pensions and savings of the founders. The financial report for the first year (to 14 May 1962) lists loans to the party from S. K. Ningkan (M$1,724), Bediman Ketit (M$851), and J. S. Tinker (M$385).

A year later the Central Executive Committee, though changed a little, was still entirely Iban with one exception—Maurice Krisha Menon, a former Shell employee. Though an Indian, he was married to an Iban and lived in Betong, administrative headquarters of the Saribas district.

SNAP formed its first branches in the first, second, fourth and fifth divisions—within those divisions almost all the branches were located in predominantly Iban districts. The fourth and fifth division branches were in the areas where Ibans had migrated from the second division. In 1962, SNAP extended to the third division, but confined its branches to the northern Mukah, Oya and Balingian districts—areas which were also linked by migration from the second division.

In the period 1963 to 1965, SNAP consolidated its branch structure in the second and fourth divisions. The party, though including other races, remained predominantly Iban through 1965—introducing the first two Chinese to the eighteen-member Central Executive Committee in 1964, and adding one more Chinese in 1965. No Malays were yet included, a factor related in some measure to the history of antipathy toward Malays in the Saribas District, from which the original founders of SNAP came. The dramatic changes in SNAP took place in 1966, stimulated by its ejection from the ruling Alliance government. These changes will be discussed as we consider the Sarawak Alliance Party.

Initial policy statements by SNAP suggested an 'input' from various directions, for the party stressed Sarawak nationalism, advancement of native interests, and conservative economics. The first two elements can be viewed as a reflection of Iban leadership, and the communal interests of that race; support for conservative economics is more likely a reflection of tutorship by Shell Oil Company personnel.[73]

---

[73] A senior Shell officer is said to have personally guided Stephen Kalong Ningkan during his years in Brunei. A Shell lawyer drafted the party's constitution. The first two 'internal' policies to be followed by SNAP were listed as: '1. A balanced budget' and '2. A reduced national debt'. Neither of those planks were stressed in subsequent party policy statements.

Party Pesaka anak Sarawak (PESAKA)

The Ibans have also been divided in the course of history. Rajah Charles Brooke employed second division Ibans (Sea Dayaks), principally from the Saribas district, in his efforts to pacify Ibans of the Rejang River, third division. The animosities aroused by those campaigns still persist. The Brookes also allocated exclusive territory to particular Christian Missions. The second division was an Anglican (SPG) preserve and that Mission established schools in the Dayak areas—most notably St Augustine's, Betong, in the heart of the Saribas district. The Rajah permitted the Methodist and Catholic churches to proselytize in the third division. During the Brooke period both those churches chose to locate their schools in the predominantly Chinese and Malay town areas. The Ibans of the second division had thus been exposed to government, and to education, longer and more thoroughly than those of the third division. The historic cleavage, born in battle, was cemented on a more durable base. For this reason, the formation of SNAP had very little impact throughout the whole length of the Rejang and its watershed. The only areas of the third division where SNAP developed significant support were the Mukah, Oya and Balingian districts—areas linked by comparatively recent migration from the second division.

The Dayaks of the third division were fragmented politically. Some were members of SUPP, others had followed Temenggong Jugah and joined PANAS, and those in the northern district had joined SNAP. Numerically they were of critical importance to the future of Sarawak, particularly under the tiered electoral system. The third division has the highest population of any division, and the Ibans are a clear majority of its population. By mid-1962, those with a broader view could see that the British government was intent upon forging ahead with the formation of Malaysia, thus substantially accelerating the drive toward independence. It was also clear that although the third division Ibans were in a pivotal position, they were so split as to be rendered politically ineffectual, and could be 'swamped' within Malaysia.[74]

A senior expatriate officer initiated unofficial efforts to form a party that would unite the Rejang River Dayaks, and thus create a bond that would enable them to become politically potent and stand on their own feet. The key Dayaks in the formation of this new Party PESAKA were Penghulu Masam anak Radin, T. R. Francis Bujang anak Manja, Penghulu Francis Umpau, Pengarah Banyang and Penghulu Chundi anak Resa. The first three lived in the Kanowit district and the fourth in Sungei Aup, Sibu district. Penghulu Masam and Francis Bujang had served as trackers with the Sarawak Rangers during the Malayan Emergency. Penghulu Umpau was a brother-in-law of Francis Bujang, and they had both been primary school teachers. Another important

---

[74] Pengarah Banyang and Penghulu Umpau, announcing their intention to form a political party, stressed that unless the Dayaks 'could present a common and united front, they would be completely overwhelmed'. They went on confidently to assert their belief that 'future leadership would, of course, rest with the Dayak people'. *Sarawak Tribune*, 18 June 1962.

Iban was soon to leave SUPP and join PESAKA—Jonathan Bangau, who had been both a school teacher and an enterprising businessman.

Though Penghulu Umpau was a member of the PANAS Central Committee, he was quite willing to step down and form a new party. The same was not true for Temenggong Jugah, then a vice-chairman of PANAS, who seemed to value the 'old boy' character of PANAS. In mid-July 1962, the Temenggong was confronted by the four founders, and their many supporters, at the Sibu airport. A passionate argument ensued with Jugah relenting in the end and agreeing to proceed to Kanowit. Drafting of the inaugural statement and constitution and the selection of officers took the following four days and nights. Party PESAKA limited its membership exclusively to Dayaks, and its objects among others included:

> To assist all Dayaks to unite in pursuing the common aim and interest with the object of promoting and presenting an unifying [sic] approach to problems which affect their people in the successful government of this country.

> To preserve the heritage of Sarawak having regard to the necessity of promoting the political, social, economical and cultural advancement of the Dayaks in a constantly changing world.

> To ensure by all constitutional means the Dayaks have a rightful say in the government of the territory.[75]

Temenggong Jugah became the founder president of the new party.

By contrast with SNAP, more than half of the Central Executive Committee members of PESAKA were of the rank of penghulu or above.[76] This remained true until 1966, and PESAKA has often been criticized by SNAP members as a 'penghulus' party'. The situation is attributable to the relative absence of educated alternative Dayak leadership in the third division, a state of affairs which is rapidly changing.

Some 40 per cent of all successful PESAKA Councillors (in 1963) held the rank of penghulu, pengarah or orang kaya pemancha. The comparable proportion for SNAP was 23 per cent. As with SNAP, PESAKA councillors were overwhelmingly Iban (85 per cent and 91 per cent respectively), though in 1963 PESAKA picked up its extra support from the 'other indigenous' category of peoples. SNAP found its residual support from the Land Dayaks. Almost two-thirds of the councillors of both parties were Christian (61 per cent of PESAKA and 67 per cent of SNAP), though Anglican was the religion for SNAP and Roman Catholic or Methodist for PESAKA. The remaining SNAP and PESAKA councillors were nearly all animist. Age differences between councillors of the two parties are not statistically significant, but the level of education of those educated is appreciably higher in SNAP than PESAKA. There is an inter-

75 *Sarawak Tribune*, 20 July 1962.
76 The term 'penghulu' has been used in Sarawak to designate an Iban holding a position of trust from the government. The penghulu was appointed as a superior headman who would exert authority over many longhouses, throughout whole river segments. See R. Pringle, *Rajahs and Rebels*, Cornell University Press, Ithaca 1970, pp. 33, 157, 158.

esting and influential group of eight PESAKA councillors who have served in the armed forces—most of them having been members of the Sarawak Rangers unit sent to Malaya during the Emergency. These men have played an important leadership role in the party.

As with the two Chinese parties and the two Islamic parties the common ethnic origin of PESAKA and SNAP was not a sufficient basis for maintaining political unity. Differences mainly of locality, but also of the type of Iban attracted to each party, also promoted political division among the Dayak peoples.

Conclusion

For the first two years, formal party politics was the exclusive province of two parties, both initially created under the auspices of elite groups. SUPP was founded by a hard core of Hokkien business interests and PANAS by the Kuching Malay Abangs. But *élite* control could not be adequately maintained, for a challenge was mounted from within SUPP and from without PANAS, a challenge that severely circumscribed each *élite's* capacity to establish and maintain its hegemony over one whole race. The creation of a series of parties, each based upon a segment of one major community, set in motion a process that threatened to displace the established leadership in each community. *Élite* displacement is in fact positively correlated with its inability to form a dominant communal party, and the ensuing challenge to its ruling position from those of the same race.

Maurice Duverger has related the origins and growth of political parties to the advent of parliaments and an extension in the size of the electorate.[77] This sequence is apparent in Sarawak, though often it is inappropriate as a description of political evolution in Asia. In those states where gaining independence involved militant struggle, parties characteristically antedated extension of the popular franchise and introduction of meaningful parliamentary institutions. There was an element of this experience in Sarawak during the abortive struggle against Cession (1946-9), when both the Malay National Union and the Barisan Pemuda Sarawak performed most of the functions of a political party.

However, in general, Sarawak party formation in the period under consideration (1959-63) was stimulated by extension of the electorate and introduction of responsible parliamentary institutions. However the principal motivating force for all but the first two parties (SUPP and PANAS) was the impending grant of independence within Malaysia in 1963. In a process that gathered momentum, each group perceived that this was the moment when they must jockey to establish and preserve their claim to power—hence the ensuing proliferation of parties.

Duverger distinguished 'internally-created' from 'externally-created' parties, the latter emerging from outside the existing group of legislators and involving a challenge to the ruling group. SUPP was at its inception an 'internally-created' party, a creation of those who were already legislators. It was followed by another such party, PANAS, and later both

[77] Maurice Duverger, *Political Parties: Their Organization and Activity in the Modern State*, Wiley, New York 1963.

PESAKA and SCA, too, were such creations. For instance, the number of Council Negri members from the period 1955-9 who joined each party was: PANAS 8, SUPP 5, SCA 4, and PESAKA 3. By contrast only one joined BARJASA and one gave his support to SNAP. At the inception of BARJASA and SNAP, their leaders emerged from outside the Parliament and represented a challenge to the previously-appointed group of legislators. They were the two 'externally-created' parties.

Although internally-created, the functioning of a democratically organized party structure soon changed the character of SUPP. As influence began to flow reciprocally in two directions, those lower down in the network soon learned to manipulate the party in order to change its essence,[78] as understood by party founders. By 1963, SUPP was recruiting most candidates from outside the realm of the previously-elected leadership. If we take all district councillors elected in the 1963 election and identify them by the party which they joined (even if not directly elected under its auspices), we find that the proportion of councillors elected for the first time was highest in SUPP (69%), with all other parties ranked in the following order: SNAP (62%), BARJASA (55%), PANAS (50%), PESAKA (33%) and SCA (0%). This is a fair indication of the ranking from external to internal creation.

Once SUPP had clearly identified itself as hostile to the colonial government, and SCA had been created in its stead to pursue the conservative stance, each major community had two parties—each striving to represent that community plus whoever else could be attracted its way. For every major ethnic group one party could legitimately claim official support, namely PANAS, PESAKA and SCA. The other three, BARJASA, SNAP and SUPP sought to usurp power from the influential leadership, as represented by the former three parties. Campaigning energies and bitterness were principally directed inward, within each ethnic group. This trend was especially true for the Malay and Chinese communities, where the subsequent election campaign caused serious social division.

The very cleavages that militated against communal unity created a multiplicity of disagreements which in fact promoted conflict resolution through a process of flexible realignments. Rather than making racial blocks more rigid, as occurred elsewhere in Malaysia, this political division within racial communities provided a ready basis for compromise, forcing the factions to seek allies outside their community in the quest for political power.

---

[78] See Frederick W. Frey, *The Turkish Political Elite,* M.I.T. Press, Cambridge 1965, especially p. 375.

2

THE ENTRY INTO MALAYSIA
AND FORMATION
OF THE FIRST GOVERNMENT

The Role of the Colonial Government in Securing
Sarawak's Entry into Malaysia

The inclusion of Sarawak within Malaysia was accomplished with very little support or opposition from the mass of the population. The only persons with prior political experience were a relatively small number of Malays who had their political initiation at the time of Cession, and some Chinese who were involved either in government or in militant opposition. The Dayaks had little experience with either politics or administration, yet it was their acquiescence in British plans that permitted the latter to claim that the majority of the population wished to have independence through Malaysia.

By and large the Islamic communities were enthusiastic in their support for Malaysia and the Chinese were opposed to it. The Dayaks as a whole were ill-equipped to assess the merits of the scheme; the minority Kenyahs and Kayans were quite hostile to it.[1]

The key 'ascertainment' of opinion was carried out by a commission of enquiry headed by Lord Cobbold, former Governor of the Bank of England. The Commission was appointed *after* Harold Macmillan and the Tunku had agreed upon the desirability of Malaysia. The members of the Cobbold Commission were hardly bipartisan, and were: Dato Wong Pow Nee, the MCA Chief Minister of Penang, Malaya; Mohd Ghazali bin Shafie, the Permanent Secretary, Ministry of Foreign Affairs, Malaya; Sir Anthony Abell, the former British Governor of Sarawak; and Sir David Watherston, the former British Chief Secretary of Malaya.

The Commission held hearings in camera throughout Sarawak during the months of February and March 1962. It concluded that one-third of the population was strongly in favour of entering Malaysia, one-third insisted upon conditions (safeguards), and the other third was opposed. The Commission was preceded by widespread dissemination of government propaganda stressing the twin dangers of communism and predatory

---

[1] Historically the Kenyahs and Kayans have feared Iban encroachment, and relied upon the British to draw and enforce a line beyond which the Iban were not permitted to farm or settle. As a small minority in an independent state they feared for the future.

neighbours.[2] District officers were instructed to travel throughout their districts to discuss the government white paper (cited above). The uncertain future of Sarawak outside Malaysia was continually contrasted to its rosy prospect as a member of the federation.

The Commission cast aspersions on much opposition evidence, caricaturing it as communist-influenced, but it did not critically assess the submissions in favour of Malaysia. It did not particularly concern itself with the depth of understanding of those supporting Malaysia and failed to question the representative character of the meetings of chiefs who purported to speak for 112,000 Ibans, and to whose opinions the Commission attached very great weight. In retrospect the Cobbold Commission can be said to have functioned as an important 'cover' to legitimize the British decision to withdraw from Sarawak without having first granted self-government, as promised at the time of Cession and as embodied in the nine Cardinal Principles.[3] There was pathos in the Dayak who answered a question from Lord Cobbold with the reply, 'Whatever you advise, Sir'.

The expatriate officers did attempt to secure a period of reprieve before the full impact of federal control would be felt. They knew that in the long run the federal government would insist upon tight central control, as in Malaya, but for the moment they wished that the Dayaks especially be given a feeling that they had some measure of control. (This became essential at the height of confrontation when Dayak loyalty was critical to the repulsion of Indonesian raiders.) A good many expatriate officers were most unhappy with the role they were instructed to play, but generally felt that it was their job to make the best of the situation.

Once the Colonial administration was firmly set in its determination to bring Sarawak into Malaysia, and SUPP had expressed its opposition to the proposed scheme, a basic clash was inevitable. Despite British construction of a three-tiered electoral system designed to hamper any mass party and despite their patient persuasion that finally resulted in the formation of a shaky right-wing Alliance, SUPP appeared set to sweep the polls. It had mass Chinese support, this was patently clear. But it was also very strong amongst the Kedayans and pro-Brunei Malays of the fifth division, Land Dayaks of the first division and Ibans in the third. Under the existing system SUPP could win the election if it obtained a majority in the first and third divisions, which was quite possible. The colonial government did its best to publicize communist influence within SUPP, but those efforts appeared insufficient to stem the trend. Any drastic measures would be tested in court and to prove subversive intent was a slow and tedious process fraught with possibilities of legal reverses. With the passage of time the British did all within their power to undercut SUPP as a multi-racial nationalist party and to limit its support base to the Chinese. By this approach they sought to stop one strong inde-

[2] Sarawak, *Malaysia and Sarawak,* Government Printing Office, Kuching, January 1962.
[3] *Report of the Commission of Enquiry, North Borneo and Sarawak,* Government Printer, Kuala Lumpur 1962, p. 105.

pendence movement becoming politically predominant. The prime focus of the colonial authorities was upon dissuading natives from joining SUPP or remaining with that party.

Government power was exercised at two levels, locally and through state-wide restrictions. The district officers exercised as a matter of course extensive discretionary powers at the local level, unchecked except when major abuses of privilege occurred. Day-to-day the district officers would determine on the basis of his personal appraisal of the man appearing before him whether that individual should receive a shotgun permit and cartridges, whether he should be allowed access to another district or be given permission to engage in any one of a number of regulated activities. In addition, in all the smaller centres the district officer was a magistrate and would hear a wide range of lesser offences.

Given the essentially paternal relationship between European district officers and the Dayak peoples, the district officers were bound to exert inordinate influence in a direction unfavourable to SUPP. Though most of those officers consciously sought to remain scrupulously fair as polling day approached,[4] their preferences were known and were influential in a state where any edict from the 'D.O.' had always been tantamount to law. For the British officers had been instructed to promote Malaysia, not to be neutral on the issue.

Many efforts were made to intimidate SUPP cadres, the most intensive of these occurring in the Simanggang district where the district officer became famous for his zeal in undermining Dayak support for that party. An example is the account given by Bauk anak Lang of his conversation with the District Officer, after having been brought to Simanggang at gunpoint.[5]

District Officer: "You won't leave the party?"

Bauk: "I am not prepared to leave the party as the membership is now over 51,000 and my people look up to me as one of their leaders."

District Officer: "If you don't resign, you are head of the communist and you are fighting the government [sic]."

---

[4] The Chief Secretary sent a memorandum to all District Officers (C/2089/63 of 26 March 1963) impressing upon them the importance of complete impartiality in connection with the general election. Though conceding that native chiefs (who were not debarred from taking part in politics despite their receipt of a small government salary) might have engaged in certain acts of intimidation, the Chief Secretary argued that there was no systematic campaign of victimization directed against SUPP supporters. He alluded to the way SUPP supporters had withdrawn credit and engaged in social ostracism and business boycotts against their political opponents, to demonstrate that all powers of intimidation were not exclusively exercised by one side. At the local level the government specifically complained that SUPP communications have offered Dayak members free transport and expenses when coming to party meetings, and 'other things' such as funeral expenses for members and relatives. *Sarawak Tribune*, 29 November 1962.

[5] Bauk, an Iban, was vice-chairman of the SUPP Engkilili branch. The conversation took place at 9.30 a.m. on 12 December 1962. This account has not been verified by the district officer, but a wealth of other evidence authenticates the general drift of questioning.

Bauk: "It is never my intention to fight the government, because there is nothing in our party policy to say that we will fight the government. SUPP carry out its policy in accordance with the aims and objects of the party and by constitutional means. And to achieve self-government as and when we are ready, and ultimate independence."

The Resident then spoke telling me to go home. I stood up and proffered my hand to the Resident and when I turned to offer my hand to the D.O. he turned away and called me a *munsoh* (enemy).

A familiar approach employed by government officers actively opposed to SUPP was to dispatch armed security forces and dramatically escort a prominent local SUPP leader to the district headquarters. After waiting for some time he would be asked whether he intended to resign from the party. If the answer was affirmative a letter of resignation was characteristically typed out then and there (on government paper), copies being sent to the police superintendent and to Radio Sarawak. Were the answer negative the leader could be called in repeatedly for questioning and he might well find that his movements were restricted.

The other form of discrimination against the left wing was state-wide and grew out of a series of ordinances framed to deal with the exigencies of the new era of competitive party politics. The most important of these ordinances were:

The Restricted Residence Ordinance (1961). If in the Chief Secretary's opinion, a person's acts were likely to prejudice peace, order and good government, or maintenance of essential services he could be restricted to reside in any area or place. Such a decision was not open to challenge in a court of law. Two types of restriction orders were in use: (a) An order restricting a person to an area within three miles of his home for a period of six months, with the obligation to report to the police once a month. Under this type of restriction order the restricted person was free to exercise all his political and civic rights within a three mile area. By August 1963, 117 persons were restricted under this type of order, the government claiming that all had once been members of the TNKU, a paramilitary organization formed to effect the Brunei revolt. (b) An order restricting a person to an area within three miles of his home for a period of one year while requiring that he report to the police every day and remain inside his house between 6 p.m. and 6 a.m. Under this type of restriction order individuals were prohibited from taking part in any political activity other than the exercise of their right to vote. By August 1963, 47 persons were so restricted, the government contending that they were all members of the 'Clandestine Communist Organisation'.[6]

The Public Order Ordinance (1962) provided for the prohibition of any meeting of five or more persons in any public place to discuss matters of public interest without permission. From July to November 1962 the Chief Secretary invoked this ordinance prohibiting any such meeting in the Kuching district without permission.

---

[6] United Nations, *Malaysia Mission Report,* Government Printer, Kuala Lumpur 1964, pp. 67-8.

The Local Newspapers Ordinance provided that the licences of printing presses were liable to be cancelled if they printed any seditious matter, that is, articles which brought the government (or that of other colonies) into contempt or caused public alarm or despondency. Under this ordinance two Chinese language newspapers were banned and the licences of the printing presses revoked for reprinting articles from Singapore critical of the PAP government.

The Societies (amendment) Ordinance, the Trade Union (amendment) Ordinance and the Preservation of Public Security Bill each conferred powers to act against 'subversive' influences without declaring a state of emergency. Introducing the Preservation of Public Security Bill, the Attorney-General stated:

> The declaration by proclamation of a state of emergency has a very unsettling effect in any country. . . . Under the existing Emergency Regulations Ordinance, when such a proclamation has been made all the powers needed for dealing with the most serious type of disorder are immediately conferred upon the Governor, including, despite the fact that they may be quite unnecessary and there may be no intention to use them, powers of detention without trial.[7]

The new bill provided a two tier system of emergency powers so that the Governor could invoke certain of its provisions merely by notification in the *Gazette*. No longer did the government need to 'unsettle' the populace before it could detain without trial. A month after its passage four SUPP Central Committee members were detained and left the country on deportation orders.[8] In July three more from the Central Committee were placed under Restriction Orders.[9]

The Brunei revolt

SUPP gained a good deal of support from Muslims in the fourth and fifth divisions, particularly from those who would have joined the Party Rakyat had they resided in the Brunei Sultanate. The Party Rakyat (the People's Party) was modelled on the left-wing Malayan Party Rakyat and enjoyed widespread popular support throughout Brunei.[10] This residual support for SUPP came from the following two groups. (a) The Kedayans residing along the coast as far west as the Sibuti subdistrict, who were disenchanted with their lack of representation and second class status in relation to the Brunei Malays. Tom Harrisson observed that 'the whole area covered by the 1962 rebellion can be placed on the map and closely fitted in with the distribution of Kedayans'.[11] (b) The Brunei Malays of the Limbang district who felt remote from Kuching

---

[7] Sarawak, Council Negri, *Official Report,* Government Printing Office, Kuching 1962, Debate of 1-3 May 1962, cols. 77-78.
[8] *Sarawak Tribune,* 4 July 1962.
[9] Ibid., 30 July 1962.
[10] For further information regarding that party see Donald E. Brown, *Socio-political History of Brunei, a Bornean Malay Sultanate,* unpublished PhD dissertation, Cornell University, 1969, especially pp. 254-9.
[11] See Tom Harrisson, *Background to a Revolt, Brunei and the Surrounding Territory,* Light Press, Brunei 1963, p. 21.

and wanted their district to be reunited with Brunei. This is the district that intersects Brunei, dividing the Sultanate into two parts. Most external relationships of its inhabitants are consequently with Brunei rather than with the rest of Sarawak. SUPP was willing to act as a conduit for all those opposed to the *status quo* and greatly appreciated the presence of an important Islamic component within its ranks.

Though the top SUPP leaders were aware that the Party Rakyat was contemplating an extra-constitutional course of action, they argued against such a course in the belief that a revolt would only jeopardize the future of the Brunei party—that party just having won 22 of the 23 contested seats in the Legislative Council. SUPP leaders still wished to act within the bounds of legality.

At the central level SUPP had agreed to join with the Party Rakyat in order to make common cause to the United Nations against the Malaysia plan. Four SUPP leaders were to leave for New York together with the Party Rakyat delegation whose leader, Azahari, insisted that they meet first in Manila (on 8 December 1962) and travel together from there.

The snag to Azahari's plan came when a member of the SUPP delegation, Tahir bin Hassan, missed his plane connections from Limbang. Stephen Yong decided to wait in Kuching as Tahir had never before been overseas. That night (8 December) the Party Rakyat mounted an armed insurrection involving some 2,000 rebels (many trained and in uniform) directed against police stations and oil installations. The avowed aim was to liberate not only Brunei but Sarawak and Sabah too. The revolt spread to northern Sarawak, the rebels taking the towns of Limbang and Sibuti. The key Brunei oil centre of Seria was quickly overrun.

Insurgent strategy failed when a crowd of some 300 armed rebels were kept from the Sultan by an expatriate officer and his lieutenants, for only the Sultan could hope to abrogate the treaty with Britain and prevent the arrival of British troops to quell the revolt.

Had the SUPP delegation been with Azahari in Manila they would probably have been persuaded to join in an appeal to the United Nations to intervene or call a halt to hostilities, and SUPP could then have been declared an illegal insurrectionist organization.

In retrospect it appears that the armed coup was originally planned in twenty towns of Brunei and Sarawak to coincide with the frivolity of Christmas eve and the onset of monsoon conditions—factors that would militate against effective British response to such a general takeover. Action was precipitated by the British arrest of a number of rebels in Sarawak, and a consequent fear that the government knew of the plot and was closing in. The British and Gurkha troops took more than a week to regain full and firm control, and there were some bitter experiences.

Many questions concerning the revolt remain unanswered. The extent of Indonesian complicity is a subject that warrants careful investigation. Suffice it to say that the Sultan himself was convinced of Indonesian inspiration and assistance and later terminated all intercourse with Indonesia, even by his most trusted cabinet ministers. Expecting Indonesian help, many rebels reportedly cleared the runway of all obstructions on the assumption that the first British planes ferrying Gurkha troops from Singapore were in fact Indonesian.

Immediately following the outbreak of hostilities in Brunei and in northern Sarawak a state of emergency was declared throughout British Borneo. The Preservation of Public Security Ordinance was gazetted forthwith and empowered the government to issue far reaching and legally unchallengeable regulations. The most immediately important provision was the power to order the detention of any person for a period of up to two years. Such 'preventive detentions' were not challengeable in the courts.

Within a fortnight the government had arrested 49 Chinese engaged in militant anti-government activity, who were thus *prima facie* subversives. These arrests were over and above those of the Kedayan and Malay members of the SUPP Sibuti and Niah sub-branches, who were charged with complicity in the revolt and could be tried in court under the broadly-construed anti-subversion laws described above. A number of pro-Indonesian Sarawak Malay members of the 'North Borneo National Army' (TNKU) were likewise arrested. Some 62 persons were still detained under the Preservation of Public Security Regulations at the end of May 1963, and that number had risen to 103 at the end of June 1963. The three most critical left-wing Chinese language newspapers (strategically located in Kuching, Sibu and Miri) were abruptly proscribed under the powers conferred by these regulations.

SUPP leaders certainly believed that the government used the pretext of security as an excuse for obstructing legitimate activities of SUPP merely because SUPP was opposed to the Malaysia Plan. The United Nations Mission of enquiry concluded that such obstructions were not on a scale sufficient to have made a material difference to the results of the election.[12] But, as will be evident from later analysis of the 1963 election results, a small increment of Dayak support for SUPP might well have altered the whole outcome of the election, and perhaps even prevented the entry of Sarawak into Malaysia.

The vital consequence was that the revolt precipitated Dayak resignations from SUPP. Hundreds resigned and each resignation was given wide publicity by Radio Sarawak and the Sarawak Information Service Iban language weekly magazine—both of which exercised a monopoly of the media in the Iban (Sea Dayak) language. The government media constantly reiterated the theme of large-scale resignations from SUPP with a view to lowering the morale of native SUPP members. Many British officers used questionable pressure to quicken the flow of defections. As early as 16 December (1962) the Secretary-General of SUPP angrily charged that 'many of the former members of SUPP who have recently resigned had done so under vile threat and intimidation'.[13] British Member of Parliament, A. Fenner Brockway, after touring Sarawak, observed in the House of Commons: 'I am very sorry to say

---

[12] *Malaysia Mission Report*, p. 48.
[13] Stephen Yong, on Radio Sarawak evening news, 17 December 1962.

this, but I gathered the very strong opinion that the influence of British officials during the election was quite partially exerted against the United People's Party'.[14] A series of broadcasts on the evils of communism were prominently featured and their effects on the opinion leaders should not be discounted. Reflecting upon the events leading the election the SUPP chairman said,

> The British ensured the victory of the Alliance because they were committed to Malaysia and we opposed it. We lost among the Dayaks because of intimidation by the government and the chiefs—penghulus etc.—who are paid by the government. They simply put across the line that SUPP is communist and Chinese and made a few arrests. Many Iban had fought in the Malayan Emergency against the communists who were plainly identified as the enemy. There was also chicanery, such as the returning officers telling SUPP voters to put X against the people you do not like.[15]

The initial Indonesian attacks at Tebedu and Gumbang, on 12 and 23 April respectively, could not have been better calculated to damage the prospects of SUPP. They fully authenticated government propaganda concerning the dangers facing Sarawak in general and the Dayaks in particular. These attacks, together with the allegations that a thousand SUPP youths (all Chinese) were crossing to join the Indonesian terrorists, served to galvanize Dayak hostility to SUPP. On 19 April all Chinese were ordered to surrender their shotguns and in one or two outlying districts Dayak hostility and Chinese fears grew in intensity.

Constitutional developments

In 1962 and 1963 the Colonial authorities promulgated two successive measures designed to increase markedly the elected representation in the Council Negri and to prepare the way for a ministerial government, which would accompany the forthcoming independence through Malaysia. The first change (May 1962) hardly affected the twenty-four elected members. It reduced the number of *ex-officio* Council Negri members from fourteen to three,[16] but at the same time the number of other government-nominated members was increased from four to fifteen. This change gave the government flexibility, because it could choose representatives from those groups which it considered to be inadequately represented. The government intended that

> at an appropriate time, some unofficial members of Supreme Council (the Cabinet drawn from members of the Council Negri) would be associated with the formation and presentation of government policy on certain subjects.[17]

---

[14] *The Times,* 18 July 1963. He declared further: '. . . I have documents and even a poster which was displayed during the election on British authority and which said—"Do not split the vote".'
[15] Interview of the writer with Ong Kee Hui, Kuching, 3 September 1964.
[16] The *ex-officio* members who retained their seats were the Chief Secretary (later known as the State Secretary), the Attorney-General and the Financial Secretary. The other eleven were the Residents of the five divisions and six other government officers, characteristically heads of departments.
[17] Sarawak, *Annual Report for 1961,* Government Printing Office, Kuching 1962, p. 210.

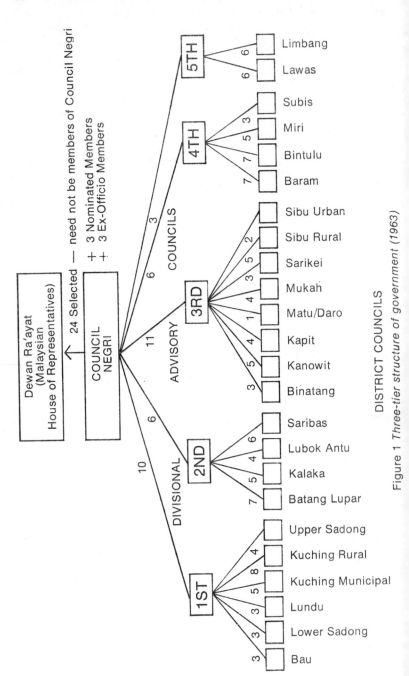

Figure 1 *Three-tier structure of government (1963)*

However events moved too fast and the government was persuaded to reduce the number of nominated members by twelve, increasing those elected to thirty-six.[18] A ministerial system was to be introduced with delay after the 1963 election.

The government decided to hold the 1963 election of the Council Negri on the three-tier system, by which district councils and, in turn, divisional advisory councils acted as electoral colleges. Figure 1 gives the structure of elective government that had developed by the end of the colonial era. The Council Negri had existed for nearly a century as an appointed body that advised the Rajah. Elected district Councils were a British colonial innovation. The colonial authorities sought to link these two levels of government by creation of the divisional advisory councils. In this way it was thought that government would remain close to the people who could exercise electoral choices at a level they would understand. Continued use of this form of indirect election, based on strong and fairly well developed local government, was justified on grounds that it:

> Makes for unity between town and country . . . (and) helps ensure that those finally elected . . . are persons having the widest support of the representatives of all communities.
> A system of direct elections might encourage the appearance of the worst type of political opportunist. . . .[19]

The Inter-Governmental Committee Report on Malaysia[20] expressed the official intention that this would be the last such indirect election. Based upon its experience in the 1959 elections, the government also made a number of other procedural decisions which could not help but influence the result of the forthcoming electoral contest.

In 1959, seven civil servants had been authorized by the Chief Secretary to stand for election, but permission was granted 'only if there was no other suitable candidate in the ward concerned'.[21] As the 1963 nomination date approached, the colonial government decided to widen this provision and permit civil servants to stand for election *and* to allow defeated candidates to re-enter government service. This ruling allowed a much broader reservoir of trained, 'reliable' conservative talent to be tapped, and again was of particular benefit to the parties of the right. This policy was important too for the non-Chinese. In the absence of widespread commercial and professional opportunities, trained natives almost invariably joined the government service.

---

[18] Largely by Ong Kee Hui and Stephen Yong who foresaw a denial of the Council's representative functions if the legislature were stacked with government nominees.

[19] Sarawak, Council Negri, *Electoral and Constitutional Advance,* Sessional paper #2 of 1961, Government Printing Office, Kuching 1961, p. 4.

[20] Sarawak, Council Negri, *Malaysia, Report of the Inter-governmental Committee, 1962,* Sessional paper #1 of 1963, Government Printing Office, Kuching 1963, p. 12.

[21] Sarawak, Council Negri, Sessional paper #1 of 1960, *Report on the general elections to District Councils, Divisional Advisory Councils, and the Council Negri held during the period November, 1959 to March, 1960,* Government Printing Office, Kuching 1960, p. 2.

The government in addition took several steps designed to prevent excessive vote-splitting. No deposits had been required for the 1959 council elections, except for the urban Kuching and Sibu Councils. It was observed that, once one or two candidates were nominated for a particular ward, a good many others would often then come forward. No less than twenty-five candidates were actually nominated for one ward of the Kanowit District Council. In 1960, the government had suggested that requiring a deposit would prevent such occurrences, though at the time it felt that the sum of $50 required by the Kuching Municipal Council and the Sibu Urban District Council was excessively high for rural areas.[22] But in the light of the political realities of 1963, the government decided that the necessity to limit the number of candidates far outweighed the risk of discouraging worthy rural dwellers from standing and established a standard $50 deposit that would be forfeited should the candidate not muster 5 per cent of the total vote in his ward. The relatively small number of candidates (998) standing for the 429 seats, an average of only 2.3 candidates per seat, indicates the success of official efforts. Moreover, there were allegations that in one area, the returning officer, a European district officer, publicly refused to accept valid nomination papers filed by dissident members of the Alliance party, on the grounds that only one Alliance party member should stand in each ward.[23]

As campaigning began, the government information service instituted a publicity campaign designed to discourage vote-splitting. It widely disseminated 40,000 copies, in eight languages, of a booklet entitled *The Countryman's Guide to Politics* whose final injunction, in bold print, said:

THE BIGGEST DANGER YOU HAVE TO FACE IS THAT OF ALLOWING PERSONAL DIFFERENCES WITH YOUR NEIGH-BOURS TO SPLIT YOUR VOTE AND SO TO ALLOW PEOPLE YOU DO NOT LIKE OR WANT TO BE ELECTED AS YOUR REPRE-SENTATIVES [sic].[24]

Another information service booklet, entitled *What You Must Know About the Elections,* also warned against vote-splitting.

The central contest was being fought between a highly-organized SUPP and a proliferation of smaller parties and independent candidates, and thus SUPP had everything to gain if votes were split between its many opponents. The government feared just such an eventuality and was working to prevent a SUPP victory.

The composition of the electorate

Throughout Sarawak the qualifications for electors were progressively liberalized to include all ratepayers in 1959 and by the time of the 1963

---

[22] Ibid., p. 4.
[23] This instance was in the Kanowit district. See SUPP, 'Aide-memoire for the United Nations Team of Investigators', mimeo., Kuching, 20 August 1963.
[24] Sarawak Information Service, *The Countryman's Guide to Politics,* Government Printing Office, Kuching 1962, p. 23.

district council elections they included virtually all resident adults—irrespective of the voter's country of citizenship. In fact any person was eligible who had attained the age of twenty-one years, had been normally resident in Sarawak for seven of the preceding ten years, and was resident within the limits of the particular district council for which he intended to vote.[25] The actual constituencies were district council wards, characteristically single-member, though in the towns there were some multi-member constituencies. The overall district council boundaries were coterminous with the limits of administrative districts. The only exceptions to this rule were that two councils were formed in each of the following districts: Kuching, Sibu, Miri and Binatang.

Utilization of pre-existing administrative boundaries reduced much of the scope for gerrymandering, or any systematic attempt to limit representation of any particular segment of the populace. The only real point of controversy was the representation accorded to each district council at the next level of government—the divisional advisory councils. The most blatant anomaly, on a pure numerical basis, was under-representation of the Sibu Urban District Council in the Third Divisional Advisory Council. It nominated only two representatives, which meant that the votes of its populace were significantly undervalued compared with neighbouring districts. Two of these, Sarikei and Binatang, had smaller populations than Sibu, but each nominated one more representative to the divisional advisory council. The three-tiered system has since been abolished, and direct election using single member constituencies substituted.

The following table gives an analysis of the registered electorate, by ethnic group, as at the qualifying date for the election (1 November 1962).

Table 6

Registered Electorate for the 1963 Election by Ethnic Group

Ethnic group	Registered electors	Population aged 21 years and over	Total population June 1962	Registered electors as % of age 21 and over
		(percentages)		
	(1)	(2)	(3)	(4)
Malay/Melanau	25	24	23.5	89
Dayak	51	48	44	90
Chinese	24	27	31.5	75
Other non-native	—	1	1	—
	100	100	100	

[25] *Sarawak Gazette,* 31 August 1963, p. 174.

Overall voter registration was an extremely high proportion for any society, particularly as both registration and voting were voluntary exercises. Why then were the Chinese so markedly under-represented, particularly as their geographical dispersion made them more accessible to registration teams than were the Dayaks? The lower average age of Chinese accounts for the difference between columns 2 and 3, but does not act as an explanation for the discrepancy between columns 1 and 2.

Citizenship was not a pre-requisite for registration, thus Chinese were not excluded on those grounds. The only disability that would tend to affect Chinese more than other ethnic groups was the requirement that each voter had been normally resident in Sarawak for seven of the preceding ten years. Recent immigrants would thus be excluded. However, the influx of Chinese was terminated effectively following the assumption of control on the Chinese mainland by the Communist régime. Thus it would appear that proportionately fewer Chinese chose to register as voters, as indicated by the proportion in column 4, and perhaps the government was less rigorous in its efforts to induce Chinese registration than it was with other more scattered communities. Allegations that the government had arbitrarily omitted certain qualified persons from the voting register were not subsequently substantiated in detail, and certainly were not sufficiently widespread so as to constitute grounds for challenging the validity of the election results.[26]

The Formation of the Sarawak Alliance and the Structuring of Political Parties Preparatory to Electoral Contest

The developing proliferation of parties described in Chapter I reflected the absence of all-pervasive societal cleavages. There were, however, dangers in the process; for the narrower the base of each party, the more specific became its demands.

The splintering of parties, each representing an important segment of a major community, might well have proceeded further[27] had it not been for the efforts of the Colonial government which clearly foresaw a monolithic, well-organized SUPP sweeping the polls against its fragmented opposition. Some native leaders had not yet appreciated the point that more parties did not necessarily mean greater strength. Personal differences proved to be a serious block to any electoral understanding, and these difficulties were compounded as there was yet no way to assess the relative bargaining strength of each party.

The first projected coalition was between BARJASA and SNAP on the initiative of Stephen Kalong Ningkan. Representatives met at the end of June 1962, but negotiations floundered when SNAP demanded two-thirds of all offices and control, on the basis of their claimed membership. However, the following month SNAP and PESAKA did tentatively

[26] United Nations, *Malaysia Mission Report*, pp. 37-9.
[27] The Land Dayaks were to form their party and the Melanaus were discussing a similar move. See *Sarawak Tribune*, 5 December 1962.

agree to form an alliance.[28] The idea of a multi-racial Alliance party, based on the Malayan model, was expressed in the inaugural statement of SCA, three months later.

Agreements 'in principle' were one matter but the actual bargaining was beset by mutual suspicion. BARJASA leaders had never held exalted opinions of the SCA leadership and were quite suspicious of those members who had defected from SUPP. The Datu Bandar (PANAS) held a 'different' view of his party's rightful share of the influential posts and future spoils, and SNAP leaders were not characterized by meekness. Then there was the ever-present cleavage between BARJASA and PANAS. The British authorities, the Malayan Chinese Association and the United Malay National Organization (of Malaya) all worked to forge a modicum of agreement, their efforts becoming more intense as the impending election drew nearer.

The 'Sarawak United Front' was launched on 22 October 1962 with much official pomp and promotion. It was transformed into the 'Sarawak Alliance' the following month,[29] thereby acquiring a rather more respectable nomenclature. Its election manifesto declared that:

> the best way of achieving inter-racial harmony and understanding, we believe, is for all racial problems to be settled by the various representative racial political bodies, and then reconciled within an alliance of such racial political bodies. . . . The Sarawak Alliance is a living example today, young though the organization is, of inter-racial harmony and understanding.[30]

The Alliance structure of political party organization was the result of a temporary electoral arrangement in the Malayan capital. Just prior to the 1952 municipal elections in Kuala Lumpur, the United Malay National Organization and the Malayan Chinese Association formed an 'alliance' against the non-communal Independence of Malaya party. The arrangement was so successful that it came to be repeated throughout Malaya. In due course liaison committees were formed and the Alliance Party superimposed upon its components, was institutionalized.

The Malayan Alliance was characterized by: (1) Unification of each race under the leadership of its own distinct communal party: Malays led by the United Malay National Organization (UMNO), Chinese led by the Malayan Chinese Association (MCA), and Indians led by the Malayan Indian Congress (MIC). (2) Inter-communal cooperation and compromise was achieved by a coming together of each ethnic group in the

---

[28] Ibid., 16 July 1962. This 'Alliance' was officially consummated in Kuching on 22 October. See also ibid., 16 and 23 October 1962.

[29] *Sarawak Tribune,* 30 November 1962. The five parties that composed the Sarawak Alliance were: PANAS, BARJASA, PESAKA, SNAP and SCA. The three Malayans who helped their Sarawak counterparts achieve final agreement were Senator T. H. Tan, Syed Ja'afar Albar and Yap Kon Chon. See ibid., 29 November 1962. A month earlier an UMNO delegation to Sarawak was composed of Azahari Taib, Shafie bin Haji Abdullah and Abdul Ghani bin Ishak, an MP. An MCA delegation present at the same time was led by Dr Lim Swee Aun, and included Senator T. H. Tan. See ibid., 11 and 12 October 1962, and the *Sibu District Annual Report for 1962,* mimeo., Sibu 1963.

[30] Ibid., 4 June 1963.

Alliance where immediate conflicts of interest were resolved. In essence the Alliance has been a pan-ethnic structure on top of basically ethnic parties. This gave Alliance politicians the best of both worlds. They would continue to rely upon essentially ethnic identity to mobilize voter support, whilst effecting necessary compromises away from public scrutiny, behind closed doors. (3) The pre-eminent position of UMNO within the Alliance party, with its ability to dictate the terms of agreement when deemed essential to the Malay interest.

The Alliance structure purports to recognize the reality of communalism (the primordial loyalties) and then strive to mitigate its ill effects facilitating inter-racial communication. Thus a *modus vivendi* between the races is achieved at the top level of leadership. But the Alliance is structurally unable to cope with the exigencies of rapid social transformation, for it is essentially a conservative (status quo) coalition. The fragility of the Alliance structure has been exhibited whenever the temperature of political controversy has risen sharply. Then the moderates are in danger of losing control over their more excitable followers, who can readily outbid the 'compromisers' at their own game, the communal appeal. During the 1959 election campaign a stiffening of Chinese resistance to Malay dominance in turn exacerbated Malay feeling and led to the expulsion of Chinese opposition groups from the Malayan Chinese Association. In 1965, just prior to the expulsion of Singapore, tension rose to high levels within the Alliance. The tragic communal violence that followed the reversal of Alliance fortunes in May 1969 was another instance of the Alliance leadership temporarily losing control over its militant supporters.

This Alliance approach is in stark contrast to the aims of a multi-racial (non-communal) party which strives to integrate and achieve compromise at the lowest levels within the party. This important difference of political party organization, a multi-racial versus a communal basis, was perhaps the central dilemma of Malaysian parliamentary politics. The continued failure of all efforts by non-communal parties seriously to whittle away the Alliance electoral following served to authenticate the realism of this approach in Malaya, until 1969. No ideology was able to transcend ethnic solidarity.

The difficulty was that in Sarawak the *substance* of the Alliance, as understood in Kuala Lumpur, was missing or present only in part. With reference to the essential characteristics of the Malayan Alliance (as outlined above) we may note: (1) The first successful parties in Sarawak were multi-racial, and most of their leaders had not accepted the desirability of confining their efforts solely to one community. (2) Thus simple inter-communal compromise could not readily take place if there were rival leaders purporting to represent the same community. Individual communities were themselves internally divided. (3) Due to the much smaller proportion of Malays in the population of Sarawak, no Malay party could readily dictate the terms of co-operation to Chinese or Dayak components of an Alliance.

In a coalition which incorporates a number of small parties, aggregation and compromise of sub-culture or clientele demands must take place between rather than within parties. The chief obstacle to the Sarawak Alliance functioning as a coalition was the direct competition between BARJASA and PANAS. This clash was epitomized in the extreme personal animosity between the chairmen of the two parties, Tuanku Bujang and the Datu Bandar.[31] In 1962-3 SNAP and PESAKA clashed only at the margins due to the essentially geographic sphere of Dayak support for each party. SCA had to compete with SUPP for Chinese support, but SCA was never really troubled by the vicissitudes derived from mass popular backing.

The loose Alliance organization proved incapable of containing both PANAS and BARJASA. For PANAS sought to play a dominant leadership role within the Alliance akin to that of UMNO in Malaya. The Datu Bandar constantly sought to convey the unmistakable impression that PANAS had the support of the Malayan Prime Minister and that PANAS was to be the branch of UMNO in Sarawak.[32] This impression was persuasive enough for the Tunku to send an emissary to disavow the contention.

> The Claim made by the leader of Party Negara Sarawak, Datu Bandar Abang Haji Mustapha, that he and the Tengku had made a "secret pact" was false and aimed at deceiving the people of Sarawak. I tell the people of Sarawak that the Tengku had never made any such pact. He [the Tunku] wants me to tell you that.[33]

The Alliance split as soon as serious discussions began as to how prospective seats and portfolios in the new Alliance government (if elected) might be allocated. On 15 April 1963 PANAS angrily withdrew, the Datu Bandar declaring that:

> PANAS has a principal policy which differs from those of the other political parties. PANAS has not decided who will be Governor, the Chief Minister and other officials.[34]

Temenggong Jugah suggested that PANAS leaders were disappointed because, among other things, their chairman was not elected to chairman of the Alliance.[35]

The break in the Sarawak Alliance came at a critical moment, for polling commenced that very month. Two weeks after the split four Malayan Alliance delegates arrived to assist the Sarawak Alliance election campaign.[36] They understood the danger of splitting the pro-Malaysia vote between the Alliance and PANAS and allowing SUPP to win by default, and chose to take the initiative, vigorously attacking both PANAS and SUPP. According to the PANAS publicity chief, Abang Ikhwan Zainie, 'the Malayan Alliance delegation has not acted like the

---

[31] For some time neither leader would speak to the other, and all dealings were through a third person. The hard feelings between the two had been exacerbated by their mutual recriminations following the Japanese occupation.

[32] *Sarawak Tribune,* 16 May 1962.

[33] Ibid., 18 June 1963.

[34] *Sarawak by the Week,* Week No. 17, 1963.

[35] Ibid., Week No. 18, 1963.

[36] They were Khaw Kai Boh, T. H. Tan, Yap Kon Chan and Syed Ja'afar Albar. *Sarawak Tribune,* 25 April 1963.

good mediator. Instead, they have declared war on PANAS'.[37] 'Malayan intervention' became a most explosive issue in the ensuing campaign. One effect was that the recriminations within the Malay community were more bitter than at any time since the height of the Cession dispute.[38] PANAS attributed this to BARJASA's dependence upon Malayan help.

> The Malays of Sarawak had once suffered a bitter blow because of the difference in politics over the Cession. . . . If that same history repeats itself in Sarawak, it will be because of the Malayan Alliance delegation.

> That ancient flame of hatred was rekindled by BARJASA as we can very well witness today, at a time when unity among the Malays is vital.

> It all began with the visit of Syed Ja'afar Albar and his colleagues.[39]

Far from unifying the Muslims and binding them to Kuala Lumpur, a substantial segment of that community was alienated by Malayan support of BARJASA. The pre-existing cleavage within the Islamic community was thus exacerbated.

The Results of the 1963 Election

Polling took place from April to June 1963, with teams of officials taking the ballot box to the voter as they toured the larger districts. Table 7 gives a proportionate breakdown of the votes received[40] by each major

---

[37] *Utusan Sarawak,* 21 May 1963. Abang Ikhwan Zainie, the editor of *Utusan Sarawak,* was also the publicity chief of PANAS. His was the only Malay-language newspaper published in Sarawak.

[38] Abdul Rahman Ya'kub, the force behind BARJASA, complained: 'Party Negara apparently is not only waging a filthy campaign politically, but has also brought politics into social life. Some of my friends in PANAS no longer want to speak to me.' *Sarawak Tribune,* 19 June 1963. Relationships within the Muslim community had once again descended to the point where basic social intercourse was interrupted.

[39] *Utusan Sarawak,* 2, 16, and 23 May 1963.

[40] A voting analysis cannot simply be based upon tabulation of the votes actually cast for the candidates of each party. Due account must be taken of the filling of one-sixth of all vacancies by unopposed candidates, for the uncontested seats were not allocated evenly amongst the various parties. The party distribution of the unopposed candidates was as follows: Alliance 34, Independents 28, PANAS 6 and SUPP 5. Thus to ignore these constituencies and simply tabulate votes cast would accord both SUPP and PANAS an unrealistically high share of the vote. On the other hand, simply to add to the votes of each party the total electorate in each ward where its candidate won without a contest, would weight the final proportions in the opposite direction. The course taken here has been to determine requisite weight by reducing the number of electors in uncontested wards by the percentage poll throughout the appropriate district, then adding the resultant more realistic uncontested vote to the actual votes cast for the particular party in each district. For instance, in the Lower Sadong District eight PANAS candidates received 2539 actual votes. But three other PANAS nominees were elected unopposed, the total number of electors in their wards totalling 2622. To ignore the latter would produce a gross distortion, yet to simply total both figures would accord an unrealistically high vote to PANAS, as only 65% of all electors actually voted in the Lower Sadong district. Thus we reduce the number of electors in the uncontested wards by that proportion (2622 x 65% = 1699) and then derive a realistic total of 4238 'votes' for PANAS in the Lower Sadong district. The totals and proportions derived from these adjusted tabulations will be the basis of our discussion following.

party, and the broad communal composition of the electors in each of the twenty-four districts. Notes are appended explaining the ethnic categories in greater detail.

Table 7

Proportion of Votes Received by Each Party in the
1963 Election and Ethnic Composition of the
Registered Electorate in Each District

District Council	Proportion of votes received by party				Ethnic group of registered voters		
	SUPP	PANAS	Alliance	Independent	Chinese	Malay/Melanau	Dayak
				(percentages)			
Lundu	21.5	30.0	37.0	11.5	22.4	35.9	41.7
Bau	40.0	13.5	33.0	13.5	34.5	6.9	58.6
Kuching Municipal	53.2	15.3	26.9	4.6	71.0	26.6	1.9
Kuching Rural	30.6	39.1	15.7	14.6	34.5	43.2	22.2
Upper Sadong	17.2	26.5	32.4	23.7	13.5	8.9	77.5
Lower Sadong	12.0	70.0	12.0	6.0	10.1	55.4	34.5
First Division	31.4	32.8	22.9	13.0	34.9	31.9	33.1
Batang Lupar	9.9	18.0	56.8	15.2	10.5	16.6	72.9
Lubok Antu	23.1	—	60.4	16.4	9.2	1.1	89.7
Saribas	5.6	30.6	36.7	27.1	7.5	42.5	49.9
Kalaka	9.1	12.6	56.0	22.4	6.1	30.2	63.6
Second Division	10.6	17.2	52.0	20.1	8.6	24.3	67.1
Sarikei	38.0	3.2	26.0	32.7	51.7	27.7	20.6
Binatang	42.2	4.6	35.4	17.9	47.6	16.4	36.2
Matu/Daro	3.7	—	42.6	53.7	7.7	92.0	0.2
Mukah	—	—	—	100.0	8.0	38.6	53.3
Sibu Urban	55.5	5.5	24.8	14.3	73.6	24.9	1.5
Sibu Rural	32.5	—	18.1	49.2	50.6	6.5	42.8
Kanowit	10.3	0.3	65.0	24.2	10.9	1.0	88.1
Kapit	17.6	—	70.8	11.8	3.6	0.6	95.7
Third Division	23.0	1.2	39.0	36.8	26.3	17.4	56.2
Bintulu	8.4	20.9	49.2	21.4	9.0	23.2	67.7
Subis	10.1	—	10.2	79.7	12.0	42.6	45.4
Miri	42.0	18.2	29.9	9.9	54.9	38.3	6.5
Baram	—	—	—	100.0	10.9	5.6	83.4
Fourth Division	14.2	10.5	22.4	53.0	20.3	23.1	56.5
Limbang	—	—	6.9	93.0	9.4	48.9	41.6
Lawas	—	—	42.3	57.7	11.0	53.0	35.9
Fifth Division	—	—	23.2	76.7	10.0	50.7	39.2
Grand Total	21.4	14.3	34.2	30.2	24.0	24.9	51.1

Notes on the Ethnic Composition of the District Council Electorates

The following notes expand the simple 'Chinese, Malay/Melanau, Dayak' categories employed in Table 7.

DISTRICT

First Division

Lundu	Two-thirds of Dayaks are Land Dayak, the other third being Iban. Hardly any Melanau live in the first or second divisions—almost all the Islamic group are Malay. Hakka (Kheh) predominate amongst the Chinese.
Bau	Nearly all Dayak are Land Dayak and the Chinese are Hakka.
Kuching (Rural and Municipal)	Three-quarters of the Dayaks are Land Dayak, the remainder being mainly Iban. A number of dialect groups make up the municipal Chinese population. Ranked in order of numerical significance they are: Hokkien, Teochew, Hakka, Henghua, Cantonese and Hailam. The Hakka predominate amongst the rural Chinese, with Hokkien and Cantonese performing a commercial role.
Upper Sadong	The Dayak population is overwhelmingly Land Dayak. The Chinese are again Hakka agricultralists with Hokkien and Teochew entrepreneurs. The Malays include a pocket of Javanese.
Lower Sadong	The Dayak are overwhelmingly Iban, and very few Land Dayaks reside east of the first division. Nearly all the Chinese are Hakka.

Second Division

Batang Lupar	The Dayaks are Iban, and the Chinese are Teochew, Hakka and Hokkien in that order, with a new Foochow settlement near Simanggang.
Lubok Antu	The Dayak are Iban, and the Chinese are Hakka and Teochew.
Saribas	The Dayak are Iban, the Chinese are Hakka, Teochew and Hokkien in that order (numerically).
Kalaka	The Dayak are Iban, the Chinese are Hokkien, Hakka, Foochow, Hailam and Cantonese.

Third Division

Sarikei	Nearly three-quarters of the Malay/Melanau category are Melanau. The Dayak are Iban and the Chinese are predominantly Foochow and Cantonese.
Binatang	Some three-quarters of the Malay/Melanau classify themselves as Melanau. Dayak are Iban, and the Chinese are Foochow with some Cantonese and Hokkien.
Sibu Urban	Most of the Malay/Melanau are Malay. The Dayak are Iban, and the Chinese are overwhelmingly Foochow with significant Hokkien representation and some Cantonese.

Sibu Rural	Some two-thirds of Malay/Melanau are Malay. Dayak are Iban, and the Chinese are Foochow, with some Cantonese, Henghua and Hokkien in that order of numerical significance.
Mukah	The Melanau predominate in the category Malay/Melanau. Dayak are Iban. The Chinese are Hokkien, Foochow, Teochew and Cantonese, in that order.
Kanowit	The Malay outnumber the Melanau two to one. The Dayak are mostly Iban, and the Chinese are Cantonese, Foochow and Hokkien.
Kapit	The Iban predominate, but a sixth of the Dayaks are Kayans, who live in the Belaga sub-district. The Chinese are Hokkien, Cantonese and Foochow.
Matu-Daro	Almost all Malay/Melanau are Melanau. The few Dayaks are Iban, and Chinese are Foochow and Hokkien.

Fourth Division

Bintulu	The Dayaks are mostly Iban (8/9), with some Kayan. The Melanau outnumber the Malay three to one, and some other Muslims are Penan. The Foochow and Teochew are the best represented Chinese.
Subis	The Dayak are Iban, the Malay/Melanau are largely Kedayan, with some Malay, 'Orang Miri' and Penan, and the Chinese are Hakka, Hokkien and Cantonese.
Miri	The Dayak are Iban, four-fifths of the Malay/Melanau are Malay. Though the most numerous Chinese group are Hakka farmers, the Cantonese are very important in commercial circles and better represented than the Hokkien.
Baram	The Malay/Melanau are mainly Malay. One-third of the Dayak are Iban, the Kayan and Kenyah composing the other two-thirds. The Foochow are the most numerous Chinese dialect group and are the business rivals of the Hokkien, even though the latter are somewhat fewer in number.

Fifth Division

Limbang	Those listed as Malay/Melanau are Brunei Malay and Kedayan. The Dayak are Iban and Bisaya. Throughout the fifth division the Hokkien are commercially and numerically the predominant dialect group. There are also some Hakka and Cantonese, a growing colony of Foochow, and representation from most of the other dialect groups.
Lawas	The Malay/Melanau are nearly all Malay, with a few Kedayan. Most of the Dayak are Sarawak Murut (Tagal) —not to be confused with the Murut of Sabah, who are ethnically distinct.

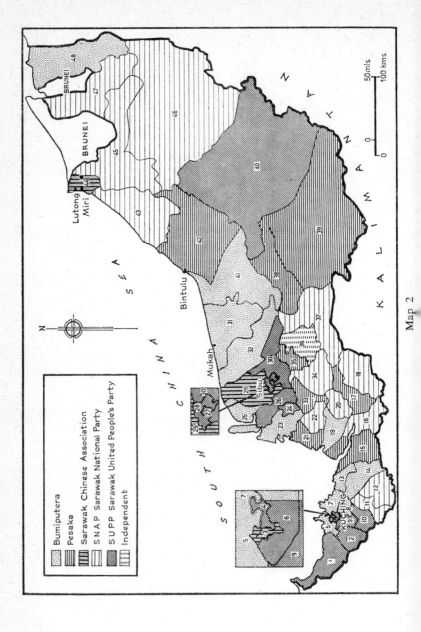

Map 2

In very general terms one may characterize the election results as having established that the Chinese supported SUPP, Malays backed PANAS, Melanaus BARJASA, Ibans SNAP and PESAKA, Land Dayaks distributed their favours widely, with PANAS and SUPP picking up the greater part, and the other indigenous ethnic groups voted for independent candidates.

Table 8

Coefficient of Correlation[a] Between Ethnic Composition
of Constituencies and Votes Cast for Each
Political Party: 1963

Ethnic Composition of Constituencies	Votes for Each Political Party		
	SUPP	PANAS	Alliance
Malay/Melanau	—0.28	0.74	—0.47
Dayak	—0.47	—0.37	0.70
Chinese	0.91	—0.28	—0.46

a. The measure employed in the Personian (product moment) coefficient of correlation, which prescribes the strength of association between the two variables. The coefficient ranges from $+1.00$ (perfect positive correlation) to $—1.00$ (perfect negative correlation), with the value of 0.00 inferring the absence of any association.

The strongest positive correlations were between: (1) Chinese voters and support for SUPP. A very strong 0.97 coefficient was found in the urban districts and a somewhat weaker 0.82 in the rural areas. (2) Muslim voters and support for PANAS. This was strongest in the three urban centres: Kuching, Sibu and Miri. In those three towns a significant positive correlation (0.64) was also found between Muslim voters and Alliance support. Elsewhere (in the rural districts) that relationship was reversed and became a negative (—0.51) coefficient. (3) Dayak voters and support for the Alliance.

Moderately strong negative relationships exist (especially in the urban districts) between SUPP and the Malays, Melanaus and Dayaks, and between the Alliance and Chinese.

A close scrutiny of the figures for each district permits separation of the Malay voters from the Melanau and of the Iban from other Dayak groups, and an examination of the many exceptions to the broad overall pattern are shown in Table 9.

The share of votes received by PANAS was markedly higher than the proportion of Malays in four districts: upper Sadong and Bau districts where PANAS attracted substantial numbers of Land Dayak votes, the lower Sadong district where PANAS received most of the Iban votes, and the Bintulu district where the Melanau tended to back PANAS

On the other hand PANAS made no inroads amongst the Brunei-oriented Malays of the fifth division, and their votes went to BARJASA and the independent candidates. PANAS also lost a good part of the Malay vote in

Table 9

The 1963 PANAS Vote and Malay Electors: The Proportion and Rank
Order of Each for the 24 Districts of Sarawak

District	Proportion of votes cast for PANAS (rank)		Proportion of electors who are Malay (and rank order of that %)[a]	
	%		%	
Lower Sadong	70	1	55.5	1
Kuching Rural	39	2	43	4
Saribas	30.5	3	42.5	5
Lundu	30	4	35.9	6
Upper Sadong	26.5	5	8.9	12
Bintulu	20.9	6	8	13
Miri	18.2	7	30	8
Batang Lupar	18	8	16.5	11
Kuching Municipal	15.5	9	26.5	9
Bau	13.5	10	7	15
Kalaka	10.5	11	30	7
Sibu Urban	5.5	12	25	10
Binatang	4.5	13	4	18
Sarikei	3	14	7	14
Kanowit	0.5	15	0.5	21
Lawas	—		53	2
Limbang	—		49	3
Baram	—		5.5	16
Sibu Rural	—		4	17
Lubok Antu	—		1	19
Kapit	—		0.5	20
Mukah	—		—	
Subis	—		—	
Matu-Daro	—		—	

a. The Melanau have been excluded from the Malay category, thus as we
   move into the third division the proportion will be much smaller than
   that of the Malay/Melanau total in Table 7.

the Kalaka and Saribas districts of the second division. PANAS only
received little more than one-fifth of the Malay vote in the Sibu district.
Its loss there was not simply a function of the urban environment, but
was also attributable to a Sibu Malay leadership that had historically
rivalled the Kuching PANAS Malay aristocratic leaders. Thus the Sibu
aristocracy threw its weight behind the rival party, BARJASA. Urbanized
Malays, including those of Kuching and Miri towns, tended to support
BARJASA in much greater numbers than did the rural Malays. PANAS thus
became the party whose core base of support was the rural Malays of

the first and second divisions—except for the Kalaka district, which was influenced more from Sibu than Kuching. The party garnered important additional backing from Land Dayaks and Iban of the first division, Melanau of the Bintulu district, and more than half of the urban Malays of Kuching and Miri. As the party of the Kuching Abangs it commanded respect amongst those who had traditionally looked to the Abangs as leaders.

There is a strong correlation between voter support for SUPP and the Chinese proportion of the electorate, though in most cases SUPP received a lower proportion of votes than warranted by the proportion of Chinese residing in the electorate. This was most striking in the Kuching, Sibu and Miri urban districts and in the Sarikei and Sibu rural districts where

Table 10

The 1963 SUPP Vote and Chinese Electors: The Proportion and
Rank Order of Each for the 24 Districts of Sarawak

District	Proportion of votes cast for SUPP (rank)		Proportion of electors who are Chinese (and rank order of that %)	
	%		%	
Sibu Urban	55.5	1	73.5	1
Kuching Municipal	53	2	71	2
Binatang	42	3	47.5	6
Miri	42	4	55	3
Bau	40	5	34.5	7
Sarikei	38	6	51.5	4
Sibu Rural	32.5	7	50.5	5
Kuching Rural	30.5	8	34.5	8
Lubok Antu	23	9	9	18
Lundu	21.5	10	22.5	9
Kapit	17.5	11	3.5	24
Upper Sadong	17	12	13.5	10
Lower Sadong	12	13	10	16
Kanowit	10	14	11	12
Subis	10	15	12	11
Batang Lupar	10	16	10.5	15
Kalaka	9	17	6	23
Bintulu	8.5	18	9	19
Saribas	5.5	19	7.5	22
Matu-Daro	3.5	20	7.5	21
Lawas	—		11	14
Baram	—		11	13
Limbang	—		9.5	17
Mukah	—		8	20

SUPP 'lost' from 13 per cent to 18 per cent of the Chinese voters, probably more. Yet these were the districts where Chinese were in an absolute majority, and a split in Chinese votes was a luxury that could be afforded, for SUPP still gained control of each of those councils. The Alliance component, SCA, was the beneficiary in the first four of those districts, and independents picked up the 18 per cent residual Chinese support in the Sibu rural district.

SUPP gained quite significant Dayak support in three districts. In the Kapit district more than 80 per cent of all SUPP votes were cast by native voters, in Lubok Antu the figure was in excess of 60 per cent and in Bau that proportion was around 10 per cent. (a) In the Lubok Antu district a small community of former Hakka Chinese goldminers, who arrived there in the last century, have intermarried extensively with Dayak farmers. The history of close Iban-Chinese relations facilitated SUPP propagandizing in the district and has created latter-day security problems for the government. This is the type of problem which led Indonesian military authorities to instigate Dayak attacks upon Chinese settlers in adjacent areas of Indonesian Kalimantan, so as to clear the Chinese from the area and to destroy the existing patterns of close relationships. (b) The SUPP party chairman, Ong Kee Hui, has worked steadily and effectively to build up a grass roots native based party organization in the Kapit district. The first 'all-native' SUPP branch has been established in that district. Ong Kee Hui had served as an agricultural officer in Kapit before the war and his familiarity with the people facilitated contact with the Iban in general and the Kayan of Belaga sub-district in particular. (c) In the Bau district the Land Dayak voters distributed their ballots amongst candidates of all the major parties, and there has been a fair amount of spatial intermingling between the Chinese and the Land Dayak—which facilitates SUPP contacts.

The solid bulk of Alliance votes came from Iban areas, though in nearly all districts where Iban were strongly represented the Alliance vote was a good 10 per cent less than the Iban proportion of the population. The districts where the Alliance clearly received many votes from other than Iban were the three urban areas and Sarikei, where the Alliance components parties BARJASA and SCA polled relatively well. BARJASA also polled well amongst Melanau of the Matu-Daro district and Brunei Malays of the Lawas district. In addition BARJASA gained much support from the Land Dayak of the Bau and Kuching rural districts, and SNAP extended from its second division Iban base to win the allegiance of many Land Dayaks in the adjacent Upper Sadong district.

The Ibans generally supported PESAKA in the third division, and SNAP in the second and fourth divisions. In Lubok Antu district BARJASA captured majority Iban support, a state of affairs related to the existing antipathies between Ibans of the upper Lubok Antu district (Ulu Ai) and those of the Saribas district, antipathies which made it difficult for both groups to happily co-exist within any one party. Subsequently, once PESAKA established itself in the second division (1965), those who had supported BARJASA transferred their allegiance to PESAKA.

The support accorded to independent candidates is indicative of the absence of penetration by political parties. Recruitment to elective office independent of party is a politically significant fact, even though most independents did subsequently align themselves with one party or another. The label 'independent' did not invariably mean that the candidate did not belong to a party. He may well have simply been by-passed and another party member officially nominated for the seat. In Mukah district official party symbols and letters of accreditation were not on hand by the close of nominations, hence all candidates were declared to be independents. In some other areas candidates considered overt party affiliation a liability and did not broadcast their allegiance until after polling had been completed. But by and large, independents were independent of any one particular party.

Table 11

The 1963 Alliance Vote and Iban Electors: The Proportion and Rank Order of Each for the 24 Districts of Sarawak

District	Proportion of votes cast for Alliance (rank)		Proportion of electors who are Iban (and rank order of that %)	
	%		%	
Kapit	71	1	80	3
Kanowit	65	2	88	2
Lubok Antu	60.5	3	90	1
Batang Lupar	57	4	73	4
Kalaka	56	5	63.5	5
Bintulu	49	6	60	6
Matu-Daro	42.5	7	—	23
Lawas	42.5	8	2	20
Saribas	36.5	9	50	8
Binatang	35.5	10	36	11
Bau	33	11	—	24
Upper Sadong	32.5	12	7	17
Miri	30	13	6.5	18
Kuching Municipal	27	14	1	22
Sarikei	26	15	20	14
Sibu Urban	25	16	1.5	21
Sibu Rural	18	17	43	10
Kuching Rural	15.5	18	6	19
Lower Sadong	12	19	34.5	12
Subis	10	20	45.5	9
Lundu	7	21	14	16
Limbang	7	22	15	15
Baram	—		28	13
Mukah	—		53.5	7

The proportion of votes cast for independent candidates steadily rose as one moved eastward.

Table 12

Proportion of Total Votes Cast for Independents by Division: 1963

	Division				
	First	Second	Third	Fourth	Fifth
Percentage of vote cast for independent candidates	13	20	37	53	77

The vote for independents was quite low in the three urban districts: 5 per cent for Kuching Municipal, 10 per cent for Miri and 14 per cent for Sibu Urban district. The independent vote was uncharacteristically high in districts where the 'other indigenous' groups were statistically important. In this category are included all Dayak who are neither Iban nor Land Dayak. The 'other indigenous' groups (principally Kayan, Kenyah and Murut) seem to have almost entirely cast their support behind independent candidates. But independent candidates also received support from some of all strata, and their share of the vote is a reflection of the ineffectiveness of party proselytizing.

Table 13

The Independent Vote and Other Indigenous Electors: 1963

District	Proportion of votes cast for independent candidates	Proportion of electors who are 'other indigenous'
	%	%
Baram	100	60
Limbang	93	28
Lawas	58	36

The conventional wisdom of political science suggests that 'the more competitive the parties, the greater the likelihood of high rates of participation' (i.e. voting).[41] Applying that hypothesis to the Sarawak situation one might expect to find a positive relationship between voting for political parties and voting *per se*—that the more important political parties were in a given district (the greater their share of votes) the higher the rate of active political participation (voting). In fact there is no such relationship, positive or negative.

[41] Lester W. Milbrath, *Political Participation*, Rand McNally, Chicago 1965, p. 96.

Table 14

Voter Participation and the Independent Vote in the 24 Districts
(districts arranged in rank order)

		Voter turnout (% poll)	
		Highest 12 districts	Lowest 12 districts
% vote received by Independents	Highest 12 districts	6	6
	Lowest 12 districts	6	6

To what then does one attribute higher or lower turnout to vote? When the members of a population perceive their vote as of vital significance, then they will be highly motivated to cast their ballots. In order to achieve this, it is necessary that they be able to choose between clearly differentiated alternatives. If there are no alternatives presented, the converse then applies and voter turnout is likely to be significantly lower.

The four districts where voter turnout was lowest (between 48 per cent and 64 per cent of all eligible electors voting) had one feature in common. Each was composed of an important Iban *and* an important Malay/Melanau component, and none had significant (more than 12 per cent) Chinese representation. By important we mean that both the Iban and the Malay/Melanau component exceeded 40 per cent, except in one district where the Melanau accounted for 23 per cent of the electorate.[42] Voter turnout was highest in the districts where Chinese were well represented and lowest where the mix was Iban with Malay/Melanau. Why was this the case? The 1963 election was a crisis election, the crisis being the independence of Sarawak as a component part of Malaysia. The broad political pattern that emerged was: Malay/Melanau active support for Malaysia, expressed through PANAS and the Alliance; Chinese organized opposition to the plan, expressed almost entirely through SUPP; Dayak uncertainty, but with their established leadership committed to Malaysia and aligned within the Alliance.

Widespread Dayak support was perceived as numerically critical, and SUPP on the one hand, and the Alliance and PANAS on the other, worked steadily to win Dayak votes. SUPP access to the Dayaks appears to have been precluded and Dayak support to have been pre-empted by the pro-Malaysia parties in those Districts where both the Iban and the Malay/

---

[42] Alternatively, if we take the ten districts where voter turnout was less than 70%, this remains the predominant pattern in seven of those districts, though in one the Dayak are not Iban but are a mixture of Murut and other indigenous groups. Of the remaining three districts with a low turnout one is overwhelmingly Iban, another is Kayan, Kenyah and Iban, and only one has a combination of Chinese and Land Dayak.

Melanau dwell in important numbers. Thus the political relaxation, or apathy as measured by voter turnout, of those mixed areas was due to the relative absence of SUPP opposition. For those districts 1963 was not a crisis election.[4r] In all other districts, the stronger the SUPP challenge the higher the voter participation tended to be.[44] This was patently true for seven of the nine districts which had the highest voter turnout. In summary form all districts can thus be classified as in Table 15.

Table 15

Voter Participation and the SUPP Vote in the 24 Districts: 1963
(districts arranged in rank order)

| | | Voter turnout (% poll) | |
		Highest 12 districts	Lowest 12 districts
SUPP vote (%)	Highest 12 districts	9	3
	Lowest 12 districts	3	9

Thus the high stimulus to vote was contingent upon the challenge of SUPP which provided a stark alternative focusing upon the Malaysia question. In those districts the marginal value of a vote was perceived as quite high, and the other party organizations then worked equally hard to win support.

[43] Perhaps the political relaxation in those areas was shared by Colonial officials who may have been somewhat less energetic in urging those opposed to SUPP to exercise their right to vote.

[44] Erik Allardt and Kettil Bruun found that in Finland a strong challenge from the Communist party in a constituency tended to increase voter turnout significantly. See their 'Characteristics of the Finnish Non-voter', *Transactions of the Westermarck Society,* III, pp. 55-76.
   One of the districts which is recorded as having a high SUPP vote and low turnout is Kapit, but as the rank order is 14 and 11 respectively, the difference is not significant. However the difference is significant for two other districts, Bau and Miri, and there is no immediate explanation for the low voting in those areas.
   One of the three districts where SUPP received a low vote but there was a high voter turnout, Kanowit, is hardly statistically significant. There is a difference in rank order of only four, and that district had a large number of uncontested seats. In the Matu-Daro district almost half of all seats were filled without contest, so although there was a high turnout for the contested seats so many other seats were decided without voting that for this district one must be careful in using voter turnout as an index of political participation. The other district where voter participation was relatively much higher than the SUPP vote would have led us to expect was Kalaka. That district was on the borderline between the PANAS and BARJASA spheres of prime influence, and there was close competition between those two parties for votes. In addition, five unauthorized SNAP members, who had not received official Alliance backing, stood as candidates.

The translation of votes into councillors was of particular interest. The election results left the Alliance party with a plurality of votes and elected councillors, but far from a majority of either. The average number (arithmetic mean) of votes taken to elect a councillor for each party over the whole state was as follows in Table 16.

Table 16

Average Number of Votes per Councillor Elected by Party: 1963

	SUPP	PANAS	Alliance	Inde-pendent	Total
Number of councillors	115	59	138	117	429
Number of votes received	46,776	31,210	74,878	66,252	219,126
Average number of votes per councillor elected	407	528	542	567	511

Thus at this stage SUPP had a much greater number of councillors elected than was warranted by the proportion of votes received by the party throughout the state. At the other extreme independents were markedly under-represented, but that was to be expected for in many electorates various independent candidates were nominated by close acquaintances and small living units. Each of the political parties at least only nominated one candidate for a vacant seat.

A more detailed analysis by division (Table 17) demonstrates that over-representation of SUPP councillors, in relation to votes polled, was

Table 17

Proportion of Votes Polled and Councillors Elected by Division of Sarawak: 1963

Political Party	Division of Sarawak					Total
	First	Second	Third	Fourth	Fifth	
SUPP						
% vote	31.5	10.6	23.0	14.2	—	21.4
% councillors	41.4	11.1	31.1	20.6	—	26.8
PANAS						
% vote	32.8	17.2	1.2	10.5	—	14.3
% councillors	33.6	19.4	0.7	7.9	—	13.8
Alliance						
% vote	22.9	52.0	39.0	22.4	23.2	34.2
% councillors	16.4	55.6	37.8	25.4	23.3	32.2
Independents						
% vote	13.0	20.1	36.8	53.0	76.7	30.2
% councillors	8.6	13.9	30.4	46.0	76.7	27.2

Table 18

Councillors Elected June 1963, Classified According to their
Formal Party Allegiance

District Council	All councillors elected					Alliance councillors by their component party			
	Total	SUPP	PANAS	Indep	All'ce	BARJ	SNAP	PES	SCA
Lundu	12	2	5	2	3	—	3	—	—
Bau	16	7	1	2	6	5	1	—	—
Kuching Munic.	27	21	6	—	—	—	—	—	—
Kuching Rural	34	14	15	3	2	2	—	—	—
Upper Sadong	15	2	4	3	6	—	5	—	1
Lower Sadong	12	2	8	—	2	—	2	—	—
1st Division	116	48	39	10	19	7	11	—	1
Batang Lupar	19	1	5	2	11	—	11	—	—
Lubok Antu	15	4	—	2	9	9	—	—	—
Saribas	20	2	7	2	9	1	8	—	—
Kalaka	18	1	2	4	11	4	7	—	—
2nd Division	72	8	14	10	40	14	26	—	—
Sarikei	17	8	1	7	1	—	—	1	—
Binatang	15	7	—	1	7	2	—	5	—
Matu-Daro	13	1	—	5	7	6	—	1	—
Mukah	19	—	—	19	—	—	—	—	—
Sibu Rural	22	11	—	7	4	1	—	3	—
Sibu Urban	21	16	—	1	4	3	—	1	—
Kanowit	24	3	—	5	16	—	—	16	—
Kapit	17	—	—	—	17	—	—	15	2
3rd Division	148	46	1	45	56	12	—	42	2
Bintulu	14	2	3	1	8	1	6	1	—
Subis	13	1	—	10	2	—	2	—	—
Miri	19	10	2	1	6	4	2	—	—
Baram	17	—	—	17	—	—	—	—	—
4th Division	63	13	5	29	16	5	10	1	—
Limbang	15	—	—	14	1	—	1	—	—
Lawas	15	—	—	9	6	6	—	—	—
5th Division	30	—	—	23	7	6	1	—	—
Total for Sarawak	429	115	59	117	138	44	48	43	3

Table 19

Distribution of all Councillors July 1963 According to the Parties they
Supported, with the Backing of Independents

District Council	Disposition of all councillors					Alliance component parties			
	Total	SUPP	PANAS	Indep	All'ce	BARJ	SNAP	PES	SCA
Lundu	12	3	6	—	3	—	3	—	—
Bau	16	7	2	—	7	6	1	—	—
Kuching Munic.	27	21	6	—	—	—	—	—	—
Kuching Rural	34	15	16	—	3	3	—	—	—
Upper Sadong	15	2	5	2	6	—	5	—	1
Lower Sadong	12	2	8	—	2	—	2	—	—
1st Division	116	50	43	2	21	9	11	—	1
Batang Lupar	19	1	5	1	12	—	12	—	—
Lubok Antu	15	4	—	—	11	11	—	—	—
Saribas	20	2	7	1	11	2	9	—	—
Kalaka	18	1	2	1	14	4	9	1	—
2nd Division	72	8	14	2	48	17	30	1	—
Sarikei	17	10	1	1	5	3	—	2	—
Binatang	15	7	—	—	8	2	—	6	—
Matu-Daro	13	1	—	2	10	9	—	1	—
Mukah	19	—	—	2	17	7	9	—	1
Sibu Rural	22	12	—	1	9	2	—	6	1
Sibu Urban	21	16	—	1	4	3	—	1	—
Kanowit	24	3	—	1	20	—	—	20	—
Kapit	17	—	—	—	17	—	—	15	2
3rd Division	148	49	1	8	90	26	9	51	4
Bintulu	14	2	3	—	9	1	7	1	—
Subis	13	2	—	1	10	5	5	—	—
Miri	19	10	2	1	6	4	2	—	—
Baram	17	2	—	3	12	—	4	8	—
4th Division	63	16	5	5	37	10	18	9	—
Limbang	15	—	—	8	7	3	4	—	—
Lawas	15	—	—	6	9	8	1	—	—
5th Division	30	—	—	14	16	11	5	—	—
Total for Sarawak	429	123	63	31	212	73	73	61	5

true in each division. PANAS was over-represented by its councillors in the first and second divisions, but under-represented in the third and fourth divisions, ending up with a 0.5 per cent under-representation. The Alliance was over-represented in the second, fourth and fifth divisions and under-represented elsewhere, ending up with a 2 per cent deficit when one relates councillors to votes. The Independents lost in every division except the fifth, where they just drew even.

The overall Alliance vote plurality was not transformed at the district council level into a higher proportion of seats, in fact quite the contrary applied.

The councillors who were elected and the party which nominated them for the election are listed in Table 18. Alliance councillors have also been identified by the Alliance component party to which they chose to adhere. This latter information was obtained initially from the Alliance headquarters and amended where necessary after discussion with the councillors themselves.

As outlined earlier there was a distinct geographic character to the voting, and it seems appropriate at this stage to look more closely at the support given to each of the Alliance component parties. PESAKA councillors were concentrated in the third division and SNAP in the second. SCA, though receiving many votes, was overwhelmed by SUPP and forfeited most of its significance as only three councillors were elected as its nominees. BARJASA suffered from the geographic dispersion of its areas of strong support—three main pockets located in three divisions of Sarawak.

Formation of the First Fully-Elected State Government

The final results of the district council election were declared during the week ending 24 June 1963. Neither the number of votes received, nor the total number of councillors elected, was the critical variable for the next stage of government building. The decisive factor was actual control of each district council as they were all to meet between 1 July and 5 July to elect their representatives to the next tier of elective government, the divisional advisory council. Each divisional advisory council would later meet to select from amongst themselves the members of the Council Negri, the state legislature. Figure 1 (p. 48) shows the representation elected by each district council to the divisional advisory council, and from the five divisional advisory councils to the Council Negri.

The configuration within district councils was such that independent councillors could tip the balance in exactly half of all the district councils, and thus determine what party would control the selection of representatives to the divisional advisory councils. The Alliance parties were the prime beneficiaries of independent support, for of the 117 independent councillors 74 aligned with the Alliance, 4 with PANAS and 8 with SUPP. (See Table 19, p. 71.) This re-alignment was quite comprehensible in terms of shared characteristics, for as a group the independent councillors resembled those of the Alliance much more closely than they resembled the PANAS or SUPP councillors. The pre-eminent characteristics of the elected councillors of each major party are expressed in Figure 2, a diagram that graphically underlines the exclusive nature of the characteristics of SUPP nominees and the close resemblance between independent members and the Alliance councillors.

The independent councillors throughout the state also tended to align with the party that was dominant in their particular district. Two-thirds of the independents who joined parties in the first division linked with PANAS and SUPP, the leading parties in that division. Throughout all other divisions the Alliance component party which had initially elected the most councillors obtained preponderant support from the majority of those independents who aligned with one party or another. The only two special cases were the Mukah and Baram districts, where all councillors elected were formally independents. In Mukah more independents joined SNAP than any other party, in contrast to the predominant position of PESAKA elsewhere in the third division. The pattern was reversed in the Baram district, with PESAKA the principal beneficiary of independent support, in contrast to SNAP-Alliance pre-dominance elsewhere in the fourth division.

A vigorous scramble ensued to win the allegiance of several crucially placed independent members, with all types of inducements offered to win their support. The Alliance, with its powerful governmental and private backers, had rather more largesse to spread than did SUPP or PANAS and was conspicuously more successful in winning their alle-giance. Once aligned with a party the politics of individual independents ceased to be of consequence, and the focus shifted to manoeuvring between parties.

Various coalitions were mooted at that time, as each party sought to improve its own position. After failing to wean SNAP from the Alliance fold,[45] PANAS joined SUPP in a temporary coalition of convenience (on 1 July 1963). This coalition was an effort to win a majority of seats in the Council Negri through control of the first and third divisional advisory councils, or at the very least to avoid total parliamentary oblivion for either party.

Both SUPP and PANAS had polled very well throughout the first division and promised to be quite evenly matched in the divisional advisory council. The critical district council was the Kuching Rural District Council which selected eight representatives to the divisional advisory council. In the Kuching Rural District Council were three independents, and each aligned himself with one of the major parties, leaving the respective party strengths as PANAS 16, SUPP 15 and Alliance

---

[45] Ever since PANAS withdrew from the Alliance it had sought to take SNAP with it, and shortly before polling was due to commence SNAP had sought to call an Alliance meeting, where it was about to announce its withdrawal from the Alliance—according to opposing sources. That meeting was not held. The secretary-general of SNAP was quite uncertain of his own position within the second divisional advisory council, and thus also hesitated to risk a break from the Alliance immediately after the election results were known.

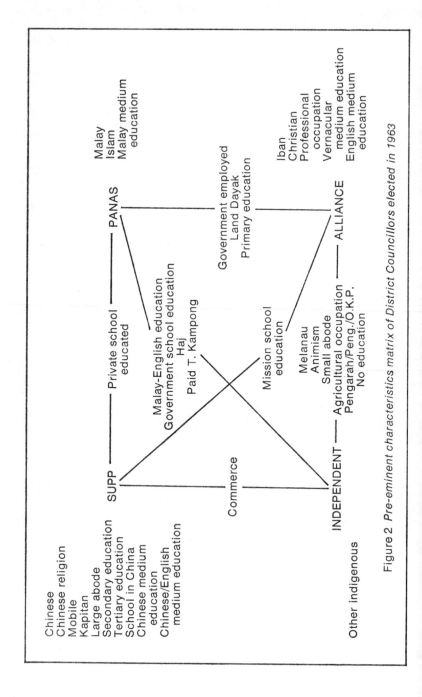

Figure 2 Pre-eminent characteristics matrix of District Councillors elected in 1963

3. This time the Alliance could tip the balance either way and while the SCA wished the Alliance councillors to vote for PANAS, many BARJASA members prevailed upon them to vote for SUPP and thus be rid of PANAS once and for all. The three Alliance members, each of whom belonged to BARJASA, were furtively hidden in order that they might not be wooed by PANAS. Leaders of PANAS asked why, if the three Alliance councillors were going to support PANAS, BARJASA should have taken the trouble to hide them. PANAS leaders suggested that

> There are indications that the BARJASA is trying to stop PANAS so that its councillors will not be represented in the Council Negri. People can say that BARJASA has an attitude "it is better to let the bone become white than to let the eyes become white".[46]

PANAS feared that BARJASA would prefer to have no Malay representation than to have councillors elected who belonged to PANAS. That was the reason PANAS agreed to form a working coalition with SUPP.

Consequent upon their agreement SUPP and PANAS easily dominated the first divisional advisory council, but were at a disadvantage in the third divisional advisory council. Although SUPP could deliver ten votes from the Sibu Urban[47] and Rural councils and from Sarikei, the Alliance could also count on a certain ten votes from Kanowit, Kapit and Matu-Daro. The remaining two councils were Mukah (with four DAC votes), all of whose members were nominally independent though leaning toward the Alliance, and Binatang (three DAC votes) where the Alliance and SUPP ran neck and neck (seven councillors each) with a sole independent member holding the balance and able to determine all of that council's representation to the Third Divisional Advisory Council. SUPP and PANAS were fairly sure that *if* they could only capture the allegiance of that Binatang independent or induce an Alliance councillor from Binatang to defect, then obtaining the vote of one independent from Mukah would be little more than a formality. For at that stage SUPP and PANAS would together have had a clear majority in the Council Negri. The only snag to this plan was that before the sun rose on the morning after the results were announced the chairman of SCA had dispatched Ting Tun Ming[48] to Binatang with

---

[46] *Utusan Sarawak*, 6 and 9 July 1963. The old proverb 'Dari pada perputih mata, eloklah perputih tulang' means that it is better to die than to continue yearning for something (unattainable).

[47] The Sidu Urban District Council was significantly under-represented on the third divisional advisory council. It was assigned only two seats, which meant that the votes of its population were significantly undervalued compared with neighbouring districts two of which, Sarikei and Binatang, had smaller populations but one more representative. As it happened this under-representation was a crucial block to SUPP's aspiration to govern the state.

[48] Ting Tung Ming was a popular young SCA Foochow who came within a handful of votes of election to the SUPP dominated Sibu Urban District Council. He subsequently was appointed political secretary to the Chief Minister, a position of considerable influence and responsibility. But the flow of influence is usually reciprocal and in time he came to be personally identified rather more with SNAP than with his old party, SCA. He was replaced by Charles Ingka (an Iban) when he left to study law in the U.K.

instructions to take the independent member and all Alliance councillors on a grand tour of Malaya. There they were fêted, safely beyond the reach of an anguished SUPP and PANAS. They returned together under the watchful eyes of Alliance officials, cleared customs and were taken to the decisive meeting of the Binatang District Council without even being allowed to speak with their waiting families. Though denied voter support the leadership of SCA did not lack political acumen.

Though the PANAS-SUPP coalition failed in its aim to capture control of the state government it did preserve the representative character of the Council Negri. Without this coalition the legislature would have been severely unbalanced. For had PANAS nominated its councillors for all of the ten first division seats, then the Council Negri would have had no elected Chinese from any of the major towns of Sarawak. Alternatively, had SUPP nominated its members for the ten first division seats, the whole Malay community would have gone unrepresented, for the Alliance did not include any Malays amongst its nominees to the Council Negri. To deny representation completely to either the Malay or the Chinese community would have augured ill for the future of elective government.

Both parties were quick to play down any effects that the coalition might have upon their respective ideological positions and adroitly sidestepped the Malaysia question by agreeing that the issue

> be determined by a referendum conducted by the United Nations and . . . that the referendum should be held before the implementation of Malaysia.[49]

This compromise aroused some anger within the Malay community, and more than a hundred posters appeared in Kuching, some of which read:

> History repeats itself—in July 1, 1946 Malays were sold to the British, and now in July 1, 1963 Malays were sold to the Chinese![50]

Though the Datu Bandar attributed the posters to BARJASA and its Malayan advisors, PANAS was embarrassed by the appearance of having aligned itself too closely with SUPP. The PANAS Chairman who had always been proud of his leading role as a proponent of Malaysia, took the first opportunity to reiterate his party's support for the earliest possible formation of Malaysia, and dropped his request for a prior referendum. He clarified his position by stating that the coalition was a means by which each party could secure seats in the Council Negri, and each of the two parties was at liberty to carry out its own policy.[51]

A month after the formation of Malaysia, the Datu Bandar renewed his efforts to transform PANAS into a branch of UMNO, an act that resuscitated his credentials as a Malay leader and caused a number of Chinese and other members to resign from the party for fear that it would in

49 *Sarawak Tribune,* 2 July 1963.
50 Ibid., 6 July 1963.
51 Ibid., 16 August 1963.

future have a racially-exclusive orientation.[52] The Prime Minister appointed the Datu Bandar a Minister-without-Portfolio in the federal cabinet, even though he was still in the opposition and very much at odds with the Malay leadership of the Sarawak Alliance. But the Datu Bandar died before being able to bring his strategy to fruition.[53] The leadership of PANAS was then assumed by his brother, Abang Othman, who lacked the overpowering drive of the Datu Bandar.

Once it became apparent that the Alliance would form the first fully-elected state government, the configuration within that Alliance became of rather more than academic interest. As outlined above the SCA had been routed, and BARJASA suffered the misfortune of having its supporters spread too thinly throughout each of the five divisions. The councils it did control were numerically among the least significant. The leaders of BARJASA also mistakenly had stood in the Kuching district, where they had been roundly defeated by either PANAS or SUPP. Thus BARJASA though having widespread support, suffered from these twin disadvantages (broad support thinly spread and defeat of top party leaders), liabilities that did not hinder either PESAKA or SNAP.

The second divisional advisory council (DAC) controlled by SNAP did nominate a BARJASA Iban to the Council Negri. In the third divisional advisory council representation remained so close that the dominant PESAKA needed to placate each of the Alliance component parties to preclude any defections. Thus from the third DAC came seven PESAKA, two BARJASA, one SNAP and one SCA nominee to sit in the Council Negri.

The tables were turned on SNAP in the fourth DAC where BARJASA joined with PESAKA and they split the nominations to Council Negri in the ratio 1:2, excluding SNAP completely, even though the latter could count eighteen supporters to BARJASA's ten and PESAKA's nine.

The final breakdown of Alliance Council Negri members was eleven PESAKA, six SNAP, five BARJASA and one SCA. Under the constitutional amendments promulgated in early 1963 the Chief Minister designate was empowered to nominate to the Council Negri three extra members of his own choosing. The Alliance chose to bolster the representation of its weakest link (SCA)[54] by two members, and nominated a further BARJASA member who had particularly good educational qualifications.

The remaining higher level of elective government were the twenty-four members of the federal Parliament, who were selected by the Council Negri though not necessarily from amongst themselves. Members of Parliament were nominated in numbers to accord with the proportion of seats held by each party in the Council Negri, after inclusion

[52] Three executive members of PANAS resigned from the party 'as there is every possibility that PANAS would become a branch of UMNO in Sarawak . . . UMNO of Malaya was strictly racial and there would be no place for Chinese members in the party'. Ibid., 23 October 1963. One of the three was Leong Ho Yuen, a PANAS member of the Council Negri.

[53] The Datu Bandar died on 20 January 1964. He had been appointed a federal minister earlier in that month.

[54] The chairman of SCA, whose party had underwritten PESAKA's campaigning costs, was in a very influential position with Temenggong Jugah of PESAKA.

of the three nominated members and excluding independents, who were not allowed to choose their representatives to the Federal Parliament. This was an interim procedure pending the introduction of direct elections in Sarawak at the end of the decade. The nominations to federal Parliament were an attractive way to provide rewards for the party faithful, particularly for those (Alliance) members who had not quite made their way up the elective ladder to the Council Negri. In fact half of the members of Parliament were not Council Negri members, the Alliance nominating ten of those twelve. All the BARJASA nominees were from outside the Council Negri, as were two of the three nominated by SCA. SNAP introduced two new faces and PESAKA only one.

Table 20 gives in proportionate form the relative strength of each party's representation at the various levels of elective government.

Table 20

Party Representation at Each Level of Government: 1963

Level of Government (and date)	SUPP	PANAS	BARJASA	SNAP	PESAKA	SCA	Indepen-dents
				(percentages)			
Member of Parliament	12.5	12.5	20.8	16.7	25.0	12.5	—
Council Negri	12.8	12.8	15.4	17.9	28.2	7.7	5.2
Divisional Advisory Council	23.0	13.0	13.0	23.0	16.0	1.0	11.0
District Council—July	28.7	14.7	17.1	17.1	14.3	1.2	7.0
District Council—June	27.0	13.8	10.3	11.2	10.0	0.7	27.0
Votes cast (April-June)	21.4	14.3		34.2			30.2

With the Alliance electoral victory the two groups who had the most legislative experience and highest educational qualifications, the PANAS Malays and the SUPP Chinese, were consigned to the opposition benches. Within the Alliance government Dayaks were numerically dominant, but they leaned heavily upon British expatriate and Chinese advice.

The British colonial officers at first had advocated a 'grand coalition' including the Alliance, PANAS and SUPP. This was anathema to the Malayan government, BARJASA and SCA, who were shocked by suggestions that under such an arrangement Ong Kee Hui, the SUPP chairman, might be Chief Minister. Some Malayans suggested instead Abdul

Rahman bin Ya'kub, a BARJASA leader even though he had been defeated in his local ward.[55] But, given their predominant position the only real question was which Dayak would be Chief Minister. The final agreement was that the PESAKA leader, Temenggong Jugah, would be Governor (the formal Head of State) and the SNAP leader, Stephen Ningkan, would be Chief Minister.

Though mutually acceptable within Sarawak this agreement went beyond the competence of local powers. Under the London Agreement the first Sarawak Governor was to be appointed on the joint nomination of the British Queen and the Malayan Yang di-Pertuan Agong (King).[56] The Malayan Prime Minister believed that if a Dayak was to be Chief Minister a Malay should be Governor, and he refused to accept the nomination of Temenggong Jugah.[57] This minor constitutional crisis came to a head just nine days before Malaysia was formed. The rebuff generated strong resentment amongst Rejang river Dayaks, for this post was the key part of the price exacted for their support of the Alliance. SNAP already had three members in the Sarawak cabinet, one of whom was Chief Minister. The PESAKA leader was to be Head of State. The deadlock was resolved just two days before the inauguration of Malaysia with a distinguished local Malay being appointed Governor and Temenggong Jugah being appointed to the newly created office of Federal Minister for Sarawak Affairs.[58]

The new Chief Minister, Stephen Kalong Ningkan, chose to rely upon advice from two quarters: (1) the expatriate State Secretary and the Financial Secretary, who were both then *ex-officio* members of the Council Negri and the Supreme Council (the Cabinet); (2) the deputy chief minister James Wong of SNAP, and the political secretary to the chief minister, Ting Tung Ming of SCA. The BARJASA cabinet ministers found their capacity to influence government policy severely circum-

[55] *Strait Times,* 25 June 1963.
[56] Great Britain, *Malaysia Agreement,* Annex C (Constitution of Sarawak), Section 1 and 49. The first Governor was to serve for two years, after that he was to be appointed by the King (the Yang di-Pertuan Agong) 'after consultation with the Chief Minister' for a term of four years.
[57] The Tunku's honourable intent was demonstrated when in 1970 he cabled Abdul Rahman Ya'kub from London requesting him not to try to become Chief Minister because a Malay should not be both Chief Minister and Governor. (Interview with the Chief Minister, February 1972).
[58] *Sarawak Tribune,* 14 September 1963. The Temenggong was most upset by this Malayan veto and, according to one source, he was actually cut short on his way to broadcast that the whole plan to enter Malaysia was cancelled.
    The first Governor, Tun Abang Haji Openg bin Abang Sapiee, SMN, PNBS, OBE, was the last remaining standing member of the Council Negri. In 1940 he was appointed to that body to hold office as long as he occupied a post in the government service. Tun Openg had earlier been a native officer and magistrate and spoke Iban fluently. Though he voted against the Cession of Sarawak to Britain he was appointed to the Supreme Council (1951) and became president of the Majlis Islam Sarawak, a position that he retained until his appointment as Governor. Though an aristocrat he was commonly known for his humility among his people. He died in 1969.

scribed as they continually clashed with the SCA ministers and the expatriate officials. At that point in time the federal government was exerting no commensurate countervailing influence which might at least negate that of the expatriates. The development of this dynamic balance will be explored at length in the following chapter.

3

THE DEVELOPMENT OF POLITICS
1963-6

The development of politics since Sarawak entered Malaysia can be divided into two main periods:

1. Formal independence under British tutelage (September 1963-September 1966)
2. The Malaysianization of politics (September 1966-July 1970)

Our analysis of both periods will focus upon political crises, for that is the time when power relationships are most clearly evident. Close attention is thus paid to the ways in which such conflicts are mediated, arbitrated, suppressed or resolved.

The first phase was an interim stage in which power remained essentially in British hands. For the duration of that phase all the important government departments and the Administration were under the charge of expatriate officers.[1] With Sarawak taking the brunt of armed Indonesian attacks, British forces had assumed effective day-to-day control over the maintenance of security. This had many ramifications extending throughout the civilian sphere. Thus Indonesian confrontation not only facilitated the formation of Malaysia, it also served to prolong the British presence in Borneo. This was also the period when the new and rather inexperienced Sarawak Alliance leaders turned to their former expatriate rulers for benevolent tutelage in all political matters. The

---

[1] As late as May 1966 the top civil service posts in the following departments were occupied by European expatriate officers.
State government departments:
    The Administration—State Secretary
                     State Financial Secretary
                     Establishment officer
                     Resident, third division
                     Resident, fourth division,
    Permanent Secretary to the Ministries of Agriculture & Forestry, Lands & Mineral Resources, Communications & Works
    Director of Agriculture
    Conservator of Forests
Federal government departments in Sarawak:
    Police
    Information Service
    Education
    Judiciary (Chief Justice)
Expatriate officers were also in charge of an additional 14 technical departments, such as the Medical Department.

81

developments that altered the balance of Sarawak politics germinated throughout this initial phase, but did not blossom forth until after the termination of Indonesian confrontation—the critical factor that had for three years circumscribed the development of politics in a more distinctly Malayan/Malaysian direction.[2]

Following the 1963 elections and initial government formation (described above) the first Sarawak State cabinet (Supreme Council) constisted of the following members:

Stephen Kalong Ningkan (SNAP), Chief Minister, a second division Iban

James Wong Kim Ming (SNAP), Deputy Chief Minister, a fifth division Hakka Chinese

Abdul Taib bin Mahmud (BARJASA), Minister of Communications and Works, a first division Melanau

Dunstan Endawie anak Enchana (SNAP), Minister for Local Government, a second division Iban

Teo Kui Seng (SCA), Minister of Natural Resources, a first division Teochew Chinese

Awang Hipni bin Pengiran Annu (BARJASA), Minister of State, a third division Melanau

G. A. T. Shaw, State Secretary, a British expatriate officer

B. A. Hepburn, Financial Secretary, an expatriate officer (replaced in 1964 by J. Pike)

P. E. H. Pike, Attorney-General, a British expatriate officer

The Cabinet did not include any PESAKA Alliance members as PESAKA had agreed to nominate its leader Temenggong Jugah for the prestigious office of Governor whilst SNAP nominated the Chief Minister and a cabinet member. To the chagrin of BARJASA James Wong was initially included at British behest, for reasons of 'racial balance' so that there were two Dayak, two Muslims and two Chinese in the Cabinet. Shortly thereafter he decided to join SNAP. PESAKA placed great importance upon controlling the post of Governor, hitherto the ultimate seat of both formal and real power.[3]

Sarawak representation in the federal cabinet was of a distinctly different character to that of the state cabinet. The PESAKA chairman was a full cabinet minister and the BARJASA leader Abdul Rahman bin Ya'kub (a fourth division Melanau) was made Assistant-Minister for Justice and Rural Development. Top Sarawak representation at Kuala Lumpur was quite different from that which led the government in Kuching. At the federal capital the state's representation was provided

---

[2] In August 1966 Indonesia and Malaysia formally ended their undeclared war by Treaty. (*Sarawak Tribune*, 12 August 1966.) The formula was worked out in Bangkok in May 1966 and in fact from the beginning of 1966 fighting between Malaysian and Indonesian forces had steadily subsided.

[3] The leader of USNO in Sabah, Tun Mustapha, also made a similar misjudgment of the extent of real power that could be exercised by the Governor after independence. He had to extricate himself from that position in order eventually to become Chief Minister of Sabah, the real focus of state power.

by PESAKA and BARJASA, the two Alliance parties which wielded the least influence within the state government. The apparent reasons for this different alignment were: (a) Malayan Alliance leaders had worked quite closely with the BARJASA politicians against PANAS and SUPP, and had acquired a high regard for Abdul Rahman bin Ya'kub. They had supported the abortive attempt to nominate him as first Chief Minister. Instead he was appointed to the federal cabinet and came to play an important role in West Malaysian politics. (b) A new federal cabinet post, Minister for Sarawak Affairs, was especially created in order to placate Temenggong Jugah, following Kuala Lumpur's refusal to accept him as the first governor of Sarawak. Subsequently, when difficulties developed with Ningkan, the federal government came to appreciate that it shared with PESAKA a common desire to oust SNAP as the leading component party of the Sarawak Alliance. Thus both PESAKA and BARJASA came to be more closely linked politically with the West Malaysian Alliance leadership than were other Sarawak parties.

In the first state cabinet decision-making was a three-stage process. First, the Chief Minister would meet with Tony Shaw (the State secretary), John Pike (the Financial secretary) and Ting Tung Ming (the political secretary to the Chief Minister). The political implications of all technical matters were worked through. Then this core group would meet with the three other SNAP and SCA ministers. Finally, full Cabinet meetings would include the two BARJASA ministers and almost inevitably there would be a clash as the BARJASA ministers would be unable to sway the whole cabinet.[4] The situation proved particularly irksome to Abdul Taib bin Mahmud, who by virtue of his superior education expected to wield a good deal of influence. Instead he faced the continual humiliation of 'correction' by the expatriates as he and they sought to influence the less educated SNAP Iban members of the cabinet.

With the BARJASA minister by-passed, the government came to be primarily a British-influenced SNAP and SCA combination of Dayaks and Chinese. PESAKA, BARJASA and PANAS were thus relegated to the periphery. The Muslims, the third division Iban, and their federal supporters were far from the corridors of state power.

There is an important contrast between the core groups of the predominantly Iban parties, which had direct implications for the process of coalition-building. The principal ethnic conflict in the Saribas district (the home of SNAP) was between the Iban and the Malays. By contrast along the Rejang river (the home of PESAKA) the principal Iban conflicts were with the Chinese settlers and were derived from a basic economic clash concerning the question of land usage. The very name PESAKA is translated as 'rights' and the most important of those inherited rights was land. SNAP was willing to welcome Chinese members, something that PESAKA has never done. PESAKA remained exclusively Dayak until 1965,[5]

---

[4] This account is re-constructed from interviews with seven of the nine ministers involved. The interviews took place in 1964, 1967 and 1968.
[5] The PESAKA Constitution was not formally changed until 1966.

after which it was prepared to accept all groups except the Chinese. SNAP did not exclude any ethnic group from membership, but not until the second phase (1966+) did it attract Muslims and Chinese in important numbers.

The closest allies of Kuala Lumpur were hardly in a position to determine state policy, in fact they were for the time being in a politically marginal position in Kuching. This situation was of particular concern to the Islamic groups, who had looked forward to the advent of Malaysia in anticipation of considerable improvements in their position.

To remedy the situation efforts were initiated to establish a branch of the United Malay National Organisation (UMNO) in Sarawak. Tentatively the party was to be renamed the United Malaysian Native Organisation, to incorporate all native peoples within the party. The formation of a Sarawak branch would have a dual purpose, to unite all Muslims in one Sarawak organization, and to exert Muslim leadership over 'all we natives'.[6]

Shortly after the inauguration of Malaysia, Haji Ghazali Jawi arrived to determine whether UMNO should open branches in the state or link directly with the local political parties.[7] At the conclusion of his visit officials of PANAS and BARJASA intimated that 'the gap between them is almost closed and that the Malay community in Sarawak will again be a solid bloc'.[8] Later, in October 1963, three executive members of PANAS (two Chinese and one Malay) resigned 'as there is every possibility that PANAS would become a branch of UMNO in Sarawak. . . . UMNO of Malaya was strictly racial and there would be no place for Chinese in the party'.[9]

The active role of Kuala Lumpur was hardly disguised. The Datu Bandar, upon his return from there announced the formation of UMNO, as did the then Assistant Federal Minister for Rural Development, Dato Sardon, Chairman of the UMNO Youth Section.[10]

The outcome was by no means as certain or popular as these leaders had thought. Despite assertions to the contrary, UMNO (Sarawak) had not actually come into being. In the wake of the manoeuvring non-Malay members of PANAS resigned and the Chief Minister (Stephen Ningkan) was extremely annoyed that a federal cabinet minister should

---

[6] BARJASA leaders were confident that they would in due course gain Dayak support. They regarded their estrangement from the Dayaks as the product of British 'divide and rule' policies.

[7] Haji Mohd Ghazali bin Haji Jawi was the UMNO and Alliance leader of Perak state. Following the 1964 elections he was appointed Federal Minister of Agriculture and Co-operatives. See *Sarawak by the Week,* Week No. 40, 1963.

[8] *Sarawak Tribune,* 7 October 1963.

[9] Ibid., 23 October 1963. Leong Ho Yuen, a PANAS member of the Council Negri, was speaking here on behalf of his colleagues who had resigned.

[10] Ibid., 17 and 18 January and 10 March 1964. Abdul Rahman Ya'kub (as an assistant federal minister) then played a strategic role working directly under Tun Abdul Razak in the formulation and implementation of development schemes. He was also chief executive secretary to the Malayan election committee during the 1964 campaign.

visit his state, hold consultations with a view to shaping domestic alignments within the Sarawak Alliance, and not even bother to meet him, the leading figure of that Alliance.

In April 1964 those who had left PANAS together with a few other politicians who had resigned from the other parties, formed party MACHINDA. It was an inter-racial party (MA = Malays, CHIN = Chinese, DA = Dayaks) composed of an assortment of malcontents and it lacked any real coherence. MACHINDA did establish four branches, two composed of coastal Malays, one of Land Dayaks and the other of Iban in the Saratok district. The party gained some national attention as an active participant in the PAP sponsored Malaysia Solidarity Convention meeting in Singapore. But with the separation of Singapore from Malaysia that convention was shortlived. Personal differences soon asserted themselves and within two years both the secretary and chairman of MACHINDA had resigned from the party.[11] The party was eclipsed by the events of 1966 and late that year its second secretary led a group of members to join PESAKA. MACHINDA was formally dissolved in early April 1967, with the remaining Land Dayak members joining SNAP.

In October 1964 the UMNO General Assembly decided to discourage a simple merger of PANAS and BARJASA into a branch of UMNO in favour of a new party within the Sarawak Alliance, to be formed early in 1965.[12] This was a shrewd assessment as even a united Malay party, in the absence of strong support from non-Muslims, has little chance of

[11] Four very strong and conflicting personalities filled the top echelons of MACHINDA. Michael Buma was a fiery Saribas Iban whose personal feud with Ningkan kept him from joining SNAP or accepting a position on the Public Service Commission. He was MACHINDA's first chairman.

Leong Ho Yuen was elected a PANAS Council Negri member, but resigned from that party as soon as a merger with UMNO was seriously considered. He was the proprietor of the *Vanguard,* a newspaper with separate Chinese and English editions and which has since published with an inserted Malay language page. He was vice-chairman of MACHINDA throughout its existence.

Yeo Cheng Hoe was a particularly active Kuching Chinese who had held office in a large number of educational and public service activities. He had earlier resigned from SUPP for fear that the party was coming under militant control. Yeo was Secretary-General of MACHINDA until his resignation in March 1966, after a clash with Leong.

Senawi bin Sulaiman had formerly been an active PANAS Central Committee member, and was an astute reporter employed by the *Vanguard.* With the departure of Yeo he assumed the role of MACHINDA's secretary-general.

For MACHINDA's formation and party manifesto see *Sarawak Tribune,* 19 February, 18 April and 2 September 1964. For the notice of its formal dissolution see ibid., 12 April 1967. The *Tribune* reported that a major factor behind the party's formation was that its members were against the UMNO stepping into the country 'to safeguard the interest of a certain section of the people' (21 February 1964). 'Most of PANAS members who are strongly against the party being dissolved have resigned and joined Party MACHINDA' (17 April 1964). The new party opened its first branch at Kampong Rangawan in the former PANAS Malay stronghold of Lower Sadong.

[12] *Borneo Bulletin,* 10 October 1964, and *Sarawak Tribune,* 31 October 1964. Muslims form 25% of Sarawak's population.

dominating any elected Sarawak government. It could never play a role equivalent to that of UMNO (Malaya). To do that, it had to lead the natives.

The Land Bill Crisis of 1965

Shortly after a visit by the Federal Minister of Information (Inche Senu) to Kuching, the Muslim leaders acted.[13] The issue chosen was revision of the land zoning system. The proposed change would have permitted Chinese to purchase 'native land' and was the type of inflammatory issue that could be used skilfully to elicit non-Islamic native support.

The Brooke régime had provided every native with a plot of land, the sale of which was prohibited, and had also placed a strict limit on land aggregation. Hence the 'landlord problem' does not exist. Land is classified as mixed zone, native area, interior area, and reserved. Non-natives may not acquire or legally use any but that in mixed zones. Little more than 1,000 square miles of suitable land is owned by Chinese, less than 3 per cent of the total area or one-sixth of that used by a similar number of Iban for shifting cultivation. Thus the land available to the Chinese is patently inadequate for their needs in a country with no actual shortage of land. The present land system simply prevents it from being used effectively. The dilemma is that with their present farming operations (shifting cultivation) the native peoples also consider themselves short of land. The change envisaged in these land bills was in the short run of immediate benefit to the Chinese and could exacerbate the position of some natives by making the change to intensive agriculture imperative. A 'Land Committee', appointed by the colonial government, had earlier recommended recognition of existing customary rights as ownership and the abolition of land classification. Zoning would have been replaced by the safeguard that a Native could not dispose of his land without the consent of the Resident. The criteria for such permission were not defined and there was wide scope for corruption. The purpose of the Land Bills was to put into effect the principal recommendations of the Land Committee.[14]

The Bill was to be introduced at the May session of Council Negri. It was suddenly withdrawn. Two days later the 'Native Alliance, Sarawak' was formed, a coalition of BARJASA, PANAS and PESAKA. The two notable exclusions were SNAP and the SCA. SNAP was excluded, according to

[13] The Senu visit was in April 1965.
[14] See A. F. Porter, *Land Administration in Sarawak, an Account of the Development of Land Administration in Sarawak from the Rule of Rajah James Brooke to the Present Time (1841-1967)*, Government Printing Office, Kuching 1968; Sarawak, *Land Law and Adat, a Report by A. J. N. Richards*, Government Printing Office, Kuching 1961; and Sarawak, *Report of the Land Committee 1962*, Government Printing Office, Kuching 1963.

For the text of the following land bills: Land Acquisition, Land Adjudication, and Land (Native Dealings), see *Sarawak Government Gazette*, Part III, 12 February 1964, pp. 13-76; for State Lands and Registration Bill, see *Sarawak Government Gazette Extraordinary*, Part III, 11 March 1964. pp. 87-190.

Abdul Taib, because 'it was multi-racial and therefore not qualified to be in a native Alliance'.[15]

Taib envisioned Sarawak politics as re-structured on the Malayan pattern, that is, a dominant Islamic-led native party with a more or less subservient Chinese partner. The Land Bill had become a red herring and the reaction was swift. However, in the name of Dayak unity and with strong support from Chinese members, the Chief Minister expelled BARJASA from the Sarawak Alliance and cabinet and concentrated on winning back PESAKA and its leader, Temenggong Jugah.[16] Summoned by the Tunku and Tun Razak to attend a round table conference in Kuala Lumpur, he refused point blank. With the words, 'Sarawak crisis must be settled in Sarawak', he proceeded to Sibu to meet with Dayak leaders, retorting that 'we will inform Tun Razak of our decision'.[17]

A new Alliance government was thus formed without Muslim participation. Two weeks later, after the Chief Minister had conferred with Malayan leaders, BARJASA and PANAS were admitted into the Alliance, on condition that the idea of an all-native Alliance was dead. The following three Ministers were added to the state government:

Abang Othman bin Abang Haji Moasili (PANAS), Minister for Welfare, Youth and Culture, a first division Malay

Penghulu Francis Umpau (PESAKA), Minister for Land and Mineral Resources, a third division Iban

Tajang Laing (PESAKA), Minister of State, a third division Kayan[18]

This brought the party membership of the state cabinet to three SNAP, two PESAKA, two BARJASA, one PANAS and one SCA. The racial composition was three Iban, two Melanau, two Chinese, one Malay and one Kayan. Divisional representation was three from the first and from the third divisions, two from the second, one from the fifth and none from the fourth.

---

[15] *Sarawak Tribune,* 15 May 1965.

[16] SCA and BARJASA members were bitter rivals for influence over the Chief Minister. In addition, Ong Kee Hui had promised unconditionally the six SUPP votes to the Chief Minister.

Abdul Taib bin Mahmud, the Sarawak Minister for Communications and Works, who publicly precipitated the split made two key mistakes: (a) He believed that just because each PESAKA member had signed his name to a sheet of paper he would necessarily act accordingly and not change his view. Taib initially claimed that the proposed 'United Malaysian Natives Organisation' had 22 of the 36 elected members' votes and could vote Ningkan out of office. (b) He left for Kuala Lumpur and was away from the domestic scene at the critical moment.

The moment of decision came when Temenggong Jugah chose to visit Sibu and it was demonstrated that it was not only Kuala Lumpur that could persuade.

Jugah's trip eastward to Sibu rather than westward to Kuala Lumpur (in contrast to the 1966 crisis experience) illustrated the importance of geography to local politics. Had Jugah taken the opposite direction in 1965 the outcome would probably have been reversed.

[17] *Sarawak Tribune,* 22 May 1965.

[18] The new order of precedence in cabinet was Ningkan (SNAP), Wong (SNAP), Othman (PANAS), Endawie (SNAP), Teo (SCA), Umpau (PESAKA) and Taib (BARJASA). *Sarawak Government Gazette,* Part V, 25 June 1965, p. 567.

The three expatriate officers gave up their cabinet posts in order to make way for the new PESAKA and PANAS ministers, though they continued to act as cabinet ministers and retained their seats in the Council Negri. Having provided two of the three new ministers, PESAKA was the party that had gained the most from this crisis. But PESAKA was still quite under-represented in the state cabinet in relation to its membership in the Council Negri. During 1965 two second division Iban members of the Council Negri, Pengarah Storey of SNAP and Tutong anak Ningkan of BARJASA, switched to PESAKA, giving that party thirteen of the thirty Alliance seats, in contrast to SNAP's six seats.

The land bills crisis of May-June 1965 was the opening round of efforts to re-constitute the Sarawak state government, to diminish the influence of the expatriates, SNAP and their Chinese advisors, and to substitute PESAKA and BARJASA, a predominantly Iban and Islamic combination more amenable to co-operation with the federal government.

The lines of cleavage were clarified on one question in 1965. PESAKA and BARJASA shared the belief that both Chinese and expatriate officers were exerting undue influence within the SNAP-led Alliance government. The exclusion of SNAP from Taib's native alliance because it was multiracial (i.e. included non-natives) was paralleled by the adamant insistence of Kuala Lumpur and USNO that UPKO remove all Chinese members from its ranks as a condition for continuance in the Sabah government. Apart from this question of alleged Chinese dominance from within, there were actually few real policy differences between PESAKA and SNAP.

Education and the National Language

The national language

The Malaysian Prime Minister, Tunku Abdul Rahman, in his 1966 presidential address to the United Malays' National Organisation (UMNO), declared that

> One of the duties of the people of this country is to find a rallying point from which they can unite into a single nationality. A factor which can bring about the unity of the people is the adoption of a national language, for language is the soul of the Nation. . . . A nation without its own language cannot be said to have fulfilled the conditions of a sovereign and independent nation. . . . The question of the national language is a matter which touches on the loyalty of the people, and the acceptance of the policy is the manifestation of one's loyalty to the country.[19]

Thus it is apparent that for the Tunku the national language is the soul of the nation, the very condition of sovereignty. The acceptance or rejection of that language (Malay) is a touchstone of the loyalty of a citizen. The implementation of the national language policy is of prime significance. For political opponents of non-Malay extraction the insistence upon this national language becomes a prime symbol of Malay aspiration to mould Malaysia into a Malay state, offering the other communities a junior partnership.

[19] The full text of this address is reproduced in *Suara Malaysia*, Kuala Lumpur, 4 August 1966.

Upon joining Malaysia the Borneo states accepted Malay as the national language. They did not however accept Malay as the official language, at least for the time being. After lengthy negotiations it was agreed that no act terminating or restricting the use of the English language in the Borneo courts, legislatures or for other official purposes should be applied in Borneo until 1973 and then only after enactment by the relevant Borneo State Legislature.[20] There was no requirement for the Borneo states to act in 1973. Legally they have the option to delay implementation of Malay as the official language as long as they wish.

Taking all ethnic groups into account the 1960 literacy rate per thousand in Sarawak was 98 in English and 70 in Malay.[21] In the decade since then the disparity has increased markedly as the government's English language school system has undergone rapid expansion. The Dayak literacy rate in English (1960) was three times their rate in Malay, a disparity that has since widened considerably.

Sarawak Dayak leaders have exhibited extraordinary sensitivity to any suggestions that they should alter this part of the Malaysia agreement, and introduce Malay as the official language forthwith.[22] To forestall such 'premature' discussion one of their most important leaders, Dunstan Endawie, stated

> . . . that if the Central government attempted to force the introduction of the national language to Sarawak by 1967 it violates the Inter-Governmental Committee (IGC) report and also the Constitution of Malaysia, for it was basically constituted on it (i.e., the IGC Report).[23]

[20] Article 61 of the Malaysia Act, incorporated into the Malaysian Constitution, reads (in part): 'No act of Parliament terminating or restricting the use of the English language for any of the purposes mentioned . . . shall come into operation . . . until ten years after Malaysia day.' This applies to '(a) use of the English language in either House of Parliament by a member for or from a Borneo State; and (b) to the use of the English language for proceedings in the High Court in Borneo or in a substitute court in a Borneo state . . . (c) to the use of the English language in a Borneo state in the Legislative Assembly or for other official purposes (including the official purposes of the Federal Government). . . . No act shall come into operation as regards the use of the English language in a Borneo State in any other case mentioned in paragraph (b) or (c) . . . until the Act or the relevant provision of it has been approved by enactment of the Legislature of that State.' Great Britain, *Malaysia, Agreement Concluded between the United Kingdom of Great Britain and Northern Ireland, the Federation of Malaya, North Borneo, Sarawak and Singapore*, HMSO, London 1963, pp. 44-5, Command paper # 2094.

[21] Sarawak, *Report on the Census of Population Taken on June 15, 1960 by L. W. Jones*, Government Printing Office, Kuching 1962), p. 82. Sarawak has but one purely Malay language newspaper and the proprietors of the English language press are more concerned with their Chinese language offshoots. In fact, in Sarawak the most common language of literacy is Chinese. More than twice the number are literate in that language than are literate in Malay (ibid., p. 80).

[22] Recapitulating events prior to his dismissal, Stephen Ningkan said: 'On the national language issue the Tunku became so blind as to tell me—a Dayak —that there is no such language as the Dayak language. I once again challenge the Tunku to publish his letter sent to me dated the 26th March 1966, if he disputes my words.' *Sarawak Tribune*, 4 July 1966.

[23] *Sarawak Tribune*, 11 November 1965. Dunstan Endawie, then a Sarawak Alliance Cabinet Minister, was regarded as one of the most important

Considering the depth of Dayak sentiments any quick attempt to forge pan-Malaysian linguistic unity could well have been counter-productive.

Certain Malay nationalists hardly helped soothe Bornean fears with such statements as:

> It is high time that Sarawak and Sabah start having the national language week as ten years after Malaysia both countries *will be using* Malay as the national language.[24]

The Tunku asserted that 'the target date to make the national language the official language of Sarawak had been agreed upon'[25]—a statement that did not accord with local understanding. Then the Chief Minister of Sarawak, Stephen Kalong Ningkan, added fuel to the fire by stating:

> We in Sarawak shall not be ready for any change until 1973—if indeed any change is required at all—and I believe the position in Sabah is substantially the same.[26]

He thus cast in a Bornean perspective the remarks of the Tunku and Syed Nasir. He saw the question as still 'wide open' and was far from persuaded that a change to Malay as the official language in Borneo would be beneficial, even in 1973. There was a clear inference that this was a local matter which the federal government could not force, unless it was prepared to contravene the basis of the Malaysia Agreement.

Not only did he cast doubt on the rigidity of that date, he also had the 'temerity' to suggest that it would be better for any changes in language policy to be made for the whole of Malaysia at one time, and not to come into operation anywhere in Malaysia until 1973.[27] The Tunku regretted that Ningkan had made this suggestion. 'By saying that Sarawak cannot accept the national language next year, the Chief Minister seems to indicate that the people of Sarawak know English better than Malay.'[28]

Then came the quest for motives. Why had Ningkan made such a suggestion? Syed Nasir said that it was possible that Stephen Ningkan had obtained his ideas from people who wanted to split the unity of the people of Malaysia.[29] 'Ningkan has a motive behind his refusal to use the Malay language, although 90 per cent of the Dayaks can speak this language and less than 1 per cent has a good knowledge of the

---

younger Dayak leaders, one who really had an 'ear to the ground'—a feel for Dayak attitudes. He made this speech immediately after touring the second division. The statement would evoke dismay or derision from West Malaysians. The Malaysian Constitution was patently that of Malaya, amended to meet the needs of the new states. The comment does underline Bornean understanding that the Lansdowne (IGC) Report is a type of treaty, binding on all partners. Such an outlook does not take kindly any unilateral actions that would alter a part of its substance.

[24] Syed Nasir, Director of the Language and Literature Agency in Kuala Lumpur, reported in *Sarawak Tribune,* 28 June 1965 (emphasis added).

[25] *Straits Budget,* 6 July 1966.

[26] *Straits Times,* 3 May 1966.

[27] Ibid.

[28] Ibid., 18 May 1966.

[29] Ibid.

English language',[30] stated the Tunku. Those Dayaks who want English as the permanent official language are 'still influenced by the British imperialists'.[31] 'Just because the people of Sarawak had learnt English for the last few years did not mean that Malaysia should become a bastard nation.'[32]

Ningkan's removal from the post of Chief Minister was, by his own account, partly because he objected to the pace and methods of implementing the national language policy in Sarawak.[33] However, his successor was not much more tractable on this point. It is true that he did echo the Tunku's words that 'without a language of our own we cannot even truly call ourselves a nation'. Yet he was equally emphatic when he stated that it is agreed that English will remain the official language *until 1973 or later* if the Council Negri want that.[34]

Thus, whilst it is likely that Malay will become the official language throughout West Malaysia and Sabah, problems will arise in Sarawak. Electorally the Dayaks hold preponderant potential political power and no attempt to wish or coerce them into acting as Malays is likely to be productive at an early date. Linguistic unity, upon which the Tunku set such store, cannot be created by fiat in Sarawak. It is more likely to be inculcated in the school system, to which we now turn.

Education policy

Federal education policy has been consciously employed to foster national unity, first to Malaya and now to Malaysia. It is the prime instrument by which the government strives to supplant ethnic identification and loyalties with those directed toward the nation. This process of integration must be accompanied by some sharing of basic values and this requires common channels of communication. It is through the educational process that a whole new generation may be moulded, a generation who will share certain 'Malaysian' values and are able to communicate with one another in the national tongue.

Prior to World War II the Chinese, Malay and Indian children of Malaya had been educated separately in their own language medium. There were relatively few exceptions to this rule. Following the war, with increased communal passions, it became incumbent upon the colonial authorities to promote national unity more vigorously. The

---

[30] *Suara Malaysia*, 7 July 1966. This statement, though exaggerated, does have a good deal of validity. However, the Tunku had always been prone to underestimate the differences between the Dayaks and the Malays, in both language and culture. According to one study there is a 66% correspondence of homosemantic cognates between Malay and Iban. Rev. Stanley Bain 'Lexicostatistico comparison of Iban and related languages' (typescript) 1967, Appendix 1, p. 5.

[31] The Tunku as reported by Reuters, 17 May 1966. Reprinted by *The Mirror* (Singapore), 23 May 1966.

[32] The Tunku in *Suara Malaysia*, 7 July 1966, p. 7.

[33] *Borneo Bulletin* (Brunei), 9 July 1966. Ningkan: 'I also could not agree with the way the national language was being pushed down the throats of the people of Sarawak. I insisted that the guarantees promised to Sarawak should be respected.'

[34] *Suara Malaysia*, 21 July 1966.

course chosen was to promote English-medium schools as 'the best hope for the emergence of the Malayan nation'.[35] As independence approached Malay and English were placed on a par as the preferred medium of instruction. The stipulation was then added that eventually the national language would be the medium of instruction in all government and in assisted 'national type' schools. Since then public subsidies have been withdrawn from Chinese secondary schools not using English or Malay as their medium of instruction,[36] and all schools (primary and secondary) have been instructed to teach Malay and English as compulsory subjects. Cautious implementation of this national education policy in West Malaysia, due in large part to sheer lack of suitable staff and resources, has minimized friction and permitted the Chinese and Indian minorities grudgingly to accept the inevitable. The concession that parents may send their children to Chinese and Tamil secondary schools, if they are prepared to pay the fees, has siphoned off the energies of those who might otherwise have taken stronger political action. The overall objective remains 'to bring together the children of all races under the education system in which the national language is the main medium of instruction'.[37]

The Bornean delegates who met with representatives of Malaya, Singapore and the United Kingdom in the Inter-Governmental Committee were united in their insistence that the Malay language should not become the medium of instruction for their education systems until such time as they were prepared to accept this. It was agreed by the delegates who formed that Committee (which determined the basis for Malaysia) to insert in their report Article 17, which read (in part):

> Although education will be a federal subject the present policy and system of administration of education in North Borneo and Sarawak (including their present Ordinances) should be undisturbed and remain under the control of the Government of the State until that Government otherwise agrees. In particular:—(1) the present policy in the Borneo States regarding the use of English should continue. . . .[38]

No such specific clause has been incorporated into the Malaysian Constitution. However, the depth of Bornean feeling could only be ignored at great risk. In Sarawak the Inter-Governmental Committee Report was widely regarded as a treaty. It was the subject of lengthy debates prior to the April-June 1963 State elections. Bornean political leaders referred to the agreed conditions as clauses of a treaty, not as

[35] Federation of Malaya, Department of Education, *Federation of Malaya Annual Report on Education for 1949 by M. R. Holgate,* Government Printing Office, Kuala Lumpur 1950, p. 40. The preceding part of this sentence reads: 'The English schools everywhere operate to create that feeling of cohesion between the different races of the federation . . .'
[36] J. M. Gullick, 'Resolving Racial Fears', *The Times* (London), 31 August 1966.
[37] Malaysia, *Official Year Book,* Volume 4, 1964, Government Press, Kuala Lumpur, p. 537.
[38] Sarawak, Council Negri, *Malaysia, Report of the Inter-Governmental Committee, 1962,* Sessional Paper #1 of 1963, Government Printing Office, Kuching 1963, p. 5.

constitutional provisions ripe for amendment. The then Deputy Chief Minister of Sarawak stated, 'The IGC is a bible in as far as [our] entry into Malaysia was concerned.'[39] It was understood that no state or federal government had the mandate to change these conditions.

Due to Sarawakian sensitivity the mere promotion of the Malaysian education policy, with its greater role for Malay-medium instruction, had become an irritant to harmonious relations between the central government and the leaders of Sarawak.

Emphasis upon indefinite perpetuation of English-medium education in Sarawak was viewed in Kuala Lumpur as a deliberate attempt to divide the peoples of Malaysia.

> The Colonial education policy was introduced with the aim of making Oriental Britishers. The medium was to be English alone. The content was British entirely. There was very strong opposition to it from the Chinese and the Malays were opposed to a certain extent. That Sarawak still follows the Colonial policy is due largely to the perpetuation of British influence.[40]

Stephen Ningkan issued a quick rebuttal.

> We have chosen English as our medium of instruction not because the former Colonial government insisted upon it, but because of the Native peoples of Sarawak. Its adoption has been regarded as essential if we are to make rapid educational progress to catch up with our neighbours and to fit ourselves for life in the modern world. . . . We aim to encourage the teaching of Malay. . . . I am learning the language myself.[41]
> As to the use of Malay as a medium of instruction this is out of the question for the time being. . . . To try to change the medium now would be to throw away the fruits of the last fifteen years.[42]

The most serious aspect was the apparent lack of sensitivity for Dayak feelings.[43] To the economically backward Dayaks education had suddenly assumed a vital importance. It was the way they would catch up with their more advanced Chinese and Malay contemporaries. To them English represented the language of progress. Perhaps this was the result of British conditioning but they were aware that with English

---

[39] James Wong speaking in the Council Negri debate on education. *Sarawak Tribune*, 22 October 1964.

[40] Inche Abdul Rahman bin Talib, Malaysia Minister of Education, quoted from a personal interview, 27 August 1964.

[41] *Sarawak Tribune*, 9 July 1964. It is of interest to note that all members of the first Sarawak Cabinet (Ningkan's) received their education principally in the English medium. Only Awang Hipni received some years of education in Malay. In interviews even the Muslim Melanaus in that Cabinet believed that insistence upon Malay medium education caused a negative effect.

[42] Stephen Kalong Ningkan in *Sarawak Tribune*, 7 July 1964.

[43] Jonathan Banggau, an important Iban PESAKA leader from the lower Rejang, stated in federal Parliament—but four months after the formation of Malaysia—'The Central government has failed to keep its pre- Malaysia promises on education'. Because of this there was 'growing disillusionment among the majority of backward people in the State'. *Straits Times*, 1 January 1964.

they could gain overseas scholarships. Of the 11,500 Iban (Sea Dayaks) who were literate in 1960, three-quarters were literate in English, less than a half in Iban, and less than a quarter in Malay.[44] Those Iban who were literate thus have a vested interest in the English language. Of those the Iban school teachers may yet prove to be a politically pivotal group, who play a role akin to that of the Malay school teachers in West Malaysia.

Efforts to impose the Malay medium were often interpreted as a deliberate attempt to retard their advancement. In time the Malay medium of instruction in schools will probably be accepted, but not if Kuala Lumpur follows a 'collision course'. If pushed hard it will be viewed as an instance of 'Malay expansionism'.

Prelude to the Alliance Crisis of 1966

The ensuing crescendo of political activity throughout 1966 led to a situation in which SNAP and the expatriates were forced from power and the SCA members were placed in an awkward ambivalent position. The re-structuring that took place brought PESAKA and BARJASA leaders close together, split PANAS and SCA and immeasurably improved the standing of SNAP as the Sarawak *National* party, opposed to external intervention.

The resulting changes in the membership of each party in the Council Negri are recorded in Table 21 with notes explaining each of the changes. The number nominated from Sarawak to the Dewan Ra'ayat, the Federal House of Representatives, is also recorded (Table 22). Fresh nominations were submitted from Sarawak in 1964, after the federal elections which were held only in West Malaysia.

Many Dayaks complained that they had not received the promised benefits of development, that development was concentrated in the urban areas and the Chinese were benefiting to their detriment.[45] PESAKA members expressed rising Dayak dissatisfaction that government development policies were not to their advantage. Instances that received frequent mention were the allocation of timber and transport concessions to favour Chinese and the failure of the state government to invoke special privileges for natives in the civil service and in the allocation of scholarships, as was the practice in West Malaysia.

Whilst SNAP expanded on a multi-racial state-wide basis, PESAKA moved into the second division (SNAP's heartland) and sought to take

---

[44] Sarawak, *Report on the Census of Population, 1960*, pp. 78 and 82. The criteria employed is the ability to read or write a letter.

[45] Dunstan Endawie, a SNAP Cabinet Minister, was publicly critical of his government's failure to promote development for the Dayaks. Temenggong Jugah, Federal Minister for Sarawak Affairs, complained that 'development in Sarawak is concentrated in the urban areas and the rural people, particularly the Ibans, were dissatisfied. . . . [When I meet the rural people] all they now say is there is no help . . . there is no help'. *Straits Budget*, 8 December 1965. Many Dayaks complained that the Chief Minister's multi-racial political policies were to their detriment. Such general Dayak dissatisfaction had rebounded in favour of PESAKA.

over Dayak leadership there. Penghulu Tawi Sli, a SNAP leader, defected to PESAKA and the popular Dunstan Endawie was considering such a move.[46] This led to a direct confrontation between the two parties. Ningkan himself clashed personally with Alfred Mason of PESAKA.[47]

The domestic crisis was also of benefit to SUPP as it shifted attention from efforts to discredit the party as subversive and appeared to validate many of its earlier accusations of 'Malayan imperialism'. The only problem for SUPP was that a number of young English-educated Chinese who would have broadened the base of the party chose to

Table 21

Membership of the Council Negri by Party Allegiance

Political party	1963 (elected)	1963 (Oct.)	1964	1965 (July)	1966 (May)	1966 (Oct.)	1968
Alliance	23	27	27	30	32	25	26
SNAP	6	7	7	6	6	7	6
PESAKA	11	11	11	13	15	15	16
SCA	1	3	3	3	3	3	3
BARJASA	5	6	6	5	5	5	}BUMI. 7
PANAS	5	4	3	3	3	2	
SUPP	5	5	6	6	5	5	5
MACHINDA	—	—	1	1	1	—	—
Independent	3	3	2	2	1	2	2
Ex-officio	—	3	3	3	3	3	3
Total	36	42	42	42	42	42	42

Notes:

1963: Three councillors were officially nominated, two SCA and one BARJASA.
   Leong Ho Yuen resigned from PANAS and became an independent, preparatory to founding MACHINDA in 1964.
   James Wong (Independent) joined SNAP when appointed Deputy Chief Minister.
1964: The Datu Bandar (PANAS) died and the first divisional advisory council elected a SUPP member, Sim Kheng Hong, in his stead.
1965: Pengarah Storey (SNAP) and Tutong anak Ningkan (BARJASA) both left their respective parties and joined PESAKA. Both are second division Ibans.
1966: Prior to the removal of Ningkan, Tawi Sli (SNAP) joined PESAKA as did a fifth division independent, Racha Umong. SNAP gained Charles Linang (from SUPP) and Abang Othman (from PANAS), the latter after the September Alliance crisis.
1968: Kadam Kiai (SNAP) died and the second divisional advisory council elected a PESAKA member, Langgi anak Jilap, in his stead.
   At the end of 1966 BARJASA and PANAS were merged to form Party BUMIPUTERA.

The vertical sidelines indicate the component parties of the Sarawak Alliance on each of the designated dates.

[46] See *Vanguard*, 19 April 1966, and *Straits Times*, 19 April 1966.
[47] The Tunku alluded to Ningkan's behaviour during his Sarawak tour in July 1966. See *Borneo Bulletin*, 9 July 1966.

Table 22

Members of the Dewan Ra'ayat from Sarawak by Party Allegiance

Political party	Number nominated by Council Negri in:	
	1963	1964
Allianc(	18	18
SNAP	4	4
PESAKA	6	6
SCA	3	4
BARJASA	5	4 ⎫
PANAS	3	2 ⎬ BUMIPUTERA
SUPP	3	4 ⎭
Total	24	24

support SNAP. They were reluctant to join SCA because of its opportunism and big business backing, nor would they join SUPP for fear of its militant image. SNAP also provided an outlet for Dayak discontent once the party had withdrawn from the Alliance government—and SUPP was not the automatic beneficiary of those dissatisfied with the government. The first prominent Chinese to join SNAP was James Wong from the fifth division. He and Ting Tung Ming[48] had a good deal of influence over the Chief Minister. The next important Chinese was Wee Hood Teck, son of the venerable Wee Kheng Chiang and managing-director of the Bian Chian Bank. He joined SNAP in June 1966, becoming a chairman of its newly created Kuching branch. Wee Hood Teck provided the financial under-pinning to the subsequent sophisticated organization of SNAP branches and field workers throughout the state.[49] The influx of other Chinese members were not widespread until September 1966.

From 1965 onward two new leaders appeared within the top echelons of PESAKA. The first was Thomas Kana who was elected secretary-general of PESAKA and could claim more responsibility than any other for the

---

[48] Though an SCA nominee Ting in time came to be quite closely identified with SNAP. He was replaced as political secretary to the Chief Minister in October 1965 by an Iban, Charles Ingka. This was in response to wide-spread Iban criticism that Ningkan was too closely cloistered with Chinese advisors.

[49] He was also managing-director of the Wee Hood Teck Development Corporation, which was the beneficiary of a large contract to build the Pending port light industrial complex near Kuching. This was the first cabinet meeting during which the expatriate officers were instructed to leave while a decision was made. The expatriates had argued that on technical grounds (i.e. mixing of residential premises, warehouse facilities and the inclusion of two filling stations within the Port area) Wee Hood Teck's company should not be awarded the contract. However, the Cabinet decreed otherwise.

Wee Hood Teck is the third son of Wee Kheng Chiang (see Chapter 1, note 40) and the beneficiary of considerable inherited wealth. He is a Hokkien, born in 1931 and was educated in Kuching and Singapore. He is noted for his wealth and cultivation of the reputation of philanthropist.

growing and expanding confidence of PESAKA from then onward. Kana, born in Kanowit of Iban and Chinese parents, had a life experience closely comparable to the original SNAP leadership archetype except for the fact that he had been born in the third division. Following the war he worked for eighteen years as a hospital assistant for the Brunei Shell Oil Company. While there he was a long time personal rival of Stephen Ningkan and their enmity was later transferred to the party political sphere. He was nominated as a member of the federal Parliament in 1965, a position that accorded him status and remuneration with which to devote himself to full time party organizing.

The other new leader was Alfred Mason, who came from a well known Balau Dayak family which had maintained a close relationship with the Rajah's Malay officers. His father had been in charge of the Brooke Memorial Hospital (for lepers) and both father and son were somewhat involved with those who had been opposed to Cession (in the Sarawak Dayak Association). Alfred Mason trained in Singapore as a draftsman and then worked with the Sarawak government until 1953. In 1961 he became assistant-secretary of the Barisan Pemuda Sarawak and then secretary-general of BARJASA. As both Abdul Rahman bin Ya'kub and Abdul Taib bin Mahmud were government servants, they worked through Alfred Mason to shape that party prior to the 1963 election. Like most BARJASA candidates who stood in the urban districts Mason was defeated by PANAS and fell into political oblivion after Abdul Rahman and Taib assumed full-time political responsibilities. He switched to PESAKA and in February 1965 was sworn in as political secretary to Temenggong Jugah.[50] In that capacity he worked to gain local support for PESAKA, principally in the first and second divisions of the state.

These two PESAKA organizers worked closely with BARJASA leaders in an effort to displace Ningkan and his party SNAP from the leadership of the Sarawak Alliance government. But there were distinct limits to their co-operation. BARJASA leaders not only sought to unify all the Muslims, but also attempted to unite all natives under one leadership. The spokesman for BARJASA, Abdul Taib bin Mahmud, unequivocally stated this objective.

> Perhaps we can take an example from the success on the mainland where unity begins with unification on a uni-racial basis first and then co-operation and understanding is forged between these groups of disciplined uni-racial organizations. . . .[51]
>
> BARJASA believed in unity among the natives first and having achieved that unity would then closely co-operate with the non-natives . . . it is easier to co-operate with the non-natives when the natives are themselves united.[52]

PESAKA leaders were prepared to co-operate for tactical purposes, but strongly resisted any suggestions that their party be subsumed within one native political organization. Just as SNAP leaders were politically vulnerable to the charge of Chinese domination from within, so if

[50] *Sarawak Tribune,* 14 February 1965.
[51] *Straits Budget,* 23 March 1966.
[52] Ibid., 20 April 1966.

PESAKA were merged with BARJASA, Dayaks in the resultant party would be vulnerable to the charge of being under Malay domination. Even in coalition PESAKA could ill afford to be identified as subservient to BARJASA.

Efforts to unite the Malay community politically had not come to fruition, as had been forecast back in 1963. The federal leadership found most irritating the constant bickerings between rival Sarawak Malay leaders. After a week of discussions in Sarawak the Tunku declared that

> he was most disappointed and dissatisfied with the Alliance leadership in Sarawak . . . [they] had failed to co-operate with each other and settle their petty differences amicably.[53]

He warned the present generation of Malays that 'if they remained disunited they would be held responsible by the coming generation of Malays for the eventual disintegration of the race'.[54] He added that the Malays could gain the respect of the other races 'only be remaining united'.[55]

PANAS members were torn two ways: (1) by BARJASA and Kuala Lumpur to join in one united predominantly Islamic party that would advance Muslim interests in the state and nation; and (2) by SNAP to assume a stronger Sarawakian stance against the efforts of local 'up-starts'[56] who had the support of Kuala Lumpur. This appeal found a ready response from those aristocratic party leaders who were still smarting from the attacks upon them during the 1963 election campaign. It was very difficult for the older and locally distinguished Kuching PANAS leadership to accept the leadership of Abdul Rahman Ya'kub who by his ambition and ability had been promoted to a full federal ministerial position. Origins of the division could also be traced back to the time of Cession, most of the top PANAS leadership (with the exception of the publicity chief, Abang Ikhwan Zainie) had been pro-Cession.

From February 1966 onward relations between the state and federal governments steadily deteriorated. Stephen Ningkan and the Tunku exchanged none too complimentary remarks about each other. The Tunku accused Dayak leaders in Sarawak of being still under British influence.

> [They] still look to the British for inspiration and from what we have seen, it will take a long time before they can drop this colonial outlook. As long as the principal administrators there are British colonial officers, they cannot expect to cast off that influence and develop a Malaysian conscious-ness.[57]

[53] *Sarawak Tribune,* 24 February 1966.
[54] *Daily Citizen* (Kuala Lumpur), 21 February 1966.
[55] The Tunku recalled that Malaya gained independence only after the Malays were united in UMNO: 'The Malays in UMNO had enabled other races to unite and form the Alliance' ibid., 21 February 1966.
[56] For instance Ningkan included the PANAS minister Abang Othman within his inner cabinet because he was a 'Sarawak Malay'. BARJASA ministers continued to be excluded after 1965.
[57] *Vanguard,* 18 May 1966.

Ningkan's retort was very blunt and to the point:

> Our Prime Minister should think properly before making statements accus-
> ing the Dayak leaders of being under British influence. That is not fair.
> I am a very sensitive type and it is very difficult for people to influence me.
> I think the Tunku is a bit too old. . . . But I tell you this very frankly had
> it not been for the dayaks support for Malaysia there would be no Malaysia
> today because of the dayaks strong support [sic]. Mind you they should be
> careful about the dayaks because the dayaks are very sensitive. If we didn't
> support Malaysia it could not continue . . . I am not prepared to agree
> with Sukarno because *at the moment* we are quite happy in Malaysia.[58]
> (Emphasis added.)

British influence remained a major bone of contention between the two
governments. From the beginning of 1966 the two most important
expatriate officers, Tony Shaw and John Pike, had privately resolved
to limit their own political activities in support of Ningkan, for direct
intervention as in the 1965 crisis threatened to become counter-productive. However, Tony Shaw was one of the five-man Sarawak delegation
that flew to Kuala Lumpur for 'top secret' talks with Tun Razak in
April.[59] Official visitors from Malaya urged native unity and central
government leaders expressed their irritation that the Ningkan government was failing to implement national policies regarding language,
development and the speedy replacement of expatriate officers.[60] As the
federal government provided considerable funds for development and the
greater part of the expenditure on security, Kuala Lumpur expected
closer conformity with central policies. It saw local parochialism as a
drag on progressive development.

Borneanization of the Civil Service and the Role of Expatriate Officers

Borneanization of the civil service was an objective accepted by all
parties to the Malaysia Agreement. However, added to that Agreement
were mechanisms for ensuring that Borneanization would not impede
the development of a partnership within the broader entity of Malaysia.
In the long run Malaysia will be an unreal creation unless the principle
of Malaysianization is accepted. Bornean officers must play their part
in framing federal policies in Kuala Lumpur. Similarly Malay officers
in the federal civil service must be brought to view problems from a
Malaysian point of view that takes full account of the interests, anxieties
and hopes of the Borneo states. They can never do this until many of

[58] Excerpts from the transcript of the Chief Minister's Kuching Press conference held upon his return from a visit to Marudi, 16 May 1966. *Utusan
Melayu* (in Kuala Lumpur) was quick to retort: 'For what use is the
Malaysian army now stationed in Sarawak? Is it not to defend the position
of Kalong Ningkan?' (18 May 1966.)
[59] The other four were Ningkan, Jugah, Endawie and Charles Ingka, political
secretary to the Chief Minister (*Straits Times,* 23 April 1966).
[60] For instance, the Chief Minister of Malacca, speaking in Kuching, suggested
that three components of the Sarawak Alliance—PESAKA, BARJASA and
PANAS—should become one native organization (*Sarawak Vanguard,* 20 May
1966).

them have had opportunities of serving in the Borneo states and of being held directly responsible for Bornean interests.[61]

In order to facilitate the appointment of local personnel to federal posts in the Borneo states, a local branch of the Public Service Commission was established in Sabah and Sarawak. This body, responsible for all federal public service appointments in the state, was composed of the existing state Public Service Commission plus not more than two federal appointees.[62]

The Malaysian constitution, for purposes of appointment to the civil service, equates the Bornean natives with Malays.

> The reservation of positions in the public service shall apply in relation to natives of a Borneo state as they apply in relation to Malays.[63]

Sarawak has not yet invoked that clause though there have been some pressures to establish a ratio of natives to Chinese as in West Malaysia. The Constitution leaves no doubt that all Bornean natives[64] are intended to enjoy the privileges restricted to Malays on the Peninsula.

The chief problems have arisen from the role of British expatriate officers and the rate at which they should be replaced by Malaysian personnel. Kuala Lumpur was clearly disturbed by British efforts to obstruct national unity.

> If the British continue to administer Sarawak how can the people claim to be independent? I hope all the people here now realize that they are no longer British subjects and no longer under British rule.[65]

Federal annoyance and frustration were greatest when dealing with the Ningkan government. That government, until it was overturned in June 1966, refused to dispense with the services of certain key expatriates. Much to the chagrin of Kuala Lumpur the state government relied heavily upon British officials in its dealings with the federal capital. The central government repeatedly sent directives and plans to Kuching only to receive a detailed reply that, under the terms of the IGC Agreement, the central government could do a, b and c, but not d, e or f, for the latter conflicted with Section X.[66] It was obvious to Kuala Lumpur that this was not the work of Dayaks who had received a primary

[61] Sarawak, Council Negri, *Malaysia: Report of the Inter-Governmental Committee, 1962,* Sessional Paper #1, of 1963, Government Printing Office, Kuching 1963, Annex B, para. 30, p. 29.

[62] Great Britain, *Malaysia: Agreement Concluded Between the United Kingdom of Great Britain and Northern Ireland, the Federation of Malaya, North Borneo, Sarawak and Singapore,* Command paper # 2094, HMSO, London 1963, Clause 55, sub-sections (1) and (3), pp. 40-1. This provision was designed to have effect until August 1968 or until such time as the Federal Government determined otherwise. See Clause 55, sub-section (8), p. 41.

[63] Ibid., Clause 62, sub-section (1), p. 45.

[64] Ibid., Clause 62, sub-section (6), p. 46. 'In this article "native" means:—
(a) in relation to Sarawak, a person who is a citizen and either belongs to one of the races specified in (7) as indigenous to the State or is of mixed blood deriving exclusively from those races.'

[65] The Tunku speaking in Sibu, Sarawak. *Borneo Bulletin,* 9 July 1966.

[66] An interview by author with a high official from Kuching, September 1966.

school education. The expatriates gave the Sarawak government a 'backbone' with which to stand up to the centre. In this sense they were most disruptive to Malaysian unity.

The Tunku expressed his frustration and annoyance in these terms:
I am not happy that Sarawak still has an administration that is colonial in nature. I cannot do anything because under the I.G.C. it is not possible for the central government to bring the administration in Sarawak in line with the Centre.[67]

It would have been easier for Kuala Lumpur to deal with inexperienced natives, especially if West Malaysians could be seconded to the Sarawak State Public Service during this initial period of transition. Stephen Ningkan confirmed this when he noted, with reference to the Tunku

I opposed his plans to Malayanise the Sarawak Civil Service. . . . We joined Malaysia believing that Sarawak was becoming independent, but Sarawak's independence would come to nothing if Kuala Lumpur tell us our civil service must be Malayanized under the pretext of getting ride of the British.[68]

The central government had found it easier to deal with the Sabah state government. Expatriates have not played the key role in that state that they have in Sarawak. There are three main principal reasons for this.

First, the Sabah Alliance had all its important leaders elected to the State Assembly. They were then able to assume the reins of government. In Sarawak, due to opposition victories in the urban centres, nearly all the experienced Alliance leaders were defeated. Thus the new inexperienced state government found it very necessary to rely upon the advice of its public service—particularly the expatriates.

Second, allies of the centre were much stronger in Sabah. By December 1964 the chief exponent of state's rights, Donald Stephens, was replaced as Chief Minister by the more tractable Peter Lo, who looked to Kuala Lumpur for advice. A similar change did not take place in Sarawak until June 1966, and that change did not transfer power into hands as sympathetic to Kuala Lumpur's concerns as was the USNO-centred government of Sabah.

Third, high echelon expatriate officers were the first to be replaced in Sabah. The Sarawak government followed the opposite sequence, Borneanizing from the lowest administrative echelons upward. The latter approach left the most experienced expatriates continuing their decision-making, acting out their pre-independence institutional roles.

The less educated native Sarawakians have shown great sensitivity to the threat that West Malaysians, or locals of other races, will be appointed to government posts that they regard as their own by right. This fear appears more pronounced among the non-Islamic portions of the population who feel that they must depend entirely upon them-

[67] The Tunku speaking in Kuala Lumpur upon his return from his tour of Sarawak. *Straits Budget*, 2 March 1966.
[68] Stephen Ningkan, speaking in Kuching after his initial (unconstitutional) removal from his post of Chief Minister of Sarawak. *Straits Budget*, 22 June 1966.

selves.[69] Many Dayaks were quite happy to have British expatriates remain to 'fill the gaps' until they themselves received adequate training. The expatriates were more likely than any of the other Malaysian races to champion their interests.[70] The other races had privileges of their own to establish and protect. The British were dispensable and that was important. Neither West Malaysians nor other locals could be viewed in this light.

As European officers leave they appear to have been replaced by Malays and Chinese, no doubt because these people have the requisite seniority and experience. The Dayaks have only recently begun to enter the Civil Service and, lacking relative seniority, they are at a clear disadvantage when senior expatriate civil servants are replaced at an accelerated pace.

The 1966 Alliance Crisis

By mid-1966 there was thus a clustering of grievances against Ningkan, issues that had been largely suppressed throughout the period of armed Indonesian confrontation.

Matters came to a head when twenty-one of the thirty-two Alliance members in Council Negri signed a petition stating that they had lost confidence in Stephen Ningkan as Chief Minister and asking for his removal. The twenty-one who signed the petition included all fifteen PESAKA members, all five BARJASA plus one from PANAS. The Alliance members who did not sign were six SNAP, three SCA and two PANAS. Though the twenty-one were a clear majority of the thirty-two Alliance members they represented only half of the forty-two members of the Council Negri. The signatures were obtained, according to Ningkan, by calling members of Council Negri to Kuala Lumpur in ones and twos.[71]

The Tunku then stated that Ningkan would be removed from office by the Sarawak Governor under the terms of Article 7 (1) of the Sarawak Constitution which states:

> If the Chief Minister ceases to command the confidence of a majority of the members of the Council Negri, then, unless at his request the Governor dissolves the Council Negri, the Chief Minister shall tender the resignation of the members of the Supreme Council, other than ex-officio members.[72]

[69] At least the Chinese have powerful representatives of their race throughout Malaysia, and those professing Islam can depend upon leaders of the federal government to ensure that they will not suffer any severe disadvantage. The other indigenous Borneans must depend upon their own wits and bargaining strength.

[70] For the rationale of this position see Chapter I (p. 57) and also Robert Pringle, *Rajahs and Rebels,* Cornell University Press, Ithaca 1970.

[71] Ningkan also objected to the character of the communication from Kuala Lumpur demanding his resignation. In a telegram to the Tunku he complained that 'one of those demanding my resignation is a rubber stamp signature. Many of those who have signed the demand do not even understand the language in which it is couched. All the signatures are on one sheet of paper which is attached to the text of the demand'. *Sarawak Tribune,* 16 June 1966.

[72] Great Britain, *Malaysia Agreement,* Annex c, p. 113.

The Tunku believed that these conditions had been met by the submission of the petition signed by more than half the elected members of
Council Negri and that he, as head of the Alliance party, had the right
to demand Ningkan's resignation. After Ningkan refused to step down
the Tunku chose the tough Minister for Home Affairs and Justice for
the task of flying to Kuching to submit the name of the new Chief
Minister to the Sarawak Governor.[73] That choice did not go unnoticed,
and underlined the ultimate authority of the Tunku.

Stephen Ningkan at first refused to resign, declaring that the constitutional and democratic manner of dealing with a motion of no confidence was to debate it in the Council Negri. Instead the dissident
Alliance members had boycotted the meeting of Council Negri, flown
to Kuala Lumpur, and from there issued an order demanding his resignation. Ningkan wanted the question of no confidence to be brought
before the Council Negri where he had a good deal more support than
just amongst the Alliance members. The Council Negri meeting was
held with twenty-one anti-Ningkan Alliance members absent. Those who
then supported Ningkan did attend the meeting and included six SNAP,
five SUPP,[74] three SCA, two PANAS, one MACHINDA, one independent and
the three *ex-officio members,* i.e. twenty-one in all. Supporters of Ningkan, including the PANAS Kaum Ibu (Women's Group), demonstrated in
favour of his government carrying banners with slogans such as:

We support Dato Ningkan!
If Dato Ningkan toppled, we secede from Malaysia![75]

Ningkan called on PESAKA and BARJASA leaders to return home and settle
the question in the Council Negri or the Sarawak Alliance National
Council. Ningkan was dismissed the next day but filed a suit contesting
the legality of his removal.

Two basic questions were posed: (1) Who was competent to declare

[73] *Sarawak Tribune,* 17 June 1966. Dato Ismail was accompanied by the
Inspector General of Police, the Federal Attorney-General and the National
Alliance Treasurer and Secretary-General. The SUPP Secretary-General
later poked fun at the situation in a press statement. 'At the first sign of
dissension within the would be Alliance they scurried to Kuala Lumpur
for instructions and advice paying scant respect to the wishes of their
constituents. These truant Alliance members were shepherded back to
Kuching from Kuala Lumpur by the Minister for Home Affairs, the
Attorney-General, the Inspector-general of Police and the Director of
Special Branch—senior and important shepherds of such an erring flock.
They were then kept incommunicado at the Astana making themselves
inaccessible to their constituents. In fairness not all of them were at fault
here since not all of them have constituents. Nevertheless all of them
ought perhaps to have made some efforts to consult their erstwhile colleagues. . . .' Stephen Yong, signed press statement, issued on 13 September 1966.

[74] Upon suggestions that SUPP might help Ningkan form a new government
SUPP militants demanded the release of all detainees and exit from
Malaysia. Such stipulations were unacceptable to Ningkan and to the more
moderate SUPP leadership, specifically to Ong Kee Hui and to Stephen
Yong.

[75] *Vanguard,* 15 June 1966.

that the Chief Minister of a Malaysian state no longer enjoyed majority support? (2) What power did the Malaysian Alliance National Council have over its constituent parties?

The Malaysian Minister for Local Government and Housing, Khaw Kai Boh, gave the most competent explanation of his government's actions to the House of Representatives:

> The Sarawak state Constitution . . . gave the Governor powers to appoint Chief Ministers "at his discretion". He could appoint any member of the Council Negri whom he considered likely to command the confidence of the majority of members of the Council. The former Chief Minister was elected on the ticket of 26 Alliance members in the Council out of the total of 36 elected members. Of the 26 Alliance members, 21 had indicated to the Governor that they had ceased to have confidence in Ningkan's leadership. Furthermore, the Sarawak Alliance party was a member of the Alliance National Council, which exercised overall control over State parties. Quite naturally, the Sarawak Alliance had the right to refer the matter to the national Council, under the leadership of the Tunku, for a decision. Nowhere in the Sarawak Constitution was it stipulated that voting on a motion of non-confidence must take place before the Chief Minister could be replaced.[76]

Though there is no stipulation that a non-confidence motion must be first voted in the legislative chamber, there are strong precedents which have a binding power little less than the written words themselves. Also, the Sarawak Alliance had not referred the matter to the Alliance National Council. In fact, Ningkan still had a voting majority in the Sarawak Alliance of eighteen to twelve.[77] Similariy, the Council Negri members back home in Kuching could not be trusted by Kuala Lumpur. Just one year earlier those members had turned and supported Ningkan,

---

[76] *Straits Times,* 21 June 1966.

[77] The assertion by Khaw Kai Boh (above) that the Alliance National Council exercised overall control over state parties was called into question by Ningkan. Ningkan, who had been secretary-general of the Sarawak Alliance since its inception, declared that 'the state Alliance was a fully autonomous body registered in Sarawak and only affiliated to the Malaysian Alliance in Kuala Lumpur'. *Straits Budget,* 14 September 1966, p. 15. He went on to declare: 'If the Alliance leaders cannot follow their own constitution how could they be expected or even depended upon to defend the state and federal constitutions?'

Within the Sarawak Alliance National Council each of the five parties had six votes. Until July Ningkan could count on the support of his own party SNAP, PANAS and SCA, with BARJASA and PESAKA opposed to him. (*Straits Times,* 27 June 1966.) The change in alignment came with the announcement that SCA had decided to join the new cabinet. *Straits Budget,* 6 July 1966. Two days later, SNAP withdrew from the Sarawak Alliance (on 3 July 1966).

An interesting sidelight on the role of Kuala Lumpur appeared when the new Chief Minister refused to accept two SCA nominees to his Cabinet. In a wounded voice, Teo Kui Seng claimed that SCA was promised two portfolios in the state cabinet by the Tunku and Tun Razak and by the MCA leaders, Tan Siew Sin and Khaw Kai Boh. Teo claimed that he also was promised the return of his old portfolio, the Ministry of Agriculture and Forestry. These meetings were held when the Tunku visited the state early in July 1966. (See *Sarawak Tribune,* 14 July 1966.)

A SUPP speaker expressing opposition to Malaysia at a meeting in 1962.

The late Datu Bandar (left) and Abang Ikwan Zainie wait to present their views to the United Nations Mission of Inquiry, Kuching 1963. Immediately behind them is Madame Barbara Bey, an Iban leader of SUPP.

Abdul Rahman Ya'kub addressing an election rally in a Kuching Malay kampong in 1968. His stance is reminiscent of the Tunku's.

A Malay fisherman at Santubong.

Malay Kampong at Mukah.

Longhouses at Baram.
Photograph by courtesy of Malaysian Information Service.

The Sarawak Coalition Cabinet, 1970. Reproduction of a poster issued by the Malaysian Information Service.

despite the fact that Abdul Taib bin Mahmud had enough signatures on a sheet of paper in his pocket to bring about Ningkan's downfall. Thus, for strategic reasons, it was important for Kuala Lumpur to let the Alliance National Council handle the matter.[78]

The new Chief Minister, Penghulu Tawi Sli, gave every indication that he would co-operate more closely with the central government.[79] At the beginning of July the Tunku arrived in Sarawak in order to bolster the new government. He defended his role by saying that Kuala Lumpur could of course influence events, but there was no interference in any improper sense.[80]

On the day the Tunku arrived in Kuching SNAP held its annual general meeting. The meeting resolved that, because the Grand Alliance in Kuala Lumpur had consulted with but two of the five parties in the Sarawak Alliance before replacing the Chief Minister, SNAP should withdraw from the Malaysian Alliance party in Kuala Lumpur. SNAP called on PANAS and SCA to join it in a strong united front. Ningkan concluded his statement with the challenge

> If the Prime Minister thinks that he will, with the help of his puppets, succeed in making Sarawak a Colony of Malaysia, the Tunku is suffering from a terrible illusion.[81]

[78] Though there were tactical reasons for preferring to handle the matter in the Alliance National Council, that course of action raised real questions of procedure. The Democratic Action Party MP asked whether the right to dismiss Ningkan came within the jurisdiction of the Alliance party, and added: 'The Alliance party might as well claim that it supercedes the Malaysian Parliament'. *Straits Times,* 19 June 1966.

[79] Immediately after his appointment as Chief Minister, Tawi Sli announced that he was leaving for Kuala Lumpur. Asked why the new Chief Minister was going there, Dato Ismail replied, 'He must in this matter of great importance be given time to reflect very carefully'. (*Straits Times,* 18 June 1966.) This trip to Kuala Lumpur to form the new Sarawak Cabinet caused an unfavourable reaction in Kuching.

Tawi Sli defended the Malaysian government against 'unfounded accusations' by declaring that it had been 'adhering to the Malaysian Agreement very strictly and to the letter'. The Tunku declared that 'under Tawi Sli there was much better chance of the people developing a truly Malaysian consciousness'. *Straits Budget,* 13 July 1966.

Penghulu Tawi anak Sli, the second son of the Anglican (SPG) catechist Tini, comes from Banting in the Simanggang district of the second division. He obtained the highest available local English education (form 3) at St Thomas's school, Kuching. He then worked as a mission school teacher and was for three years a trainee pastor before becoming a clerk in the state government service. Upon retirement in 1961, after 23 years service, he became a petition writer. In 1963 he was appointed a penghulu and that same year he embarked upon an active political career as secretary to the SNAP Simanggang branch, was elected to the Batang Lupar District Council and to the Council Negri. In 1963 he and Stephen Ningkan were the two candidates for the position of Chief Minister considered by the state Alliance Council. Ningkan won that ballot but Tawi Sli distinguished himself as a capable district council chairman. Due to dissatisfaction over his role within SNAP he switched to PESAKA early in 1966.

[80] *Straits Times,* 7 July 1966.

[81] *Sarawak Tribune,* 4 July 1966.

However, by mid-July it appeared that the Alliance as then constituted would be able to consolidate itself in power. Both PANAS and SCA had declared their support of the new cabinet, and SNAP seemed isolated.

Prior to the crisis PANAS had three members in the Council Negri. Dago anak Randen was the first to support the PESAKA-BARJASA coalition. He was one of the twenty-one who had originally demanded Ningkan's resignation. The second to 'defect' was Abang Haji Abdulrahim who voiced widespread PANAS rank-and-file criticism of party leaders for having given rash and thoughtless support to Ningkan. PANAS then expelled Abang Haji Abdulrahim after he accepted the offer of a cabinet post in the new Tawi Sli government.[82] He was exonerated and reinstated within a month after strong branch level efforts on his behalf. This expulsion rebounded against the PANAS Chairman Abang Othman and Secretary-General, Mokhtar bin Bakip bringing about the latter's resignation from PANAS.[83]

Meanwhile SCA, with some outward reluctance, decided to join the new government, but the party was not given back Teo's earlier Natural Resources portfolio.[84]

The first Tawi Sli cabinet was composed of the following members:

Penghulu Tawi anak Sli (PESAKA), Chief Minister, a second division Iban

Abdul Taib bin Mahmud (BARJASA), Minister for Agriculture and Forestry, a first division Melanau

Penghulu Francis Umpau (PESAKA), Minister for Lands and Mineral Resources, a third division Iban

Abang Haji Abdulrahim (PANAS), Minister for Local Government, a first division Malay

Awang Hipni (BARJASA), Minister for Welfare, Youth and Culture, a third division Melanau

Tajang Laing (PESAKA), Minister for Communications and Works, a third division Kayan

Numerically PESAKA was the backbone of the new government, but its actual drive came principally from BARJASA's Abdul Taib within the Cabinet and PESAKA's Thomas Kana and Alfred Mason from without. Taib had assumed the critical portfolio of Agriculture and Forestry. The political value of the power to dispense lucrative timber concessions was indeed potent. Because of his experience Taib also guided other ministers, especially Tajang who held his former ministry. Numerous ways were explored to find a Council Negri seat for Thomas Kana, but none of the three nominated members (Taib, Teo and Ling— the latter two SCA) was willing to resign so he could be appointed.

Early cabinet meetings were attended by Thomas Kana and Alfred Mason. At first the new cabinet was pre-occupied with its anti-Chinese appearance, and with Chinese efforts to subvert its base of support.[85]

[82] *Vanguard,* 21 June 1966.
[83] See ibid., 22 and 26 June and 8 July 1966.
[84] Ibid., 1 July 1966.
[85] The cabinet meeting of 26 June discussed a telegram from Abdul Rahman

The expatriates were totally excluded from all decision-making in the Tawi Sli cabinet, advice was sought instead principally from Taib, Abdul Rahman and Kana. These three essentially formed an extra-cabinet committee that would meet first, then brief the cabinet. Two months later the cabinet was broadened to include the two SCA nominated councillors, Teo Kui Seng and Ling Beng Siong.[86] Teo Kui Seng was refused his former critical portfolio which was retained and expanded by Taib, who now became Minister of Development and Forestry, and Deputy Chief Minister. Tajang Laing was transferred to become Minister of Agriculture and Ling Beng Siong became Minister of State. He is an SCA, Foochow Chinese from the third division and is the brother of the SCA chairman, Ling Beng Siew.

Taib's creation of a new Ministry of Development and Forestry cut across the lines of responsibility in a number of departments and further exacerbated his relationship with those expatriate civil servants who were opposed to him.

The replacement of top expatriate officers in the administration proceeded at a greatly accelerated pace. The State Secretary was initially given ten days to leave the state. He refused but nevertheless departed before very long. He was replaced by an Iban, Gerunsin Lembat. The Chinese Deputy Financial Secretary was promoted to replace John Pike and Abang Yusuf Puteh became Establishment Officer, an important position which gave him considerable influence over promotions and appointments throughout the civil service.

SNAP itself gained many new members who had resigned from PESAKA and PANAS and was now stronger and more representative as a truly multi-racial party. But the alignment behind the new cabinet of Tawi Sli was quite formidable, and this government now had majority support in the Sarawak Alliance and presumably in the Council Negri.

The Sarawak Alliance had been restructured, and more closely resembled the Malayan Alliance, both in policy and composition. Temenggong Jugah, speaking at a reception for the Tunku, emphasized this when he said:

> The crisis in the Sarawak Alliance can be solved if political parties affiliated to it are run on a strictly racial basis as in the Malayan Alliance. . . . This meant that all Chinese should join the Sarawak Chinese Association, Malays either Barisan Ra'ayat Jati Sarawak (BARJASA) or Party Negara and Dayaks either Party PESAKA or the Sarawak National Party.[87]

---

who had met Ling Beng Siew (the SCA Chairman), the latter suggesting that James Wong and Dunstan Endawie be taken back into the cabinet. Abdul Rahman refused and warned against Ling's 'honeyed words'. Thomas Kana then spoke of an alleged approach to Lee Kuan Yew by Wee Hood Teck and Ling Beng Siew with a request for aid in toppling the Sarawak government. (Extracted from the Minutes of the cabinet meeting, 26 June 1966.)

[86] *Sarawak Tribune,* 23 August 1966. Teo was appointed Minister for Communications and Works.

[87] *Straits Times,* 6 July 1966.

If the Chinese mixed up with other political parties then there might be trouble.[88]

With strict separation of the races into their respective communal parties and the pre-eminence of the native components, the essential elements of the Malayan Alliance would be instituted in Sarawak. All that remained was the forging of close links between MCA and SCA, and between the native parties and UMNO. By this means local parochialism could be reduced to a minimum and regional loyalties were to be subsumed within pervasive ethnic ties, as on the Peninsula. Also, given the weak numerical position of the Malays in Sarawak, this structure was the most advantageous way for them to exercise influence in Sarawak politics. UMNO could help bolster the position of its co-religionists in east Malaysia. The centre could then use this political dependence to its own advantage.

On 7 September 1966, the High Court in Kuching ruled that the dismissal of Stephen Ningkan was unconstitutional.[89] The Court issued an injunction restraining Tawi Sli from holding office and Ningkan resumed his former post. He declared forthwith that all actions of the previous government were null and void and would be revoked. He called for immediate general elections in the state.[90] The SUPP warmly endorsed his call, even if elections had to be under the old three-tier system.

The acting Prime Minister, Tun Razak, rushed to Kuching. Tawi Sli presented to the Governor, then the Speaker of Council Negri and finally the Chief Minister, copies of a statutory declaration signed by twenty-five of the forty-two members of Council Negri. That declaration requested an immediate meeting of Council Negri and expressed no confidence in Ningkan as Chief Minister.[91]

Dato Ningkan declined to convene Council Negri, as did the Speaker, and the Governor was bound to accept the advice of Ningkan's Cabinet. There is a constitutional provision that the Council must meet once every six months, but that gave Ningkan's government three months

---

[88] *Sarawak Tribune,* 5 July 1966.
[89] The Court declared in its ruling that by the provisions of the Sarawak Constitution lack of confidence may be demonstrated only by a vote in the Council Negri. See *Vanguard, Sarawak Tribune* and *Straits Times* of 8 September 1966 for full text of the judgment. Two nights before the Court's decision was announced, Radio Malaysia had broadcast Tawi Sli's urgent appeal for all Alliance Council Negri members to go immediately to Kuching. *Vangard,* 6 September 1966.
[90] 'It is no longer the question of whether I still command the confidence of the House but rather whether the present Council Negri members still enjoy the confidence of the people of Sarawak. *Sarawak Tribune,* 9 September 1966. The rationale behind Ningkan's call for new elections was that supporters of both himself and Tawi Sli had been switching from side to side as the wind blew. If so, then Council members needed a new and clear mandate on this matter from the electorate. In terms of crude political manoeuvring it was clearly in Ningkan's interests to postpone the meeting of the Council and have new elections on the subject of federal-state relations.
[91] *Straits Times,* 9 September 1966.

grace. He was assured that he had sufficient appropriations for the government to function for that period. The Chief Minister said that he was not likely to be swayed by persuasion or threats—'People have underrated my toughness. I am prepared to resist threats and intimidation. No threats of force will make me resign.'[92] Abang Othman, the chairman of PANAS issued a personal statement supporting Ningkan. He was forthwith expelled from his party.[93] Ningkan's strategy was simply to postpone any meeting of the Council Negri and in the interim to exercise his full prerogatives as Chief Minister to win followers to his side and press for elections in the near future. He miscalculated in under-estimating the resolve of the Alliance to displace him. Also, at that time the election machinery could not readily swing into action.[94] He gave the Alliance time to secure the support of all their members of the Council Negri and to invoke emergency procedures.

Penghulu Tawi Sli claimed that members of his party had been threatened with kidnapping and physical violence and had asked for police protection.[95] The Police Commissioner, Roy Henry, was asked to

[92] Ibid., 9 September 1966.

[93] *Vanguard*, 9 September 1966.

[94] Upon his reinstatement as Chief Minister Ningkan had indicated his preference for general elections as the best solution of the recurrent crises. But the federal election commission was then preparing to delimit constituencies for the purpose of direct elections and any immediate polling would have had to be held under the former three-tier system, which would allow many non-citizens to vote and, according to Tawi Sli, 'many of them are possibly Clandestine Communist Organisation sympathisers' (*Straits Times*, 11 September 1966). But the initiative lay with the Federal election commission for in May 1966 the state government had approved extension of their jurisdiction to Sarawak, preparatory to direct general elections. The Commission was about to commence the delimitation of constituencies. It was not qute clear whether the state government could initiate interim polling under the old system, and extremely doubtful whether they could be held within six months. Following the emergency declaration Ningkan formally advised the Governor, in his capacity as Chief Minister, to dissolve the Council Negri and proclaim general elections. (Letter to the Governor dated 16 September 1966, reproduced in the *Sarawak Tribune*, 28 September 1966.) The Governor simply declined to do so until after the emergency meeting of the Malaysian Parliament.

Ningkan's final thrust on 17 September was to telegram all Residents instructing them to convene Divisional Advisory Council meetings on 26 September without fail and to include the following items in the agenda: (a) to consider the desirability of holding general elections either direct or indirect at earliest possible opportunity; and (b) to assess Divisional Advisory Council confidence in its representatives to Council Negri. Ningkan was confident that if the Divisional Advisory Councils met he would have obtained from four of them motions of confidence and support which their Council Negri representatives would have been obliged to express. The only doubtful division was the third, and even there Ningkan's support was growing.

[95] *Straits Times*, 12 September 1966. Those members supporting Tawi Sli were given armed police protection that prevented all undesirable contact with them. The 'undesirables' included any who might wish to persuade some of those 25 to support Ningkan and the members were actually held incommunicado in two Kuching houses. Tawi Sli confirmed this in his answers to the following questions.

provide protection for members of Council Negri. He applied a police-
man's criteria and replied that it was not necessary| He was directly
overruled by Kuala Lumpur who instructed his deputy J. J. Raj and the
Deputy Head of Special Branch to implement their orders. The Federal
government denied Ningkan use of the Information services and
Kuching broadcasts were 'blacking out' practically all Ningkan's statements on the crisis.[96] Tension appeared to be artificially stimulated in
order to create a situation that would require a declaration of emergency.[97] There was an illegal demonstration against Ningkan by 200
Malay Alliance supporters. That same evening stones were thrown at
the home of the Speaker, the British Information Centre reading room
and the Borneo Company showcase. But there was no evidence of
general unrest or imminent danger that violence would result from
the unstable political situation.

On 15 September the Malaysian government declared a state of emergency in Sarawak because the crisis had 'deteriorated so badly that it
now poses a very serious threat to the security of the state and the
whole of Malaysia' (Tun Razak).[98] As the Tunku explained, this would

---

Sir, do you still maintain that there were threats of kidnapping and violence
against your Alliance party members?

Tawi Sli: 'It looks like it, because we very often received telephone call
from someone who never gave his name or her name but always make a
suggestion for us to come by motor car to a certain place and even to
some sort of er some sort of threatening words being passed over in the
telephone to say that someone should do some kidnapping' [sic].

There has been a suggestion, Sir, that your members have been detained
in various houses in Kuching to prevent them being persuaded by Dato
Ningkan's supporters to change sides in Council Negri. Is this so, Sir?

Tawi Sli: 'Yes. Because our detention somewhere or, well, in a group like
this is for the purpose of what you call solidarity is one thing and also to
safeguard from being bought by people of Ningkan's party, because most of
the supporters of his side are well-to-do people, and you know some of our
people are, some are weak-minded, then when you are offered certain
amount of money to come and go on his side' [sic].

From the transcript of an interview with Tawi Sli by the Australian
Broadcasting Commission correspondent, Kuching, 19 September 1966.

[96] *Straits Times,* 10 September 1966.
[97] Syed Kechik, the former political secretary to Inche Senu, advised Tawi
and his group in formulating Alliance strategy throughout the crisis and
was responsible for drafting most of the public statements by Alliance
leaders during he crisis.
[98] According to the Malaysian Minister of Home Affairs this state of emergency was in addition to the one issued (and still in force) during Indonesian confrontation. *The Times* (London), 16 September 1966.
   The expatriate officers were asked by Kuala Lumpur to prepare a case
that a situation of heightened emergency existed. They refused and a
number of older documents were used in preparing the official publication,
The Communist Threat to Sarawak, Government Printer, Kuala Lumpur
1966, published the day the new emergency was declared.
   One cause for federal concern was that if the centre-state tension
escalated to armed conflict the Malayan troops and police were out-
numbered by the Sarawak Constabulary, Field Force and Rangers. Shortly
afterwards, the First Malaysian Rangers—a predominantly Iban and quite
highly politicized force—were transferred to Ipoh and remained in the
north of Malaya for the following three years

enable a change in the Constitution, empowering the Governor to call a meeting of the Council Negri. As twenty-five of the forty-two members of the Council Negri had declared that they had no confidence in Ningkan it would then be possible 'to establish a stable government'. It was necessary to take this course 'in face of threats from communists in Sarawak' (Tun Ismail).[99] General elections would be held 'as soon as possible'.

It is important to note here the tendency, accepted over the period of confrontation, to equate opposition with subversion and disloyalty. Thus one invokes emergency powers to deal with powerful opposition. The logic employed by Dr Ismail, in the Federal Parliament, was as follows:

1) There is an uncertain situation in Sarawak which the Communists are bound to exploit.
2) Ningkan's government has the support of SUPP, in fact it relies on SUPP support.
3) SUPP is riddled with communists.
4) Thus Ningkan is ruling with the aid of the communists.
5) But Ningkan is the head of the State Security Committee.
6) Thus there is an intolerable threat to national security.

> There were political parties who were not averse to making use of the communists to achieve their ends. . . . We have to take definite preventive measures to see at least that political stability is ensured in Sarawak.[100]

When Council Negri did meet, the Chief Minister and his followers boycotted the session, which they said had been forced to meet under 'most insulting conditions imposed by the Federal Parliament whereby the governor is given unprecedented powers even more autocratic than those of former Colonial Governors'.[101] Ningkan refused to resign, choosing instead to force the Governor to dismiss him under the new constitutional amendments. He defiantly declared: 'I shall return!'[102]

Sarawakian nationalism was aroused by the dramatic sequence, and the chief beneficiary was SNAP—the party receiving numerous pledges of support from all communities throughout the state. In opposition SNAP took the offensive, characterizing the central government in none too complimentary tones.

---

[99] *Times,* 17 September 1966. The state of emergency, under article 150 (4) of the Malaysian Constitution permits precedence of federal authority over matters normally within the legislative authority of the state. This new authority, in turn, enabled the Malaysian Parliament to pass an amendment to the Malaysian Constitution (which in effect changes the constiution of the state of Sarawak) conferring absolute discretion on the Governor of Sarawak to summon the Council Negri and to replace the Speaker should he fail to comply with the Governor's directions. The Governor was also empowered to directly dismiss a Chief Minister who had lost the confidence of the Council Negri. See *Straits Times,* 16 September 1966, and *The Age* (Melbourne), 20 September 1966.
[100] Ismail in *Straits Budget,* 21 September 1966.
[101] Ningkan in *Straits Times,* 24 September 1966.
[102] *Sarawak Tribune,* 24 September 1966. Ningkan added: 'I shall never be a party to Malay domination' (*Straits Times,* 24 September 1966).

Efforts to re-structure Sarawak politics had led to a polarization, with two basic organizational modes at odds with each other. The first is that of an Alliance based upon individual uni-racial parties, as in West Malaysia. The second, as espoused by the opposition SUPP and SNAP, is a multi-racial party within which accommodation takes place, and which is much more likely to have a distinctly Sarawakian identity.

As the best educated and most experienced minister of the Tawi Sli government, Abdul Taib was extraordinarily active and influential within the cabinet. A special committee was set up to speed the Borneanization of the over 300 civil service positions still held by expatriate officers, in order to reduce substantially their determinative role in policy formulation. Taib declared: 'Sarawak is now in the process of setting up a political government . . . and the fate of the country lies with the politicians'.[103] The cessation of Indonesian confrontation and the confluence of unresolved issues that stimulated political manoeuvre, resulted in changes that terminated the phase of British colonial tutelage and heralded the inauguration of a politicized government bent upon asserting its control over the administration—which had hitherto functioned as the principal policy making institution. The new government with its active BARJASA component was much more acceptable to the centre than was the former Sarawak oriented SNAP leadership.

[103] *Vanguard,* 3 October 1966.

4

THE MALAYSIANIZATION OF SARAWAK POLITICS 1966-70

Once confirmed in power the new government set about the process of instituting a 'political government'.

(a) All the expatriate officers in the administration were removed within a year, as were most of the top expatriates in the technical departments. The substitution of less experienced local and Malayan officers removed the main obstacle to supremacy of the politicians in decision-making.

(b) The district and divisional development committees that had formerly included full local participation, were purged of all opposition party members and re-staffed only with Alliance party politicians and civil servants. Their future role was to implement government policy without obstruction.

(c) Those who had been appointed to serve as penghulus were instructed to

> serve the government of the day loyally. . . . Those Penghulus who take part in party politics and those who fail to carry out government policies should resign, or government would take disciplinary action against them.[1]

This meant that the only legitimate political activity by penghulus was to take part in the politics of the government party, given that the Chief Minister himself was a penghulu, as was one other of his cabinet ministers and the Federal Minister for Sarawak Affairs held the office of Temenggong. An effort was made to emphasize the penghulu's role as implementer of government policy rather than as representative of his people. The following month Temenggong Jugah assisted by Jonathan Bangau, MP, respectively President and Treasurer of PESAKA, called a meeting of forty-four penghulus from the third division, the

---

[1] *Sarawak Tribune,* 11 July 1967. The statement was by the Minister of State. A few days later the Minister said that the Malaysian Information Service press release had been incorrect and that he 'merely urged penghulus and tuai rumahs to be co-operative with the government and not to make statements or propaganda against the government' (ibid., 15 July 1967). But that later clarification only changed the tone, not the substance of his message. In any case the Chief Minister quickly clarified that penghulus could not take part in politics 'but they were expected to support the government of the day, otherwise they should resign as they received remuneration from the government in power'. (Ibid., 17 July 1967).

meeting being held in the Sarawak Alliance chamber in Sibu.[2] The occasion clearly enjoyed a government-party imprimatur and the only publicized resolutions to come from the occasion dealt with a strengthening of official Iban leadership. Temenggong Jugah spoke in favour of the government simply extending the appointments of penghulus who enjoyed the popular confidence, rather than encouraging election of a new penghulu every five years.

In previous years the practice of electing penghulus had varied from one district to another. In some districts all adult males voted, in others the vote was restricted to the Tuai Rumah, that is, to the heads of each of the individual longhouses. In other districts the process was simply one of consultation. To standardize procedure the state government determined as from November 1966 that future selection of penghulus should be made through an election by secret ballot, and that only heads of families (Tuai bilek) should vote. With a heightening of general political consciousness and with the competition between two predominantly Dayak political parties, it was inevitable that the process of choosing penghulus would be politicized.[3] The only alternative was to consider them all to be permanent civil servants, as in West Malaysia.

In November 1966 BARJASA and PANAS at last agreed to merge and form one united Islamic party. The departure of the former PANAS chairman, Abang Othman, and his entry into SNAP together with a number of followers, removed the chief obstacles to merger. The new Parti BUMIPUTERA Sarawak chose as its president Abang Ikhwan Zainie, publisher of *Utusan Sarawak* and the only prominent anti-Cession leader in PANAS. Its deputy president was Tuanku Bujang, former top leader of BARJASA who was subsequently appointed Governor of Sarawak (in April 1969). The secretary-general of the new party was Abdul Taib bin Mahmud and the list of forty-three executive members also included three Dayaks and one Chinese.

After its exclusion from office and in anticipation of the promised (1967) elections, SNAP relied upon organization as the road to political power. Whilst part of the government, SNAP had only added six new branches and exhibited little interest in developing a popular base of support. By sharp contrast in 1966-7 alone SNAP opened thirty-five

---

[2] See *Sarawak Tribune* and *Vanguard*, 9 August 1967.

[3] One instance of penghulu selection involving political criteria was reported in the Bintulu district, where a candidate who received the highest vote was not confirmed by the government. He happened to be a SUPP member. Another case in the Belaga sub-district of the Kapit district was rather ineptly handled. Three successive elections were held to select a new penghulu, and in each vote the same man, Lisut Tinggang, won. As the winner was a SUPP member residing in the area of the Minister of Agriculture, the latter decided that such a form of popular election was not in accord with Kayan custom. He thus decreed that only the Tuai Rumahs could vote and only Tuai Rumahs could stand for election, which ruled out the thrice successful candidate. It is true that customarily only those Kayans from the marin (upper) class were penghulus, but the contention that consultations were historically confined to the Tuai Rumah (head of longhouse) is doubtful. Consequent upon issuance of the November 1966 standard procedures, the explanation was patently political. See *Sarawak Tribune*, 9 and 10 June 1967.

new branches, thereby doubling the number of its branches in the first, third and fifth divisions of the state. Hitherto SNAP support was derived principally from second and fourth division Ibans. Out of office, it rapidly attracted other Dayak groups, some Chinese and those Malays who did not wish to be a part of the newly merged Parti BUMIPUTERA. SNAP opened twelve new predominantly Malay branches, four branches which were mostly Chinese and many others that numbered various races amongst their influential members. A sophisticated branch level organization capped the groundswell of hostility against outside intervention during the 1966 Alliance crisis. The four contested District Council by-elections held during 1967 were each won by SNAP candidates (a Chinese, an Iban and two Malays) and the party was riding on a wave of invincibility.

Within the Alliance, Parti BUMIPUTERA exercised a leading role. In fact, judging solely from the output of the Malaysian Information Service, one might have concluded that Abdul Taib rather than Penghulu Tawi Sli was Chief Minister. Inside the Sarawak Alliance National Council Parti BUMIPUTERA had twelve representatives, SCA six and PESAKA six.[4]

PESAKA was on the defensive for its apparent subservience to Parti BUMIPUTERA and SNAP took advantage of this weakness as it moved into PESAKA's former heartland. The lack of strong PESAKA leaders within the Cabinet contributed to the general inertia and the party dithered for many months, relying upon the prestige of the incumbency of office to pull it through. As a result of its lack of initiative the position of the party steadily deteriorated during 1967 as Dayak resentment against Malay usurpation grew and was adroitly exploited by SNAP's field organizers.

Twelve months after its ouster from government SNAP was so popular amongst the Iban that it was on the verge of capturing majority support even in the Kapit district, where PESAKA had easily won virtually every seat in the 1963 election. Worried PESAKA leaders successfully prevailed upon Temenggong Jugah, and in his welcoming speech to Tun Razak he launched a scathing attack against the three Parti BUMIPUTERA ministers (Abdul Taib, Awang Hipni and Federal Minister Abdul Rahman Ya'kub) who

> were working only for the Malay community and not doing the same for the natives [Dayaks]. Large sums of money were being allocated for the building of mosques everywhere but very little were being given for development in the ulu areas where the Dayaks lived.[5]

The Temenggong's forceful advocacy of Dayak concerns was a determined attempt to recover Dayak support for PESAKA. If reinforced by action it would answer SNAP charges that PESAKA had sold out to the

---

[4] *Sarawak Tribune,* 7 June 1967.
[5] *Vanguard,* 9 October 1967. Temenggong Jugah was incensed when told that Abdul Taib had allegedly used timber cess funds to finance the building of mosques and suraus, calling them 'grants from the federal government'. Kapit district had in fact received a disproportionately high percentage of development expenditure.

Malays and to Parti BUMIPUTERA. Later that month the Sarawak Alliance National Council meeting (boycotted by Parti BUMIPUTERA) demanded a Cabinet re-shuffle, which could only mean a reduction in the primary role of Abdul Taib.[6] Adamant PESAKA demands that Taib be sacked as a Cabinet minister were fulfilled with his resignation from the Council Negri and his replacement by Ikhwan Zainie.[7] In return for the resignation Abdul Taib obtained a written guarantee that the most important of his policies, the freezing of timber licences, would be implemented. This was achieved through signed agreements between the state and federal governments and between the federal government and the UN Food and Agricultural Organization—which agreed to carry out a detailed inventory of the state's forest resources. The federal government thus came to be guardian of the terms of this agreement, due to its international character.

PESAKA could well afford to be firm as they then provided fifteen of the twenty-five Alliance seats in the Council Negri, and thus were numerically indispensible. Since 1965 PESAKA had steadily increased its representation in the Council, principally through defections from its Alliance partners.

But Council Negri membership was derived from the 1963 election results. It was the forthcoming election (though oft postponed) toward which they had to work. In the new Cabinet the omnibus portfolio of development and forestry was abolished, and PESAKA acquired more significant ministries. The membership[8] then became:

Penghulu Tawi Sli (PESAKA), Chief Minister

Abang Haji Abdulrahim (BUMIPUTERA), Deputy Chief Minister

Teo Kui Seng (SCA), Minister for Communications and Works

Abang Ikhwan Zainie (BUMIPUTERA), Minister for Local Government

Penghulu Francis Umpau (PESAKA), Minister for Lands and Mineral Resources

Tajang Laing (PESAKA), Minister for Agriculture and Forestry

Ling Beng Siong (SCA), Minister for Youth and Culture

Awang Hipni (BUMIPUTERA), Minister for Welfare

Sandom anak Nyuak (PESAKA), Minister of State (appointed on December 22, 1967)

The party representation within the new cabinet (4 PESAKA, 3 BUMIPUTERA and 2 SCA) more accurately reflected the state of the parties in the Council Negri. PESAKA held the two portfolios that dealt with resource allocation. The power to issue timber licenses was the source of seemingly unlimited largesse and control of the land ministry precluded any Chinese attempts formally to acquire land held as birthright by the Dayaks.

With federal co-operation the scheduled elections were further postponed on the assumption that (a) SNAP would run out of funds and its

---

[6] *Sarawak Tribune,* 24 October 1967.

[7] *Sarawak Tribune,* 23 November 1967.

[8] *Sarawak Tribune,* 29 November 1967.

organization crumble; (b) if SNAP remained in opposition for a considerable length of time, Malay supporters of that party would gradually re-join the Alliance, attracted by established success; (c) the issue of federal intervention during the 1966 Alliance crisis would lose significance with the passage of time.

But the two opposition parties, SNAP and SUPP, took advantage of widespread anti-government dissatisfaction and applied themselves energetically to building up party organizations to capitalize upon this discontent. The government parties responded in two ways: (1) use of political patronage to win support, and (2) invocation of security restrictions to circumscribe opposition activities.

The threat from SUPP was met principally through restrictions based upon considerations of national security, for their opposition was often equated with subversion. The government was reluctantly reconciled to Chinese supporting SUPP, but wherever that party was able to build up a branch with significant native backing the authorities would step in, arrest leading native members and occasionally proscribe the branch—thus preventing all party officers from leading any other organizations registered under the Societies Ordinance. These sweeping measures were employed to intimidate the Dayaks and to prevent SUPP from expanding its multi-racial base of support.

Despite some official suggestions that the SNAP slogan 'Sarawak for the Sarawakians' bordered on the subversive, internal security measures were not employed by the government against SNAP. The strategy chosen to weaken SNAP was chiefly intended to undermine its efficient organization and also to woo its influential supporters through the use of political patronage, specifically development funds and timber licenses. The difficulty with the latter course was that though such 'favours' might win various individuals to the Alliance side, the patently political use of public funds often served to alienate those who were not the recipients of such favours. Such use of patronage appeared to be counterproductive in a system where *élite* politics were to be checked by resort to the electoral process, with its concomitant rule of one man, one vote.

A substantial part of the funding that was used to pay SNAP staff and field workers came from Wee Hood Teck, the Kuching banker and philanthropist. His business had not flourished since the ouster of Ningkan as Chief Minister, in part because the end of confrontation and the passing of the British had reduced the demand for new housing and industrial sites.[9] In addition his bank generated relatively small profits. This could be attributed to the character of the banking business

---

[9] The Wee Hood Teck Development Corporation was awarded the large contract to build the Pending Port light industrial complex near Kuching (downriver). Early returns from this substantial investment in commercial and residential development were contingent upon the maintenance of strong demand for such sites. However, from mid-1966 onward the level of economic activity in Sarawak dipped noticeably. For instance, whereas the consumption of electricity had increased at an average rate of 19.8% per annum from 1963 to 1966, there was negligible (less than 1%) growth in the year 1967. Sarawak Electricity Supply Corporation, *Annual Report 1967*, Sarawak Press Sdn. Bhd., Kuching 1968, p. 6.

and to the exclusion of his Bian Chiang Bank from the Association of Malaysian Banks.[10]

Alliance leaders—including the Federal Minister of Finance, Tan Siew Sin—were quick to emphasize that he should leave SNAP and join the Alliance. Wee Hood Teck finally succumbed to this pressure and SNAP lost most of its financial underpinning.[11] How much support still reached SNAP through the 'back door' one will never know, for though Wee did resign from SNAP he did not join SCA.

Patronage Politics

Patronage plays a determinative role in politics as the dispenser of wealth can place certain limits upon the activities of the recipients. Within Sarawak wealth lies in the hands of the government and a small part of the Chinese community. Commerce and industry are owned preponderantly by Chinese within the Foochow, Hokkien and Teochew dialect groups. In contrast to West Malaysia, European enterprises are much less dominant in Sarawak. The one exception to this is the Sarawak Shell Oilfields which are of an enclave character.

The principal new form of wealth, apart from oil, is timber. Aggressive Foochow businessmen, led by the Chairman of SCA Ling Beng Siew, have taken a leading role in the exploitation of this resource. The granting of licences to fell timber transcended the realm of mere political patronage because it shifted control of vast economic resources to the recipients, and accorded to them the means of exerting great influence throughout the body politic. Those holding high office in the state government have in the past clearly exercised the right to allocate such timber licences on a politically partisan basis.

Other material benefits that have accrued to those close to government include the provision of opportunities for sponsored travel overseas, appointment to boards of government corporations and grants for minor rural projects.

Overseas travel

Utilizing cumulative categories each district councillor has been identified by the widest sphere in which he has travelled. The number of councillors who have travelled overseas is indeed quite high, and with the passage of time an increasing proportion have undertaken such travel.[12]

---

[10] The net profit of the Bian Chiang Bank for the year ended 31 December 1967 was M$7,551, down from M$67,876 for 1966. Donations made by the bank during 1967 totalled M$55,478 (compared to M$16,831 in 1966) drastically reducing the balance available to be carried forward to a meager M$751. (Bian Chiang Bank Berhad, Directors' Report for the year ended 31.12.67, mimeo, Kuching, 29 July 1968.)

[11] Wee Hood Teck, a Vice-Chairman of SNAP and Wee Boon Ping (the Financial Officer of SNAP) resigned effective 15 October 1968.

[12] These tables record the proportion of councillors and members who have travelled overseas since their birth or initial arrival in Sarawak. Thus a Dayak born in Indonesia, or a Chinese born in China, who had migrated with his family to Sarawak and who had not since travelled overseas would be regarded as having never been overseas, for the purposes of this table. The prime object of such a classification is to isolate the phenomena of overseas travel and distinguish it from migration.

Table 23

Overseas Travel by District Councillors by Year of Election, Political Party Allegiance and New Recruitment to Elective Office

| | Never overseas | Percentage | | | | % Data | Total number |
		W. Malaysia & Singapore	Other Asia	Haj	Rest of the world		
District Councillors							
1950-4	56	16	3	12	13	78	157
1955-9	58	19	4	10	9	79	618
1960-2	49	29	5	6	12	79	480
District Councillors 1963	41	36	3	6	14	85	429
BARJASA	33 (39)	47 (39)	— (3)	14 (14)	6 (6)	82 (89)	44 (73)
PESAKA	17 (22)	61 (55)	5 (3)	— (19)	17 (5)	95 (95)	43 (61)
SNAP	23 (37)	61 (51)	—	—	16 (12)	90 (89)	48 (73)
SCA	(20)	—	(40)	—	(40)	(100)	(5)
Alliance	24	55	2	4	14	89	138
PANAS	49 (42)	27 (24)	2 (2)	17 (15)	15 (17)	83 (84)	58 (63)
SUPP	63 (61)	20 (22)	4 (5)	—	13 (13)	69 (71)	115 (123)
Independent	47 (41)	28 (24)	4 (3)	8 (17)	14 (14)	95 (97)	117 (30)
Newly recruited	52	26	3	8	12	82	235

Note: The figures in parentheses refer to the councillors adhering to each party in July 1963, after the re-alignment of the independent councillors.

Table 24

Overseas Travel by Sarawak Dewan Ra'ayat and Council Negri Members Selected in 1960 and 1963 by Political Party Allegiance

	Percentage						
	Never overseas	W. Malaysia & Singapore	Other Asia	Haj	Rest of the world	% Data	Total number
Council Negri							
1960-2	3	23	—	—	73	91	33
1963	—	14	17	—	69	92	39
Members of Parliament 1963	—	14	9	—	77	92	24
Member of Council Negri & Parliament 1963	—	13	15	—	72	90	52
PANAS	—	—	—	—	100	100	6
BARJASA	—	13	25	—	62	73	11
PESAKA	—	23	23	—	54	100	13
SNAP	—	11	—	—	89	100	9
SCA	—	20	40	—	40	100	5
SUPP	—	—	—	—	100	67	6

Table 25

Overseas Travel by Sarawak Dewan Ra'ayat and Council Negri Members Elected in 1970 (and Candidates) by Political Party Allegiance and New Recruitment to Elective Office

	Never overseas	W. Malaysia & Singapore	Other Asia	Haj	Rest of the world	% Data	Total number
			Percentage				
Members of Parliament 1970	33 (39)	17 (27)	4 (4)	4 (4)	42 (27)	100 (88)	24 (93)
Council Negri Members 1970	34 (41)	18 (22)	14 (8)	— (5)	34 (23)	92 (86)	48 (220)
Members of Council Negri & Parliament 1970	34 (41)	18 (23)	10 (7)	1 (5)	37 (24)	94 (87)	72 (304)
BUMIPUTERA	36 (27)	7 (11)	7 (4)	7 (19)	43 (38)	82 (81)	17 (32)
PESAKA	30 (28)	20 (24)	20 (9)	— (4)	30 (35)	100 (92)	10 (50)
SNAP	48 (47)	14 (21)	— (5)	— (5)	38 (23)	100 (90)	21 (69)
SCA	— (—)	— (17)	40 (25)	—	60 (58)	100 (92)	5 (13)
SUPP	25 (50)	31 (20)	13 (9)	—	31 (22)	94 (82)	17 (56)
Independent	50 (51)	50 (32)	— (5)	— (4)	— (7)	100 (86)	2 (84)
Newly recruited	53 (57)	13 (16)	9 (7)	3 (4)	22 (16)	94 (83)	33 (162)

Note: The figures in parentheses refer to the candidates who stood for election in 1970.

The most dramatic increase occurred in travel by district councillors to West Malaysia and Singapore. This sudden jump after 1960 was a direct result of the promotional efforts mounted by the then Malayan government to win Bornean support for the formation of the Federation of Malaysia. A great many influential persons were taken on guided tours of the Malayan peninsula, specifically to visit rural development schemes. The level of sophistication of those Malayan efforts is underlined by the high proportion of PESAKA and SNAP councillors who had visited only West Malaysia and Singapore, a proportion considerably greater than for PANAS, BARJASA or SUPP. Given strong Islamic support for Malaysia and equally strong SUPP opposition to the scheme, the support of the Dayaks of SNAP and PESAKA was vital to the successful inauguration of Malaysia.

The members of the Council Negri and Dewan Ra'ayat were very well travelled, three-quarters having left Asia at least once. Such trips are generally seen as a customary perquisite of elective office.

Of those elected in 1970 the newly recruited were distinctly less widely travelled than those who had hitherto held elective office. This observation strongly supports the hypothesis that overseas travel is in large part a function of actually holding elective office. The SNAP members, having the greatest share of new recruits, were the least widely travelled of all party members, though formerly their elected members had travelled very widely.

Minor rural projects

The final responsibility for the approval of minor rural projects rests with the State Development Officer, all of whose funds come directly from the federal government, which retains control over their use.[13] Various State and Federal Ministers during their travels have 'approved' grants for such minor rural projects on the spot, in the sense that their 'recommendation' will facilitate expeditious consideration of that particular project. Whether the project will actually be implemented, as the recipients have often been led to understand, will largely depend upon the relationship of the particular Minister to the State Development Officer—who acts on behalf of the Federal government in general and Tun Razak in particular.

Alliance politicians have taken increasing care to associate themselves with these grants. For instance, a check of the published grants associated with Sarawak Ministers in 1968 reveals that ministers approved, presented cheques or declared open projects in the constituencies that they later contested (see Table 26).

Ling Beng Siong distributed more funds in his constituency than did any other minister, and added many substantial donations both from personal funds and from his timber companies. Except for Sandom

---

[13] Prior to 1966 the District Councils also advised on the distribution of such grants. The requests for such grants in 1968 totalled in excess of M$5 million. Some $1 million was actually spent, but the funds came through irregularly.

anak Nyuak, all the ministers listed in Table 26 were returned in the 1970 elections.

Table 26

Grants by Ministers for Facilities in the Constituencies they Subsequently Contested in 1969

Constituency	Minister	Project	Value (M$)
S. 7	Abang Ikhwan Zainie (BUMI)	Mosques	20,000
		Suraus	15,000
S. 15	Penghulu Tawi Sli (PESAKA)	Basketball court	5,000
		Road and bridges	13,000
		Surau	10,000
S. 25	Awang Hipni (BUMI)	Chinese temple	7,500
		Water supply and footpath	5,800
		Surau	3,000
S. 26	Sandom anak Nyuak (PESAKA)	Water supply and jetty	6,600
S. 29	Ling Beng Siong (SCA)	Paths, roads and bridges	30,200
		Playground	1,000
P. 124	Abdul Taib bin Mahmud (BUMI)	Mosques	18,000

Note: The above *i*nformation has been extracted from accounts published daily during 1968 in the *Sarawak Tribune* and the *Vanguard.* As there are likely to be certain omissions, the figures should only be treated as an indication of the trend prior to the commencement of serious campaigning for the 1969 election.

Appointments to boards of Government agencies

Appointments to the boards of statutory authorities are a familiar way to reward those close to the party in power. For instance, the political appointees to the nine-member board of directors of the Sarawak Electricity Supply Corporation changed as follows:

  1965—one each from BARJASA, SCA, SNAP and SUPP
  1966—two from PESAKA, one each from BARJASA and SNAP
  1967-70—two BUMIPUTERA, two PESAKA, one SCA and one who was
      formerly BARJASA[14]

From 1966 onward the political representatives were chosen only from the Alliance parties. Further politicization was apparent in 1967 when party appointees became a majority of the nine directors, and all were associated with those parties that formed the new Alliance government.

---

[14] Sarawak Electricity Supply Corporation, *Annual Report,* The Sarawak Press Sdn. Bhd., Kuching 1965, 1966, 1967, 1968, 1969, 1970.

Delimitation of Constituencies

Since 1963 the District Council wards have been aggregated to form 48 state and 24 federal electorates. The process of drawing boundaries for the direct elections, direct as distinct from the former three-tiered system, was begun in 1965 and concluded in late 1968 with the publication of the *Report of the Election Commission on the Delimitation of Constituencies.*[15]

The communal composition of the total electorate underwent appreciable change during the period 1962 to 1968 (Table 27). The net effect was to increase the proportion of Chinese by 4 per cent and Malays/Melanaus by 1 per cent, both at the expense of the Dayaks.

Table 27

Percentage of Registered Electors and Total Population Divided by Major Ethnic Group

Ethnic group	Registered electors			Total population		
	1962	1968	Net change 1962-8	1969	1970	Net change 1960-70
Malay/ Melanau	25	26	+1	24	25	+1
Dayak	51	46	—5	44	44	—
Chinese	24	28	+4	31	30	—1
Other non-indigenous	—	—	—	1	1	—

The rise in the proportion of Chinese in the electorate took place despite stricter franchise requirements. The minimum requirement to vote is now Malaysian citizenship, and no longer simply local residence for seven of the past ten years. Thus it is likely that there has been quite an awakening of Chinese political consciousness. The left-wing SUPP has in fact done all it could to encourage Chinese registration, in stark contrast to the policy of the Labour Party of Malaya—with whom it is frequently grouped by commentators. SUPP has by no means abandoned the struggle 'by constitutional means'.

The Constitution of Malaysia as amended in 1962, permits weighting 'to the extent that in some cases a rural constituency may contain as little as one half of the electors of any urban constituency'.[16] The extent of final variation did exceed that envisaged by the Election Commission, and was greater than 50 per cent above and 50 per cent

[15] Malaysia, *Report of the Election Commission on the Delimitation of Parliamentary and State Constituencies in the State of Sarawak,* Government Printing Office, Kuala Lumpur 1968. The delays were in large part due to political factors outside the control of the Commission itself.
[16] Ibid., p. 6.

below 'the quota'.[17] The quota of 6,944 was determined by dividing the total number of registered electors throughout the state by the number of state constituencies.

Figure 3 records the degree to which registration in each State Constituency has diverged from this quota. The electorates have been grouped according to the predominant community in each electorate. Thus there are 12 predominantly Malay/Melanau electorates (11 with a clear absolute majority, 1 with a plurality), 28 Dayak electorates (23 Dayak majority and five Dayak plurality), and 8 Chinese electorates (7 Chinese majority and one Chinese plurality).

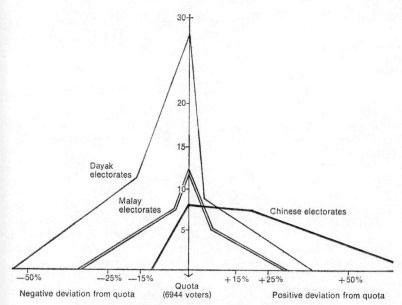

Figure 3 *State constituencies with Dayak, Malay and Chinese preponderance (1969)*

To interpret the diagram it is necessary to bear in mind that positive deviation means that each electorate has a larger number of voters, and thus each voter and his community is under-represented. The converse, negative deviation, is to the benefit of that particular group of voters.

[17] By way of explanation reference should be made to the difficulties under which the Commission operated, having no precise figures or equivalent past experience in Sarawak on which to base their estimates of eligible voters. The change in franchise requirements made predictions on the basis of eligible voters in 1963 somewhat questionable.

We can observe a strong positive deviation for the Chinese electorates, and equally strong negative deviation for the Dayak electorates, and a fairly symmetrical distribution for the Malays/Melanaus. The net effect is summarized in Table 28.

Table 28

Representation of Electors by Ethnic Group: 1969 Boundaries

Ethnic group	Proportion of constituencies dominated by that ethnic group	Registered electors	Net under or over representation (1) in relation
	(1)	(2)	to (2)
	%	%	%
Malay/Melanau	25	26	—1
Dayak	58	46	+12
Chinese	17	28	—11

The outcome can be contrasted with the situation prevailing in West Malaysia where rural weightage almost automatically serves as a euphemism for proportionately greater Malay representation at the expense of urban Chinese.

The Election Commission published its draft Report in June 1967, and invited comments from the public, As a result of its hearings the Commission slightly altered the boundaries of four State Constituencies, changes which had the following effects:

(a) A predominantly Dayak ward in S. 14 Gedong was exchanged for a predominantly Malay ward in S. 13 Semera, thus altering the electorate S. 14 Gedong from the status of Dayak majority to Dayak plurality. (It is now Dayak 47%, Malay 42% and Chinese 11%.)

(b) A solidly Dayak ward was transferred from S. 32 Oya to S. 30 Dudong. The net effect was a change of S. 32 Oya from Dayak plurality to Melanau/Malay majority.

Had the Election Commission not made these changes, as requested by leaders of Parti BUMIPUTERA, the net under-representation of the Malay/Melanau community would have risen to 3 per cent and the over-representation of the Dayaks to 14 per cent.[18]

The Chinese, because of their predeliction for concentrating in town areas, were almost certain to be under-represented. However, the extent of their under-representation could have been modified somewhat by boundary adjustments. But many simple changes of the basic constituency plan would only have increased Chinese representation at Malay expense, principally in the First Division of Sarawak. Realizing this, SUPP appealed for a basic re-drawing of boundaries throughout the Kuching

---

[18] The changes proved to be worth two seats to Parti BUMIPUTERA, as that party won S.14 and S.32 by the narrow margins of 2.4% and 3.3% respectively.

and Serian districts, and asked that one extra constituency be transferred from the third to the first division. None of its requests was granted by the Commission.

The 1969 Election Campaign

Politics since 1966 had been largely geared to the anticipation of imminent electoral contest. Even though elections had been often postponed there was little doubt in the minds of politicians that they would eventually be held accountable in an electoral reckoning. Nor was there a general expectation that there would be any tampering with the ballots once actually cast. Such popular confidence in the scrupulous fairness of electoral procedures is uncommon even in the economically most developed of nations.

A good deal of bickering persisted within the Alliance. From its dominant position in the Council Negri, PESAKA aspired to become the UMNO of Sarawak, the leading native component of the Alliance. Its efforts to recruit Malays and Melanaus provoked a direct clash with Parti BUMIPUTERA, which was seeking a solid base in those two ethnic communities. On 4 October 1968 Parti BUMIPUTERA sent a circular letter to all its members urging that

> . . . Parti BUMIPUTERA cannot withdraw one inch as to be forced to give away Malay seats to give way to PESAKA. Our basic objectives was to unite the Malays and Bedayuhs (Land Dayaks) and we would be prepared to oppose any one who becomes the tool to split our race. . . .
> The people surely remembered that at the time when we were uniting our race and struggle for our community, these people were never seen in the rural areas. . . .
> LET US STRUGGLE ON FOR THE UNITY OF OUR RACE— BEWARE OF THOSE WHO WILL OUTPLAY US IN THEIR GREED FOR SEATS.[19]

Wan Alwi bin Tuanku Ibrahim, a young Malay lawyer who became a vice-president of PESAKA and a nominated member of Parliament, was repeatedly attacked by BUMIPUTERA leaders who vilified him as one who would split the Malays and render them politically ineffectual. Parti BUMIPUTERA concentrated upon its efforts to discredit SNAP Malays and regarded PESAKA's efforts as a mortal stab. Despite protracted discussions BUMIPUTERA and PESAKA were unable to agree upon a mutually acceptable allocation of constituencies, and finally nominated candidates to stand against one another in sixteen coastal state constituencies. PESAKA decided to use its own symbol on the election ballots, whilst SCA and Parti BUMIPUTERA utilized that of the Alliance. The imagery was particularly important to PESAKA. The Alliance symbol, a sailing boat, was the possession of the 'orang laut', the coastal dwellers who were overwhelmingly Islamic. SNAP was already on the attack against PESAKA for their alleged subservience to the Malays. SNAP themselves used a

[19] Parti BUMIPUTERA Directive no. 8, signed by the Secretary-General of the party, Abdul Taib bin Mahmud. This English translation (from the original romanized Malay) appeared in the *Vanguard*, 1 November 1968.

Figure 4 *Party symbols used in the 1970 election*

SNAP

SUPP

ALLIANCE

PESAKA

shield—a much more distinctly Dayak symbol. So on 21 March (1969) PESAKA declared that they would use their own shield on the ballot. (Despite the conflict with BUMIPUTERA, PESAKA remained uneasily a nominal member of the Sarawak Alliance.)

SCA leaders were happy to use the Alliance symbol because they were heavily dependent upon 'Alliance' votes, that is, Malay and other native voters who would support SCA candidates precisely because they were nominated by the Alliance and not precisely because they belonged to the SCA. For party BUMIPUTERA the Alliance symbol evoked a positvie response from their principal base of support. Throughout the campaign, the BUMIPUTERA leadership stressed its strong links with the central Malaysian leadership—with considerably more success than had the BARJASA leadership in 1963, because it now had become clear that the support of Kuala Lumpur was indispensible to the achievement of power and prestige within the Sarawak Malay community. This was not true for any other ethnic group. To further strengthen this image of official backing the BUMIPUTERA leaders indicated that the Tunku had encouraged their party to apply for direct membership in UMNO after the election.

An organization that has been of great assistance in the task of uniting Muslims throughout Sarawak is commonly known by the acronymn BINA, that is the Angkatan Nahdatul Islam Bersatu. BINA is a religious organization whose charter precludes political activity. It propagates an orthodox type of Islam, committed to changing Muslim attitudes in order to dramatically improve their economic situation. BINA is a cadre organization with a quite select membership. All members are approved by a central committee headed by the Chairman, Dato Abdul Rahman Yakub. BINA has invoked intense loyalty from its members, who have a sense of mission. The religious and political aspects of their cause are quite indistinguishable and the zeal of BINA members has helped greatly to unify the Muslim community behind the leader of BINA, who is also the key figure in Parti BUMIPUTERA. BINA was founded (in May 1968) by four men, Dato Abdul Rahman, Al-Ustadz Anis (of the Majlis Islam) who became the secretary, Abdul Taib Mahmud, the treasurer and Ustaz Mohd Mortadza. Its work since then has been quiet and effective, within the confines of the Muslim community. One of the dangers inherent in such an organization is that it will play a role analogous to that of UMNO Pemuda in a state whose religious composition is quite different to that of West Malaysia. This dilemma was identified by one of BINA's founders who expressed a fear that in this respect BINA could be some years ahead of its time. Parti BUMIPUTERA can ill afford any over-zealous propagation of Islam amongst the Bidayuh and other Dayak groups, action which could be totally counter-productive to that party's efforts to broaden its own base of support.

There was an unprecedented broadening of political freedom during the three months immediately preceding the opening of polls in May 1969. The controls on political expression, imposed in Sarawak first by the British at the time of the Brunei revolt, were relaxed and the debate ranged freely.

The central Alliance government approached the first Malaysia-wide elections with an air of self-confidence. They had an overwhelming majority in the Dewan Ra'ayat, they had survived the test of Indonesian confrontation and the challenge of Singapore's People's Action Party, and had brought prosperity to Malaysia. Events in Sarawak were not of central consequence to the federal leadership, as long as that state was content to remain within the federation. At his birthday party (8 February 1969) the Tunku asked Stephen Yong (the Secretary-General of SUPP) about his party's stand on Malaysia. Yong replied that SUPP supports the concept of Malaysia, but opposed the manner in which the British Government brought Malaysia into being. The Tunku then asked whether Yong would put this into writing, which he did in the following manner.

> The SUPP supports the concept of Malaysia. Our party believes that as a small country Sarawak should seek regional co-operation and eventual merger with neighbouring countries with common cultural, economic and political ties so as to become part of a bigger and stronger nation.
>
> In pursuance of their belief that future security and prosperity of Sarawak lies in merger with her neighbours the leaders of SUPP had taken an active role, before the Malaysian Plan was mooted, in trying to bring about the proposed formation of the Federation of the three British Borneo Territories. We were, however, opposed to the manner in which the British Government brought Malaysia into being without giving independence to the people of Sarawak and allowing them to freely choose of their own accord the arrangements by which they would merge to form Malaysia.
>
> Our opposition to the British Plan for Malaysia has spot-lighted the attention of the world on Sarawak. In deference to world opinion the British Government had to give an opportunity to the people of Sarawak to make their views known, and, as a result, the Cobbold Commission was appointed. The SUPP then made representations to this body setting forth its views on the proposed plan for Malaysia.
>
> In order to ensure that the views of the people of Sarawak be given due and proper consideration, the SUPP submitted an appeal to the United Nations based on the principle of self determination. By this action the SUPP has enabled the people of Sarawak to get a better deal out of the arrangements for Malaysia. Certain safeguards for the people of Sarawak were incorporated in the Inter-Governmental Committee Report. However, certain terms and conditions whereby Sarawak became part of Malaysia require to be re-examined so that the natural aspiration of the people of Sarawak will be realised. The SUPP will seek to attain this by constitutional means.
>
> Since the formation of Malaysia, the SUPP has continued to work for the people of Sarawak constitutionally within the framework of Malaysia. . . .[20]

In return for adoption of this declaration as SUPP policy the Tunku agreed not to detain SUPP candidates and to allow extensive freedom to those campaigning for that party. Wearied by the constant bickering

---

[20] This phrasing adroitly castigates the British without once criticizing the central Malaysian government. It is reproduced verbatim in SUPP's election manifesto, *What* SUPP *Stands For,* Vanguard Press, Kuching 1969.

between PESAKA and BUMIPUTERA the Tunku agreed to await clear indication as to who really had the support of the Sarawak people, and was quite amenable to suggestions that he not campaign on behalf of Sarawak Alliance candidates.

Stephen Yong was placed in an invidious position as he spent the following three weeks touring SUPP branches to justify his pledging the party's support for Malaysia. However, he did manage to have his exact wording made part of the SUPP election manifesto. As a result the Tunku did not visit Sarawak and SUPP freely campaigned throughout Dayak areas where many they met thought that SUPP had gone out of existence, as it was so long since they had heard from the party. SUPP leaders were somewhat surprised at the strength of Dayak feeling against Malaysia. SUPP propaganda that penghulus were advancing their own personal interests rather than those of their anakbiak (followers) began to have some effect.

The Aftermath of the Riots in West Malaysia

Polling commenced throughout Malaysia on 10 May 1969 and the results for West Malaysia were announced the following day. The rude shock of a sharply reduced Alliance majority and the consequent outbreak of intense communal rioting in Kuala Lumpur severely shook the government and aroused it from its state of political relaxation. The central government responded by suspending the constitution and invoking sweeping emergency powers.[21] This caught East Malaysia by surprise and for a few days the implications of the suspension of parliamentary democracy were not fully apparent. Polling in East Malaysia was suspended on 15 May, all political rallies were cancelled the following day and then all party publications were banned (on 22 May). In mid-June came a wave of seventy-nine arrests under the new emergency and then suspension of the most prestigious Chinese language newspaper, the *See Hua Daily News*.[22]

---

[21] For accounts of the events of 13 May see: Tunku Abdul Rahman, *May 13 Before and After,* Utusan Melayu Press, Kuala Lumpur 1969; Felix V. Gagliano, *Communal Violence in Malaysia 1969: The Political Aftermath,* S.E. Asia Series #13, Ohio University Center for International Studies, Athens, Ohio, 1970; Goh Cheng Teik, *The May Thirteenth Incident and Democracy in Malaysia,* Oxford University Press, Kuala Lumpur 1971; Malaysia National Operations Council, *The May 13 Tragedy,* Government Printer, Kuala Lumpur 1969; John Slimming, *Malaysia, Death of a Democracy,* John Murray, London 1969.

[22] On 2 July 1969. The only 'tension' evident in Sarawak at that time concerned three curious fires that gutted the Kuching government rest house (which was slated for destruction to make way for the new Council Negri chamber), damaged the offices of the Majlis Islam and part of a classroom at the Batu Lintang Teachers College. Initially the police reported that electrical short circuits were responsible (*Sarawak Tribune,* 7 June 1969). But two days later the State Information Control Centre announced that the three fires 'were the works of members of the Sarawak Communist Organisation [SCO] who hope to create chaos and disturbance by playing on the sentiments of the various racial groups in the state. The government has now obtained concrete evidence of this but the evidence cannot be

In mid-July the State Operations Committee (SOC) was established as the supreme executive authority in Sarawak. The Chief Minister was not appointed to head the SOC as was the practice in every other state of Malaysia. Instead the former Federal Secretary was placed in the key position.[23] All members except Temenggong Jugah were civil servants. Responding to Tawi Sli's criticisms the SOC chairman explained that

> the State Operations Committee was appointed by the Director of Operations who also saw it fit that the SOC should not be headed by the Chief Minister because the powers that are given to this Committee are so tremendous that it is not in the interest of the country and the people for such powers to be vested in a Chief Minister who had not received the current mandate from the people. The powers of the Chairman are so wide that he may even put his political opponents behind bars. . . . It has been obvious right from the inception of SOC that one of its first actions was to look into the ways and means of ensuring that the State's main natural assets i.e. forestry is given out in a fair and justified manner so that it can be of benefit to the majority of Sarawakians most of who live in the rural areas. This act of SOC controlling the issue of logging licences had undoubtedly incurred the displeasure of certain group who for reasons of personal gain keep pursuing the attitude of anti-SOC . . .[24]

SNAP, SUPP and PESAKA joined in submissions to Tun Razak, Chairman of the National Operations Committee, requesting a resumption of the elections and guaranteeing that there would be no violence.[25] In the meantime all campaigning was banned by the government, in stark opposition to the free atmosphere that had earlier prevailed. The government ministers had a near monopoly of the means of communication and still toured the state and dispensed funds. However, with the SOC in command only those with close federal links had easy access to such largesse. The person most favourably placed in that regard was Abdul Rahman bin Ya'kub, who had been appointed Minister of Education in the new Malaysian Cabinet (on 20 May 1969). This was one of the most senior and responsible positions in the government, and he worked closely with Tun Razak—the Director of Operations and the Deputy Prime Minister.

By contrast the PESAKA leaders were at odds with the federal government, particularly over the question of the proposed extension of the Continental Shelf Act to Sarawak. Under this act all mineral rights

---

shown to members of the public for security reasons' (*Sarawak Tribune*, 9 June 1969). There was the suggestion that these outbreaks were deliberate attempts to create artificially a crisis atmosphere and legitimize emergency rule.

[23] Penghulu Tawi Sli was actually momentarily appointed, only to have his name deleted from the *Government Gazette* notification before publication, thus aggravating the insult.

[24] *Sarawak Tribune*, 16 November 1969.

[25] *Eastern Sun*, 14 October 1969. The BUMIPUTERA stance was that no-one could really guarantee the absence of disturbances and to have joined in the submission would have been to undermine the Tunku, whose resources were fully stretched in West Malaysia.

beyond the three mile limit but within twelve miles belonged to the central government. The Sarawak state government wanted to extend its control over mineral rights to the twelve mile offshore limit. The importance of that debate lay in the fact that most of the recent oil production and the new finds have been offshore, beyond the three mile limit.

After a brief discussion with the Minister of Finance, Penghulu Tawi Sli[26] agreed to a reduction of the federal government's 'escalating' grant to Sarawak, from M$27 million in 1969 to M$12 million in 1970. Tawi did not invoke the provision for arbitration as provided in the Inter-Governmental Committee Report of 1962. He subsequently explained that he had been given an oral assurance that Sarawak could have all the revenue from the offshore oil in return for the lower grant. There is no written record of such an understanding nor has any federal minister ever acknowledged the alleged 'bargain'. Since that time more oil has been found off the coast of the Baram and Bintulu districts. The entire Sarawak Cabinet was called to Kuala Lumpur for discussions on this matter in October 1969, but no agreement was reached. The federal government summarily abolished another $5.8 million annual grant that had been given to Sarawak since 1964 under the terms of the agreement to enter Malaysia. Since that time the Central government has simply annexed that part of the shelf under dispute, invoking the emergency regulations to do so.[27] Federal paramountcy was clearly apparent in the control of basic economic resources. Although the action lapsed when the emergency ended it is almost inconceivable that the federal government would agree to forfeit all the returns from this oil.

The 1970 Elections

Polling was resumed early in June 1970, with a strict ban on all campaigning and no new nominations permitted.[28] Each candidate was permitted to circulate one poster of a designated size with the words 'Vote for _____', a photograph of the candidate and his election symbol. All went smoothly until the last week of polling when terrorists ambushed and killed three members of a government polling team transporting ballot boxes in the Sarikei district. The militant Sarawak Communist Organisation had been urging a total boycott of the electoral process and this was apparently their way of underlining the gravity of their message. Considering the high voter turnout throughout the state, particularly in SUPP and BUMIPUTERA areas, there is little evidence that the communists were successful in their campaign to dissuade the populace from voting.

---

[26] See *Vanguard,* 18 December 1968.
[27] See two articles on this issue by Bob Reece in the *Far Eastern Economic Review,* 12 March 1970 and 30 October 1969.
[28] The only exceptions were in two constituencies (S. 10 and P. 135) in each of which one of the candidates had been killed—in a motor accident and a fire-fight respectively. The deceased candidates in both seats were simply replaced. All the votes cast back in 1969 were destroyed and fresh ballots printed.

The results of the contest for the Council Negri were as follows:

Table 29

Votes Cast and Members Elected to the Council Negri by Political Party:
1970

Political party	Total number of votes received	Proportion of votes cast (%)	Number of members elected	Number of votes cast per member elected
SUPP	72,196	28.9	12	6,016
SNAP	61,210	24.5	12	5,101
BUMIPUTERA	36,992	14.7	12	3,083
PESAKA	34,351	13.7	8	4,294
SCA	26,676	10.7	3	8,892
Independent	19,108	7.6	1	19,108
Total	250,533	100	48	Av. 5,219

Parti BUMIPUTERA was able to exert particularly strong party dis-
cipline, as exemplified by the results in the two parliamentary seats
where the Alliance candidates had earlier been disqualified by the Election
Commission for technical reasons.[29] In both those seats Party BUMI-
PUTERA advised its followers to vote for the Alliance state candidates,
but to cast blank ballots for the parliamentary contest. In Bandar
Kuching 5,113 such spoilt votes were cast (compared with a total of
508 spoilt votes in the two component state seats) and in Miri-Subis
there were 3,684 such invalid ballots (compared with 860 spoilt state
votes). In each seat this represented at least a quarter of all votes cast,
and demonstrated the effectiveness of Parti BUMIPUTERA in mobilizing
sympathetic voters.

The constituency boundaries appear to have been drawn primarily with
a view to the desired state representation, and little attention was paid
to the political effects of joining each pair of state constituencies to
form one parliamentary seat. The simultaneous election for members of
the Dewan Ra'ayat and the Council Negri resulted in ratios of votes
cast per member of parliament elected which were quite different from
those that pertained for the members of the Council Negri. This was
an adequate demonstration of how the precise determination of constituency boundaries can play havoc with the process of translating votes
into legislators. SNAP won all except one of the second, fourth and fifth
division parliamentary seats. It also picked up a seat from the first and
from the third division. SNAP gained a small but comfortable majority
in each of the second division parliamentary seats, where a coastal

[29] Lee Swee Hiok (SCA's candidate in Bandar Kuching) failed to sign his
nomination forms and T. K. Muip bin Tabib (BUMIPUTERA's candidate
in Miri-Subis) also failed to complete all necessary formalities.

Malay state constituency was joined with an interior Iban one. As was evident in the above table, at the Council Negri level the parties could be ranked in the following order—from the least to the highest number of votes cast per member elected: BUMIPUTERA, PESAKA, SNAP, SUPP and SCA. However, the rank order of votes cast per member of parliament elected was quite different.

Table 30

Votes Cast and Members Elected to the Dewan Ra'ayat by Political Party: 1970

Political party	Total number of votes received	Number of members elected	Number of votes cast per member elected
SCA	10,520	2	5,260
SNAP	64,583	9	7,176
BUMIPUTERA	41,835	5	8,367
SUPP	72,751	5	14,550
PESAKA	30,765	2	15,382
Independent	20,514	1	20,514
Total	240,968	24	Av. 10,032

Whereas at the Council Negri level SNAP representation was in proportion to votes received, at the parliamentary level its representation was much more favourable. BUMIPUTERA still received relatively more seats than votes. For SUPP the relationship was again noticeably reversed with the party receiving a much greater share of votes than seats. This was in large part because the majority of SUPP supporters were concentrated in urban environs, and the constituencies were heavily weighted toward the rural seats. The ratio of seats to votes was very favourable for SCA at the parliamentary level, but considerably worse for PESAKA.

In order to appreciate the political development taking place in Sarawak during the past decade the 1963 election results have also been analysed on the basis of the constituencies delineated for the 1970 elections. The primary units for 1963 (the District Council wards) have been aggregated to accord with the boundaries of the 48 state constituencies, as description on that basis permits comparative analysis. The accompanying ethnic breakdown is derived from the electoral registration of 1968, with additional clarification from the kampong count undertaken by the author during that year. (See Table 31.)

Ethnicity and voting in the 1970 election

The strength of association between ethnicity and voting for each party is described in the following pages. Additional comments pertaining to election results by constituency have been added, primarily to facilitate the comparison of voting in the 1970 election with that in 1963.

Table 31

Percentage of Votes Cast in the 1970 and 1963 Elections for Each Constituency by Party and the Percentage Ethnic Composition of Each Constituency

State Constituency	1970 Voting %						1963 Voting %				Ethnic composition %		
	SUPP	BUMI	SCA	PES	SNAP	Indp	SUPP	PANAS	All.	Indp	Malay	Dayak	Chinese
1. Lundu	28.6	22.9		24.4	21.2	2.8	21.3	30.	37.2	11.4	32.8	48.6	18.5
2. Bau	37.5	16.2		10.6	28.7	7.	40.2	13.9	32.4	13.5	6.1	58.6	35.
3. Kuching Barat	38.		50.2		10.	1.8	19.9	52.	26.6	1.5	52.6	2.	44.3
4. Kuching Timor	80.5		10.6		6.8	2.2	73.4		19.6	7.	5.7	1.2	92.4
5. Semariang	16.4	54.5			8.9	20.3	15.1	62.7	20.6	1.7	75.1	7.4	17.5
6. Sekama	58.4		29.5		9.7	2.4	51.9	23.2	11.3	13.6	28.	4.3	67.6
7. Sebandi	24.1	59.1		16.8			10.8	64.4	13.	11.8	73.3	7.2	19.5
8. Muara Tuang	29.5	46.3			17.2	7.	24.9	57.6	8.5	9.5	46.7	23.9	29.1
9. Batu Kawah	54.1		22.1		23.8		58.2	14.5	15.6	11.6	18.	26.8	53.8
10. Bengoh	41.9	5.4		11.6	35.7	5.4	42.	22.3	20.1	15.6	.6	75.9	23.5
11. Tarat	28.2		28.6		43.2		21.9	28.6	32.2	17.3	9.	71.4	19.6
12. Tebakang	30.	25.1			44.9		12.9	24.9	32.7	29.5	9.4	78.3	12.3
13. Semera	10.3	64.			25.7		15.6	71.6	11.2	1.6	69.1	19.3	11.6
14. Gedong	11.5	38.8		13.3	36.4		8.1	68.4	13.2	10.3	42.1	47.	10.9
15. Lingga-Sebuyau	19.3	11.6		35.5	31.9	1.6	8.2	23.1	57.1	11.6	23.9	65.8	10.2
16. Simanggang	26.7	14.9		10.2	35.8	12.5	14.8	12.5	60.3	12.3	18.2	63.8	18.
17. Engkilili	29.5			35.1	28.6	6.8	26.	9.1	44.4	20.5	1.4	86.2	12.4
18. Ulu Ai	18.4	2.8		31.2	32.4	15.1	9.6		68.3	22.1	.5	97.2	2.2
19. Saribas		42.5		17.2	30.7	9.9		59.1	23.2	17.7	66.6	29.	4.4
20. Layar				15.4	55.	29.5	10.9	4.5	49.1	35.5	18.5	72.1	9.4
21. Kalaka		30.5		42.6	25.2	1.8	4.8	24.4	43.6	27.2	55.3	37.5	7.2
22. Krian	17.8			18.8	63.4		12.2	3.	63.8	21.	9.7	82.7	7.7

23. Kuala Rajang	17.5	45.4	7.8	15.6	13.8	14.6	7.3	19.2	58.8	53.3	33.4	13.4
24. Repok	47.2	35.1		16.6	1.1	56.7		31.5	11.8	1.2	18.4	79.3
25. Matu-Daro	9.8	65.	11.	2.4	10.9	3.7	4.6	42.6	53.6	93.2	1.2	5.6
26. Binatang	42.9	29.9	15.2	12.		42.1	6.9	35.4	18.	19.	35.7	45.3
27. Sibu Tengal	60.1	28.2		6.7	5.1	67.4	.6	18.9	6.8	11.7	2.1	84.9
28. Sibu Luar	48.7	37.1		9.2	4.9	47.5		15.7	36.1	21.7	9.	69.3
29. Igan	40.7	53.3		3.5	2.5	18.7		21.2	60.1	15.6	46.1	38.3
30. Dudong	36.7		31.4	25.	6.9	19.4		26.5	54.7	1.7	70.	28.3
31. Balingian	17.6	32.	16.2	17.	17.2				100	51.1	38.3	10.5
32. Oya	9.3	28.8	25.1	25.5	11.3				100	50.9	41.7	7.4
33. Pakan			31.2	27.8	41.			35.4	64.7	.2	98.	1.8
34. Meluan			35.1	38.2	26.7	9.2		88.7	2.2	.3	94.3	5.4
35. Machan	36.3		56.2	7.4		21.2		63.4	15.4	3.8	68.	28.2
36. Ngemah	13.8		21.2	19.4	45.6	9.8		74.4	15.9	.2	92.4	7.
37. Song	29.3		31.5	39.3		15.7		77.4	6.9	1.6	94.8	3.6
38. Pelagus	33.7		43.8	22.6		14.7		67.4	17.9	3.7	79.8	16.5
39. Baleh	16.9		40.9	31.9	10.3	21.6		69.4	9.		99.9	16.5
40. Belaga	36.2	30.	32.2	3.1	28.4	16.3		65.3	18.4	28.3	99.9	13.8
41. Tatau	18.5	26.8	9.3	26.7	15.5		20.7	63.4	15.9	28.3	57.9	13.8
42. Kemena	17.		31.7	19.6	4.9	10.7	21.8	39.6	27.9	20.7	71.1	8.2
43. Subis	26.5		15.5	32.2	25.8	24.2	5.9	10.	60.	37.4	47.6	14.9
44. Miri	36.1	41.4		18.1	4.4	40.5	16.7	31.9	11.	32.8	12.2	54.6
45. Marudi	18.7		17.8	61.3	2.2				100	9.2	72.8	18.
46. Telang Usan			21.1	48.2	30.7				100		98.	1.9
47. Limbang	23.2			63.7	13.1			7.	93.1	39.5	49.1	11.3
48. Lawas	39.		24.2	33.8	3.			42.2	57.8	51.4	38.1	10.5
Av.	28.9	14.7	13.7	24.5	7.6	21.4	14.3	34.2	30.2	26.	46.	28.

Table 32

Coefficient of Correlation of Ethnic Composition of State Constituencies
with Votes Cast for Each Political Party: 1970

Ethnic com-position of constituencies	Votes for each political party				
	SNAP	PESAKA	BUMIPUTERA	SCA	**SUPP**
Malay/ Melanau	—0.23	—0.39	0.91	0.52	—0.40
Dayak	0.53	0.44	—0.91	0.06	—0.36
Chinese	—0.47	—0.19	—0.08	—0.40	0.87

As in 1963 SUPP was more closely correlated with Chinese voters in
the urban than in the rural districts. In the three towns a strong negative
relationship was evident between votes received by SUPP and the proportion of Malay voters and also of Dayak voters. In the rural districts
SUPP's negative relationship with Malays persisted but, as its strength
of association with Chinese dropped, so it became neither positively nor
negatively associated (—0.1) with the Dayak proportion of the constituency. In nearly all the rural constituencies contested by SUPP the
party's share of the vote was significantly higher than the proportion of
registered Chinese voters. Thus it is reasonable to suppose that SUPP
received a good deal of other support, principally from the Dayaks.
However, in the towns of Kuching, Sibu and Miri Chinese votes were
split and went in considerable number to other parties, as they did also
in the coastal Semariang and Semera constituencies, and in Sekama.
These were all constituencies where the SNAP share of votes polled was
distinctly greater than the proportion of registered Dayak voters. SUPP
lost Chinese votes to the SCA in the Binatang and Repok (Sarikei)
districts. The overall SUPP percentage of the vote rose from 21.4 per cent
in 1963 to 28.9 per cent in 1970. The vote received by SUPP rose in all
but seven of the forty districts it contested.

Support for the SCA was positively correlated with the presence of
Muslims and negatively with the presence of Chinese. In the three major
towns, where SCA won two of its three seats, the strength of association
with Muslims was +0.91 and with Chinese —0.95, a striking dependence
upon Muslims for a party that purports to represent the Chinese. This
fact alone is adequate demonstration of the electoral benefit for SCA of
its Alliance partnership with Parti BUMIPUTERA. Ling Beng Siong did
win the Igan constituency through his own efforts. It is a mixed Dayak
and Chinese area and, as a State Minister, Dato Ling had been most
attentive to the material needs of his people. The two other successful
urban SCA candidates gained the solid backing of Malays. In Kuching
Barat Malays seem to have supplied some four-fifths of the support for
SCA, defeating Ong Kee Hui[30]—the popular former President of the

---

[30] Ong's trawling activities, in conjunction with Japanese interests, had caused
a shortage of prawns—thus strongly alienating local Henghua and Malay
fishermen. See *Chinese Daily News,* 17 January 1968 for their statement
of grievances.

Kuching Municipal Council and Chairman of SUPP. Cheng Yew Kiew, the successful SCA Council Negri member has since become a Muslim, and taken the name Shahbuddin Cheng.[31] In Miri a strong performance by the well-regarded SNAP Chinese candidate further split Chinese votes and facilitated the victory of the SCA candidate, who had relied upon Malay votes. All parliamentary seats were formed by combining a pair of state constituencies. Of the two parliamentary seats won by SCA P. 132 Sarikei was composed of state BUMIPUTERA and SUPP seats and P. 141 Bintulu was a state pair each won by BUMIPUTERA and PESAKA. The role of Parti BUMIPUTERA in delivering the vote for SCA should again be emphasized, as should the latter's resultant dependence upon BUMI-PUTERA.

Parti BUMIPUTERA candidates stood only in rural seats and a very high proportion of their support came from the Malay and Melanau communities. Voter support for the party showed a strong negative correlation with the presence of Dayaks in the constituency. In most of the twenty-two constituencies it contested Parti BUMIPUTERA received a lesser proportion of votes than would have been expected had all the Malays and Melanaus supported that party. However, in five districts other ethnic groups also clearly supported Parti BUMIPUTERA. Land Dayak candidates nominated by Parti BUMIPUTERA in the Bau and Tebakang districts appear to have received Land Dayak votes. A few Iban in Ulu Ai transferred their 1963 allegiance toward BARJASA to Parti BUMIPUTERA, and in the Bintulu district the extra margin of support could well have come from the Islamized Penan peoples. Parti BUMIPUTERA concentrated its votes more effectively than did any other party, gaining a mean of 32.9 per cent of votes cast in each of the twenty-two constituencies it contested. Comparable proportions for each of the other parties were as follows:

Table 33

Average Proportion of Votes Received by Each Party in Contested State Constituencies: 1970

Political party	Mean proportion of votes received in contested constituencies	Number of seats contested by each party
BUMIPUTERA	32.9%	22
SCA	32.4%	11
SUPP	30.4%	40
SNAP	26.4%	47
PESAKA	24.3%	33

[31] As of early 1972 there had been relatively few Chinese or Iban conversions to Islam, in contrast to the prevailing trend evident in Sabah. One group of Land Dayak in the Padawan district have entered Islam. Their change is a tangible result of the 'hearts and minds' campaign launched by the Malaysian Army.

Parti BUMIPUTERA won more than half of the seats it contested. Each of the other parties stretched themselves more thinly and none even won a third of the seats for which its candidates stood. In most first division seats Parti BUMIPUTERA did not poll as well as had its predecessor PANAS, except for Bau and Tebakang where BUMIPUTERA continued to attract Land Dayak votes. However in every other contested seat throughout Sarawak (except for Saribas) Parti BUMIPUTERA improved upon the share of votes received by PANAS in 1963. Clearly Parti BUMIPUTERA was gaining Melanaus and other Muslims throughout the state at the expense of losing the extensive PANAS (first division) Land Dayak base of support.

Party PESAKA support was correlated in a positive direction with Dayak voters and in a negative direction with the Malay and Melanau, the strengths of correlation being quite moderate with each ethnic group. The difficulties between Parti BUMIPUTERA and PESAKA had derived from the latter's quest also to represent the Malay and Melanau communities—in this it had failed dismally. The bulk of Dayak votes appear to have been split between PESAKA and SNAP, PESAKA receiving the support of a good many interior Iban. In only three constituencies did PESAKA poll more votes than there were Dayaks registered to vote. These were the heavily Muslim areas of Sebandi, Kalaka and Matu-Daro. Of the three, PESAKA was only successful in Kalaka. Its candidate there was closely related to the Malay aristocracy. Kalaka district Malays back in 1963 had been on the borderline between the Kuching and Sibu Malay aristocracies and were then quite evenly divided in their support for the two contending parties: PANAS and BARJASA.[32]

SNAP votes were also evenly distributed between ethnic groups, the strongest correlation being a positive 0.53 with Dayak electors. SNAP fielded candidates in 47 of the 48 constituencies and, more than any other party, gained the support of the Kayan, Kenyah and Land Dayak, in addition to the Iban. SNAP and Parti BUMIPUTERA were the only parties that won seats in all five divisions of the state—each of the other three parties only won seats in two or three divisions. But SNAP did not rely so heavily upon one ethnic group as did Parti BUMIPUTERA. In terms of breadth of pan-ethnic support SNAP was truly a Sarawak national party. SNAP also won a noticeable share of Chinese votes at the expense of SUPP in eight constituencies, and in the Limbang district James Wong received Dayak, Chinese and Malay votes on behalf of SNAP. There was a significant positive correlation (+0.59) between the 1963 Alliance vote and that received by PESAKA (1970) in the rural constituencies. The equivalent relationship between SNAP (1970) and the Alliance (1963) was +0.08—lacking any particular significance. Whereas PESAKA support came from areas that had hitherto

---

[32] In 1970 most Malays in Kabong and a good many in Sessang and Nyabor voted for PESAKA because they were still smarting from Abdul Taib's grant of a timber licence to four local Malays (two Tua Kampongs and two District Councillors) who were permitted to exploit communal land and immediately sub-let the timber rights to a Chinese company.

supported the Alliance, SNAP support came nearly as much from other areas as from those of the Alliance in 1963. SNAP had clearly extended its horizons much more widely and more effectively than had its former Alliance partner, PESAKA.

5

THE SARAWAK
COALITION GOVERNMENT 1970—

Formation of the New Government

The process of government formation was thrown wide open when it became known that BUMIPUTERA, SNAP and SUPP had each received twelve seats in the new 48-member Council Negri.[1] PESAKA received eight seats, with an additional independent member later joining the party. They had expected to fare much better but three of the four former PESAKA ministers went down to defeat at the hands of new candidates from SUPP and the sole successful independent. The remaining three seats went to SCA, although SCA success in two of those constituencies was principally derived from BUMIPUTERA voters.[2]

Though the Sarawak Alliance (BUMIPUTERA and SCA) had won the greatest number of seats (15) and together with PESAKA could command exactly half the Council Negri seats, discussions between these parties were quickly stalled because PESAKA (long accustomed to the leading role within the Alliance) demanded that it nominate the Chief Minister—presumably Thomas Kana—and three of the eight other ministers, as was the case prior to the election. Fresh from its success in essentially delivering fourteen of the fifteen Alliance seats, BUMI-PUTERA was not willing to be so subservient to PESAKA, a party which could only boast eight seats.

Negotiations were initiated between SNAP, SUPP and some PESAKA members with a view to formation of a government that was not to be led by Abdul Rahman Ya'kub.

These discussions covered a broad range of options, possibilities that even included dissolution of both SNAP and PESAKA and the formation of a new Dayak-based party.[3] PESAKA members appeared to be acting at cross purposes. Linggi of PESAKA wanted SUPP excluded from the new government. Sidi Munan (PESAKA) conveyed the offer of a Deputy Chief Ministership (under Abdul Rahman) first to Thomas Kana and then to any other willing Iban.

---

[1] Actually SUPP did not win its twelfth seat until the end of July, but was expected to do so in the state constituency where fresh nominations had been called.

[2] See Chapter 4.

[3] The first meeting called by Temenggong Jugat was at Sibu on Sunday, 5 July 1970. It ended inconclusively and the participants met again in Kuching the following evening, at a meeting called by James Wong.

Thomas Kana wanted to call a meeting of the Sarawak Alliance National Council and expel Parti BUMIPUTERA. Ningkan suggested a coalition of SNAP, PESAKA and SUPP (sharing portfolios 3:3:3). But there was no agreement whatsoever regarding the Chief Minister designate. At the Monday evening meeting (with Parti BUMIPUTERA and its advocates absent) James Wong suggested a grand coalition that would include all parties and would thwart any chance of Abdul Rahman Ya'kub becoming Chief Minister. As the senior lawyer present at that meeting, Stephen Yong was prevailed upon to draw up a record of the discussions that had taken place, deliberations with a view to formation of a grand coalition. When asked to sign this document Stephen Yong and Chan Siaw Hee refused and asked for time to consult their members. They said that they could not finalize an agreement without first obtaining a mandate from their party members, and also that no BUMIPUTERA representatives were present to commit their party to the grand coalition. What they did not acknowledge to the meeting was the fact of their discussions with Parti BUMIPUTERA, negotiations that bore fruit the very next day in the announcement of a Coalition government initially formed by SUPP and BUMIPUTERA.

Just prior to the announcement of the election results Tun Razak and his political secretary had enquired whether SUPP leaders might be interested in joining the government. Discussions were initiated by Tun Razak[4] early Sunday morning with a view to installing Abdul Rahman Ya'kub as Chief Minister. Initially SUPP asked for an Iban Chief Minister who would be supported by Abdul Rahman and Yong, for Abdul Rahman was not readily acceptable to SUPP members due to his uncompromising stance as Federal Minister of Education. An alternative suggestion was for another BUMIPUTERA member to be Chief Minister, but Abdul Rahman was unwilling to resign his Federal ministership merely to become one of six state Ministers.

The other immediate problem was the SCA. Tun Razak was unwilling to drop them from the Cabinet entirely as they were members of the Alliance. However, Abdul Rahman said he would handle their non-inclusion on a state level. SUPP made quite clear that their party's participation was contingent upon SCA's exclusion from the Cabinet.

Given PESAKA's intransigence and SNAP's strong Sarawak nationalism, these negotiations represented the only course left open to Parti BUMIPUTERA if it wished to be in a position to lead the new government. The deep personal animosities that had developed between Wan Alwi and Kana of PESAKA on the one hand, and the leader of BUMIPUTERA on the other, precluded any real possibility of a Sarawak Alliance Government (BUMIPUTERA, SCA and PESAKA) being reconstituted under the leadership of Abdul Rahman.

SUPP was led to understand that were an opposition (SNAP-SUPP)

---

[4] Tun Razak stayed across river in the Astana to oversee negotiations during those crucial three days. Another figure particularly active in Kuching at this juncture was Syed Kechik, former political secretary to Inche Senu and then Tun Mustapha. Syed Kechik has also been an active participant during the 1966 Sarawak Alliance crisis.

government formed then there would be no early return to control by an elected government. The State Operations Committee would simply remain in control. The alternative governmental arrangements were quite vague, whereas with BUMIPUTERA it was possible to hammer out a firm agreement, lawyer with lawyer.

SUPP leaders were fearful of the reaction from their rank-and-file members and of domination by the powerful leader of BUMIPUTERA, Abdul Rahman bin Ya'kub. Therefore they drew up the following document stipulating the terms under which both parties would agree to enter into a coalition government. This agreement was signed on behalf of BUMIPUTERA by Abdul Rahman Ya'kub and witnessed by Senu bin Abdul Rahman on behalf of Tun Razak. Stephen Yong signed for SUPP in the presence of Ong Kee Hui, and the agreement was dated Tuesday July 7th, 1970.

POINTS OF UNDERSTANDING

The signatories hereto representing their respective parties have agreed to abide by the following points of understanding for the establishment of a clean and efficient state government of Sarawak.

1. A nominee of Party BUMIPUTERA shall be the Chief Minister, a nominee of the Sarawak United People's party shall be the Deputy Chief Minister and one elected member of the Iban race shall be the other Deputy Chief Minister;

2. Major issues and matters involving Government policy and measures affecting the interest of the state and parties hereto shall be agreed to mutually before decision can be made;

3. Appointment of other State Ministers and allotment of portfolios shall have the unanimous decision of the signatories hereto;

4. The pledges made by the parties hereto during the election as far as possible shall be implemented by the State Government.

This signed agreement between BUMIPUTERA and SUPP permitted SUPP to exclude any SCA members from becoming Ministers. It also allowed SUPP Ministers to claim to be honouring their pre-election pledges particularly: (a) to make land available for cultivation by the landless, and (b) to urge the federal government to release or speedily bring to trial all political detainees, and to ameliorate conditions in the three controlled villages (Beratok, Tapah and Siburan).

The Dayak members of SUPP did not actively participate in the deliberations leading to this agreement, nor was the accommodation actually approved by the SUPP Central Working Committee.[5] SUPP entered into a coalition government primarily as a Chinese party, fearing the consequences that might arise from the near complete exclusion of Muslims under the SNAP-PESAKA-SUPP, that being the Dayak and Chinese alternative. Troops were on the alert and the lessons of 13 May

---

[5] SUPP leaders did meet with candidates and various members of the Central Committee during Monday, 6 July 1970. They also met with the Chairman of SCA, Ling Beng Siew, the latter urging SUPP not to support Abdul Rahman as Chief Minister.

1969 had not been forgotten. SUPP leaders also claimed to have believed that the terms of their agreement with BUMIPUTERA were more favourable than those they could have obtained from the Ibans. The Ibans would find difficulty in conceding land as the wealth of the Dayak peoples is their land, very little of which has been alienated to non-natives. SUPP was also concerned over the extent of uncontrolled corruption that they expected under the alternative governmental arrangement.

The Federal government also indicated its willingness to accept into the Cabinet an additional Member of Parliament from Sarawak. In due course the Coalition government nominated the chairman of SUPP. Ong Kee Hui was appointed as Minister for Research, Technology and Local Government and thus became the first non-Alliance Federal minister in Malaysian history. The appointment of Ong Kee Hui became the focus of much resentment from within SUPP. In contrast to the formation of the State coalition government, the party had neither agreed to Ong's appointment nor did members expect him (as one amongst twenty other federal ministers) to play an influential role within that government.

One important bargaining chip in the possession of SUPP was the five parliamentary seats won by the party. Though formally in the opposition SUPP promised that in so far as matters affecting the national interest were concerned, and if the party was consulted in advance, its members in the Dewan Ra'ayat would not oppose the Alliance.[6] This undertaking was of great importance to the Central Alliance leadership for at that critical juncture it facilitated achievement of the desired two-thirds majority in Parliament, a majority with which the Alliance could then amend the constitution whenever it so desired. The representation of each party in the Dewan Ra'ayat after the Sarawak election results were announced was as follows:

Alliance (West Malaysia)	66
Alliance (Sabah)	16
Alliance (Sarawak—including PESAKA)	9
Total Alliance	91
Democratic Action Party	13
Pan Malayan Islamic Party	12
Sarawak National Party (SNAP)	9
Gerakan Ra'ayat Malaysia	8
Sarawak United People's Party (SUPP)	5
People's Progressive Party	4
Independent (from Sarawak)	1
Undecided (West Malaysia)	1
Total number of seats	144

The two-thirds majority (96 out of 144) was exactly achieved with the addition of the five SUPP votes to the total Alliance figure.

[6] *Sarawak Tribune,* 18 July 1970.

The other interesting effect on the national level is that the central Malay leadership has been able to work effectively in Penang and in Sarawak with Chinese other than those represented in MCA, in fact a rather broader and more representative segment of the Chinese community. In 1972 remnants of the Gerakan, led by Dr Lim Chong Eu, followed the Sarawak precedent and formed a Penang state coalition government. The Penang state Alliance (and UMNO) leader, Mohd Khir Johari pointed out that the coalition government in Sarawak was 'working out nicely'[7] and tried to reassure local MCA members that there would indeed be a role for them within the Gerakan-Alliance coalition. Such wider participation by predominantly Chinese opposition parties allowed a necessary broadening of political representation. Two months later a Perak state coalition government was announced. It included eighteen members of UMNO, one of MCA and twelve from the People's Progressive Party.

In Malaysia the formation of coalition governments has resulted in a co-optation of the 'moderate' parliamentary opposition, leading to an isolation of all those residual opponents who may then be deemed to be 'extreme' and consequently suppressed as a subversive danger to the nation.

On the state level all was not resolved by the SUPP-BUMIPUTERA coalition agreement. The appearance of Dayak support was quite crucial to the two major participants in the coalition government. There was an element of comic opera to the capturing of Penghulu Abok, the first Iban to waver from the fairly solid PESAKA front. After being kept isolated from all other PESAKA members (in the Palm Hotel) he was brought by his bodyguards across river to the Astana. A day later Simon Dembab Maja[8] was persuaded to support the new government and was appointed Deputy Chief Minister. The leader of PESAKA and Federal Minister for Sarawak Affairs Temenggong Jugah, shortly thereafter visited Kuala Lumpur and was presented with the choice of either declaring his party's support for the new coalition government or resigning his cabinet post.[9] He chose the former, much to the alarm of many PESAKA members.

---

[7] See *Straits Times,* 6 November 1971 and from 14 February 1972. The Penang Coalition government was formed on 15 February 1972. In 1969 the MCA had failed to elect any members to the Penang State Assembly.

[8] Simon Dembab is an Iban from Engkilili. He was thirty-three when appointed a minister, was educated in both Chinese and English and had been School Affairs Officer of the Lubok Antu District Council. Alfred Mason is his brother-in-law, a factor that made him rather more accessible to those working on behalf of Dato Abdul Rahman. In 1963 he had been a member of BARJASA.

[9] *Straits Times,* 8 July 1970 reported Tun Razak's statement that the post of Minister for Sarawak Affairs was now vacant, and rumours were rife that Ong Kee Hui would be appointed forthwith to fill the vacancy. Temenggong Jugah's influence has tended to diminish with the passage of time, to the extent that by January 1972 Federal grants to Christ Hospital in his hometown of Kapit were being presented not by the Temenggong but by the Secretary-General of his Ministry, Wan Sidek— a senior West Malaysian civil servant. (See also *Sarawak Tribune,* 15 January 1972.)

The Coalition state cabinet consisted of the following six members, listed in order of precedence:

Dato Haji Abdul Rahman bin Ya'kub (BUMIPUTERA), Chief Minister

Stephen Yong Kuet Sze (SUPP), Deputy Chief Minister and Minister for Communications and Works

Simon Dembab Maja (PESAKA), Deputy Chief Minister and Minister for Lands and Mineral Resources

Abang Ikhwan Zainie (BUMIPUTERA), Minister for Welfare

Penghulu Abok anak Jalin (PESAKA), Minister of State

Sim Kheng Hong (SUPP), Minister for Local Government[10]

The new Chief Minister enlisted from PESAKA two men who had never before been leaders in government or state politics. By contrast, the top leadership of BUMIPUTERA and of SUPP hold cabinet posts.

Consolidation of Political Support

The Sarawak Coalition government possessed a rather more coherent set of ideas as to the policies it wished to implement and demonstrated its sense of direction in the implementation of those policies. This was in contrast to the reactive style of the previous Iban led governments, much of whose energies had been dissipated in their endless 'deliberations' with Kuala Lumpur. The Coalition government had the twin advantages of Kuala Lumpur's blessing and the possession of coherent political organizations equipped to implement their policies.

The Chief Minister has himself demonstrated considerable finesse in his consolidation of political support and in the changes he is steadily implementing in such highly sensitive areas as land law, education policy and language. He has not sought to dictate his will, rather he has sought to govern by consensus within the Coalition. Abdul Rahman personally acknowledges a great debt to the Tunku who caused him to change his approach from that of his early days as an Assistant Federal Minister and later as Minister of Education. He recalled with emotion the Tunku's words of guidance.

> Rahman, as a young man you like to run as fast as possible, but you cannot rush people, you must take time, you must take into consideration the whims and fancies, the feelings, cultural backgrounds, everything about men. Above all be generous in your heart.[11]

In its first two years the Coalition government placed a premium upon achieving stability (political and governmental) and respect from civil servants and the populace at large. It continued to suspend the issuance of timber licences and sought to cultivate the reputation of being a 'clean and efficient' government. A good deal of its energy was devoted to creating institutions that would facilitate future economic development—specifically to the creation of an Economic Development Corporation, a Land Development Board, a State Economic Planning

---

[10] *Sarawak Government Gazette,* Part V, 31 July 1970, p. 1517.

[11] Speech of the Chief Minister in Council Negri, 29 May 1971, and interview with the writer February 1972.

Unit and the Sarawak Foundation. All development planning was essentially long-term strategy and even that was delayed by lack of suitable personnel. The government also amended the hitherto sacrosanct land code so as to allow natives in possession of titled land to pledge their land as security for loans from such institutions as MARA, the Borneo Development Corporation and the Sarawak Development Finance Corporation. The intent of that change was to provide opportunities for fuller native participation in commerce and industry.

The Chief Minister consolidated his political position by winning over SNAP members of Council Negri, by extending the powers of his own ministerial portfolio, by surrounding himself with capable young administrators who fundamentally shared his outlook, by securing a measure of press ownership and by creating the Sarawak Foundation.

In the Council Negri the government gained the support of all wavering PESAKA members,[12] and by mid-1971 boasted a total of 38 seats—13 BUMIPUTERA, 10 PESAKA, 3 SCA and 12 SUPP. Two SNAP members defected to the Alliance[13] one of whom was subsequently named Minister for Youth.[14] The SNAP opposition was reduced to ten members of Council Negri. Some SNAP members still provide a formidable opposition to the coalition. However, the problems besetting the government are not at this stage readily apparent within the legislative arena, so long as the coalition government holds together. Were BUMIPUTERA and SUPP to part company then all options would be open once again. SNAP and SUPP together would only need to attract three members of the Council to their side to form a government. Finally, in an Alliance-SNAP government the Dayaks would greatly outnumber representatives of Parti BUMIPUTERA and there would then be considerable internal pressure for a change of Chief Minister.

Coincidentally with the expansion of Cabinet the Chief Minister incorporated into his own portfolio the critical ministries of Lands and Mineral Resources. Hitherto those responsibilities had been the formal province of Simon Dembab, who was retained in the Cabinet as Minister for Agriculture.[15]

The Chief Minister has round him a group of capable, relatively young advisers—both civil servants and politicians. Abang Yusuf Puteh has been promoted to the post of Deputy State Secretary, in addition to his former duties as Establishment Officer. He exercises day-to-day control

---

[12] Thomas Kana was also appointed a senator as from December 1971. Some two months after the election he decided to declare his support for the government believing that he could do more for his people were he within the government, and that his party would be irremediably divided were he to remain in opposition.

[13] Ngelambong anak Bangau an Iban from Song sub-district joined PESAKA and Nelson Kundai anak Ngareng, a Bidayuh from the Serian district, aligned with BUMIPUTERA. The only other defecting legislator was a SNAP member of federal Parliament, Penghulu Abit anak Angkin (Kapit), who also joined the Alliance, thus reducing to eight the number of SNAP members in the Dewan Ra'ayat (out of Sarawak's twenty-four).

[14] *Sarawak Government Gazette,* Part V, 15 October 1971.

[15] The only other changes that took place in 1971 were that Abang Ikhwan became Minister for Culture and Penghulu Abok Minister for Welfare.

of the whole State Civil Service and is also the Director of the Sarawak Foundation.[16] Civil Servants have always regarded Abang Yusuf with a mixture of awe and apprehension. He has rigorously maintained standards within the bureaucracy. His formal superior, Gerunsin Lembat, is a more relaxed person who has suffered a good deal of illness and has had to delegate responsibilities to his deputy. Abang Yusuf is a man with clear ideas and both the will and the power to implement them. Bujang Mohamad Nor, Financial Secretary, was a university colleague of Abang Yusuf, and shared many of the same aspirations. Another interesting figure is Safri Awang Zaidell, who is 'doing special duty in the Chief Minister's Office'.[17] Safri is also secretary of the Community Service Council, an organisation of top civil servants, chaired by the Chief Minister (with both Deputy Chief Ministers and Temenggong Jugah also members) which is able quietly to implement various government policies.[18]

The press in Sarawak was almost completely owned by local Chinese businessmen. However, through an out-of-court settlement of a $90,000 libel action the Chief Minister indirectly secured control of the *Vanguard*,[19] publisher of a Chinese newspaper and one of the two English language newspapers in Sarawak. Abdul Rahman also obtained control of the state's Malay language daily, *Utusan Sarawak*. Prior to the state election he appointed as editor Ahmad Boestaman, the former Chairman of the Malayan Partai Ra'ayat and an ex-detainee. The newspaper was formerly owned and edited by Abang Ikhwan Zainie, the Minister of Culture. *Utusan Sarawak* ceased publication late 1971, and appears to have been replaced by a Malay language page in the *Vanguard*. Not only must other newspaper proprietors reckon with new-found competition from the Chief Minister, they must also avoid discussing all 'sensitive issues' under the terms of the sedition laws.

In the May 1971 session of Council Negri a bill was presented pro-

---

16 See p. 107.
17 Sarawak *Staff List,* 1971, Part 1, Government Printing Office, Kuching 1971. Safri has always been a highly politicized person, having played a role in the formation of SUPP (see p. 14), and being quite close to Ahmad Zaidie (p. 28). During the period of British control (until 1966) they did nothing to accelerate his promotion within the civil service. His wife is the Personal Assistant to the Chief Minister.
18 Other members of the Council were the State Secretary and his Deputy, the General-Officer-in-Charge, East Malaysia, Commander of the 3rd Malaysian Infantry Brigade, Head of Special Branch, Secretary of the Security Committee, Commissioner of Police and the Federal Secretary.
19 Dato Abdul Rahman explained to Council Negri that 'in fact while the present shares were as a result of a court case that he took against the Vanguard for libel he had not a single share in it, because under the constitution Chief Minister could not engage in business . . . what had happened was some of his shares were taken by Tuan Haji Shahbuddin Cheng though there was no money transition involved in this, and the others were transferred to his son who was working there', *Sarawak Tribune,* 16 March 1972. The libel suit was the culmination of a long-standing animosity between the Chief Minister and Leong Ho Yuen. It dated from 1963 when the latter successfully sought to have PANAS leave the Alliance and contest the election against BARJASA.

viding for the establishment of the Sarawak Foundation. This organization has a broad charter, its resources being pledged to 'promoting and providing educational and other facilities for the peoples and citizens in the state and Malaysia as a whole, and promoting a Malaysian consciousness, national unity and national loyalty amongst the peoples in Sarawak'.[20] The idea of setting up the foundation was first publicly mooted by Thomas Kana,[21] not long after the Ningkan government was defeated. It appeared to be modelled upon the Sabah Foundation, an organization that had proved to be quite functional to Tun Mustapha's winning the state election. However, nothing more was heard of the idea until 1971.

In its first six months, the public had given the Sarawak Foundation some M\$300,000.[22] A large part of these funds came from wealthy companies and individuals whose donations received wide publicity on radio and through the government information service. The Chief Minister also announced that about 200,000 acres of forest land had been reserved for the Foundation.[23] The Foundation has been given the responsibility of administering the Timber Cess Fund. At its second meeting the Foundation approved 360 scholarships, 160 financed by the Foundation and 200 under the Timber Cess Fund.[24] The Chief Minister is the Chairman of the Foundation, Abang Yusuf Puteh its Director and the Board of Trustees consist of members of the State Public Service Commission—all civil servants who are bound to support the government of the day.

On the party-political level BUMIPUTERA quietly and effectively built up its power, consolidating its base first amongst the Biduyah. Dago was appointed to head the Public Service Commission and constantly referred to as 'the Bidayuh National Leader'.[25] The SNAP Bidayuh who defeated

[20] *Sarawak Government Gazette*, Part III, 10 May 1971, p. 38.

[21] *Sarawak by the Week*, Week No. 30, 1966, p. 12.

[22] *Sarawak Tribune*, 25 December 1971.

[23] On 24 November 1971. See *Sarawak Gazette*, December 1971. No precise location has been allocated. Based on the forthcoming FAO Report it is assumed that some 200,000 acres can be found. Such an allocation substantially reduces the area of new concessions that can be given to private timber companies.

[24] *Sarawak Tribune*, 25 December 1971. Out of the 360 scholarships 136 were for pupils to carry on their schooling in West Malaysia as part of an effort to overcome 'provincial isolationist tendencies'. Abang Yusuf, *Sarawak Tribune*, 25 January 1972. A cess of \$1 per ton of hill timber has been imposed since 1963 and the total amount collected to the end of 1970 stood at over \$4 million. Less than \$400,000 of the total sum collected had been spent during those years, leaving an unexpended balance of over \$3,900,000 at the end of 1970 (*Minutes of Council Negri*, 29 May 1971). The low expenditure was due to uncertainty as to whether funds should be spent on native peoples generally or specifically for the benefit of those from whose areas the timber was extracted.

[25] For instance, see *Sarawak Tribune*, 21 December 1971. Dominic Dago ak Randan, born in 1934, was headmaster of the Catholic Mission school at Piching and has been a district councillor since 1959. He was a nominated member of the Dewan Ra'ayat from 1963 to 1969. In 1963 he was a member of PANAS and has been a member of BUMIPUTERA since its formation.

Dago in the Serian Parliamentary constituency found himself suddenly dismissed from the position of Pengarah which he had held since 1965.[26] The Bidayuh Minister for Youth has been featured prominently in the Malaysian Information Service publicity materials.

By contrast both PESAKA and SNAP appeared to be quite dispirited organizations, even some of their Iban branch members having applied to join BUMIPUTERA. Quietly a merger of the two exclusively native parties (BUMIPTERA and PESAKA) could well be achieved in the near future. Internal Alliance memoranda were circulated in 1971 to canvass the reactions of party members, particularly those in PESAKA who felt uneasy at the threat of being subsumed by BUMIPUTERA. A constant and driving motivation of those striving for native political unity was the desire to preclude manipulation by moneyed Chinese interests, who were regarded as havng played a quite improper role prior to 1969.

PESAKA leaders were said to have accepted a merger scheme early in 1972,[27] but they had to reckon with branch-level dissatisfaction that SNAP would reap a harvest of Dayak supporters, who would transfer their allegiances away from a party alleged to be dominated by Malays. The other difficulty in such a BUMIPUTERA-PESAKA merger is that a stress upon native unity appears to SUPP leaders as an attempt to isolate that party. Alliance leaders were quick to assuage SUPP sensitivities by publicly canvassing the desirability of an Alliance-SUPP merger. Such an arrangement could well be further explored as a means of preventing the damage of pre-selection wrangles prior to the 1974 election.

The chief minister has thus been extraordinarily successful in increasing the relative power of Parti BUMIPUTERA within the coalition government, and in breaking down nodal points of opposition. He has propagated the image that his is a dynamic government, free from corruption. He has kept his links with the central government in careful and constant repair. His almost weekly visits to Kuala Lumpur serve the dual function of resolving vexed issues on behalf of Sarawak and of maintaining his own position in Malaysian national politics, for he is widely believed to have future aspirations in that sphere. At the party political level he has appeared to isolate SNAP, though he has also demonstrated an awareness that the coalition must be maintained in order to stave off the opening of a pandora's box of alternative governmental arrangements. He has created a variety of new governmental organizations designed to modernize the state, and they will also serve to bolster the position of Parti BUMIPUTERA and its supporters.

---

[26] Pengarah Rahun was one of the two Biduyah Pengarah. He was appointed 'for life' by the Ningkan government. This was not the first time this type of dismissal had occurred. When challenged in the Council Negri, Abdul Rahman Ya'kub produced evidence that as early as 1965 the then SNAP Chief Minister had vetoed promotion of O. K. P. Dukau to the office of Pengarah 'because he belongs to an opposition party. . . . It must be understood that my Government is a political government. O. K. P. Dukau to be told to retire from service. . . .' (sic). Internal memorandum signed by Stephen Kalong Ningkan, Chief Minister, 6 September 1965. Vanguard, 14 March 1972.

[27] Sarawak Tribune, 22 and 24 March 1972.

Circumscription of the Electoral Process

Popular involvement in the governmental process has been singularly limited ever since the 1970 elections. Local government is no longer determined on an elective basis and penghulus, tua kampongs and kapitans may soon become regular civil servants, appointed without elective consultation and debarred from participation in party politics. In contrast to past practice the only use of the elective process has been to fill two vacant legislative seats, one state and the other federal.

Following the procedure adopted in West Malaysia during confrontation all district council by-elections have been suspended and the question of abolishing future council elections is under review.[28] For the time being, casual vacancies are filled by appointing a person recommended by a political party of which the former Councillor was a member. If he was an independent then the government will if practicable appoint someone who is not a member of any party at the time of appointment.[29] The implication of this change is that the district councils (elected in 1963) will remain quite static in composition, reflecting the alignment of forces that existed a decade earlier. Even without having all councillors appointed, were the government desirous of changing the character of certain councils it would be in a position to do so, given that such a high proportion of councillors originally designated themselves as independents. The process of attrition and provision of incentives to resign could cause many vacancies and result in quite a change of composition. The government also decided to transfer responsibility for the administration of primary education from District Councils to the State Education Department. Such a change will take from the councils their most important responsibility, and could in due course also facilitate the process of altering the medium of instruction in primary schools from English to Bahasa Malaysia—the national language.[30]

The only formal tests of public opinion held during 1971 were two by-elections for vacated Council Negri and Dewan Ra'ayat seats. The

---

[28] *Borneo Bulletin*, 15 January 1972. The Chief Minister has left few doubts as to his feelings on the future of elective local government. Speaking in the Dewan Ra'ayat on the report of the Royal Commission on local authorities in West Malaysia he said that he 'did not see why the Opposition was harping on democracy when the Commission's report had placed democracy on the fourth order of priority after national unity, social and economic development and efficiency of administration. Apart from the Kuching Municipality, most of the other local authorities in Sarawak were inefficient and bankrupt'. *Straits Times*, 12 February 1972. The federal government decided to continue this suspension contrary to the recommendations of the Royal Commission headed by Athi Nahappan. The initial West Malaysian suspension also came at a time when PAP was on the attack against MCA.

[29] *Sarawak Government Gazette*, Part III, 7 May 1971, p. 22.

[30] There are indications that SUPP has agreed to accept conversion of the educational medium to Malay. The SUPP Chairman of the Kuching Rural District Council stated that his Council hopes to get all the primary English schools in its jurisdiction to change their medium of instruction to Bahasa Malaysia from next year. *Sarawak Tribune*, 28 July 1971.

first was in the Pelagus Council Negri constituency and was contested by two principal figures: Leonard Linggi anak Temenggong Jugah and Wesley Ajan anak Nabau. Wesley Ajan, a former SNAP candidate in the 1970 Council Negri election, stood as a Coalition Government candidate and was strongly supported by SUPP, Parti BUMIPUTERA and some members of PESAKA. However, then the Kapit branch of PESAKA, under Temenggong Jugah's patronage, nominated his son Linggi. Though the nomination papers were countersigned by PESAKA's Secretary-General,[31] the leader of PESAKA's Youth Section (Sidi Munan) objected strenuously and called for an immediate general meeting of the party. The meeting was on then off, then on and eventually was not held, despite Temenggong Jugah's wishes to hold the meeting once large numbers of his supporters had arrived at party headquarters. It became fairly clear that the Chief Minister and his supporters did not want Linggi in the Council Negri and were willing to do a great deal to block his election. Also this was the chance for Sidi's faction to oust Jugah from the leadership of the party and they did their best to do so.

Temenggong Jugah and his son were accused of disloyalty to the government. But on the other hand Linggi argued that PESAKA could ill afford to forfeit a Dayak seat to SUPP, particularly as that seat was in the heart of traditional PESAKA territory.[32] The election was particularly hard fought, charges of bribery being traded back and forth between the two camps, and a high degree of public interest apparent.[33] Linggi won the seat receiving 48.5 per cent of votes, compared to Ajan's 42 per cent. SUPP rather than BUMIPUTERA bore the brunt of the campaign against Linggi, for even the symbol of the coalition government (four inter-locking rings within two concentric circles) was quite similar to that of SUPP. The Chief Minister quickly sought to mitigate any ill effects of that campaign by arranging the appointment of Linggi as Alliance Publicity Officer, and Linggi himself chose to bide his time rather than immediately seeking to exercise a pre-eminent role amongst the Iban.

The other by-election was for the Dewan Ra'ayat. The sitting member for Bau-Lundu, Siyium anak Mutit the sole Bidayuh elected as a member

---

[31] The role of Thomas Kana, the PESAKA Secretary-General, was most ambivalent. He attended the meeting that decided upon a joint neutral coalition government candidate and voiced no objection to Ajan. But then he countersigned Linggi's nomination papers. Later he endorsed Sidi's call for a PESAKA general meeting. When the numbers were against Sidi (just two days prior to the assembly) he forfeited the police permit, for the meeting, leaving Jugah's disgruntled supporters milling around Sibu.

[32] SUPP also had good reason to field a candidate in the Pelagus constituency, for in the 1970 election it had gained a third of the votes (to PESAKA's 44%) more than half of these votes coming from Dayak supporters. If SUPP was to expand its multi-racial support, here was its opportunity and they also had reason to believe that the Chief Minister had no wish to see Linggi seated in the Council Negri. Linggi is a British-trained lawyer, is able to invoke some of the traditional sources of appeal possessed by his father and is educationally better equipped than all the other PESAKA members of Council Negri.

[33] The percentage of the registered electorate who voted was 77.3%, compared with 74.71% in the 1970 general election. *Sarawak Government Gazette*, Part V, 16 July 1970, p. 1387 and 23 July 1971, p. 1276.

of SUPP, decided to resign from that party. Prior to his election he had pledged to donate all of his parliamentary allowance (M$1,150 per month) to SUPP. In return the party gave him an expense allowance of $300 per month, hardly a princely sum for someone with few other means of support. He felt that SUPP were not interested in him or his community and he decided to resign from the party. However, he forgot that before receiving SUPP endorsement he had also signed an undated letter, addressed to the Speaker of the Dewan Ra'ayat, tendering his resignation from Parliament. This letter was held by the Secretary-General of the party to be used in just such an eventuality. Shortly after defecting from SUPP the Speaker announced that he had received and accepted Siyium's letter of resignation and a vacancy now existed in his constituency. The coalition government supported another SUPP candidate (a Bidayuh) for that constituency, and he was duly elected by a majority of 939 votes in a straight contest with a SNAP (Chinese) candidate.[34] The voter turnout was markedly low (61 per cent compared with 90 per cent in 1970), a fact related to a reduction in the number of polling places provided—76 in 1970, 29 in 1971.[35] Though justified by reasons of economy, such a reduction would result in many fewer votes being cast by the more remote Bidayuh, who might have been expected to give rather more support to SNAP than SUPP.

Popular participation in politics through the electoral process has thus been decidedly limited by government decisions to suspend all council by-elections and the pending total abolition of elective local government. Such a policy effectively prevents the development of strong institutionalized local centres of opposition to the state and federal governments. Tests of popular feeling must await casual vacancies to the state and federal legislatures.

The Economic Situation

The basic political problems rest in the dire economic situation facing Sarawak, a situation that has become clearly apparent ever since mid 1971 when the price of timber slumped. The rapid exploitation of hill timber in Sarawak provided wealth and employment (together with political patronage) sufficient to tide Sarawak through a period of steadily declining world rubber prices.[36] But since July 1971, due to a secular slackening in Japanese demand and vastly increased production

[34] Robert Sulis Ridu a young overseas trained leader of the Bidayuh National Association, nominated as an Independent and received some 424 votes. He was prevailed upon to withdraw from the contest, for despite all disclaimers his nomination appeared to be a means for BUMIPUTERA to seize a seat from SUPP. The Chief Minister was not willing to alienate SUPP and risk the survival of his Coalition government. During the campaign Nelson Kundai, the (ex- SNAP) Bidayuh member was appointed a Minister. Cotter (SUPP) received 53%, of valid votes cast, compared with 42% for Lee Nyan Choi of SNAP.

[35] *Sarawak Government Gazette*, Part V, 7 October 1971, p. 1636 and Election Commission, *General Election Sarawak (Malaysia)*, mimeo.

[36] Except for a temporary fillip in 1969, the price of rubber has fallen steadily so that by 1972 even first grade rubber was sold in Kuching for just 41 cents per picul, compared to 76 cents in 1965.

from Indonesial Kalimantan, the value of timber exported from Sarawak has dropped dramatically,[37] further exacerbating the plight of those already in a marginal economic situation caused by the low rubber price.

Table 34

Value of Principal Exports from Sarawak: 1961-71

(Value in M$ million rounded)

Year	Timber	Rubber	Pepper	Sago	Illepe nuts	Crude Petroleum
1961	42	83	29	3	—	107
1962	41	73	24	4	16	107
1963	54	70	22	6	—	89
1964	62	60	24	8	—	93
1965	82	59	42	6	—	101
1966	109	46	33	5	5	115
1967	136	32	35	5	—	133
1968	181	26	35	5	13	169
1969	187	50	53	4	—	177
1970	198	24	56	4	17	203
1971	168	17	63	3	—	391

Source: Sarawak Department of Statistics. *Quarterly Bulletin of Statistics, 4th quarter 1971,* Government Printing Office, Kuching 1972.

The economic situation need not be totally bleak and without hope, for the new oil discoveries offshore from the Baram and Bintulu districts have resulted in a dramatic rise in the value of exported petroleum products. However, such production is highly capital intensive and of an enclave character, providing considerable remuneration to the government but very little new employment for those rendered jobless by the slump in timber and rubber prices.

Projected royalties are sufficient to finance a massive programme of agricultural development throughout the state. One area which would appear to lend itself to such beneficial large-scale agricultural development and could provide considerable new employment opportunities is the Miri-Bintulu-Long-Lama triangle. The sums involved are vast, particularly were Shell to go ahead with their proposed M$3,000 million liquified natural gas plant near Bintulu. Due to the high potential remuneration the Sarawak State government has strenuously objected to the concept that offshore oil royalties should accrue to the federal government. Given that all the new oil and gas fields are beyond territorial limits, and that the wealth they contain promises to be even more lucrative than that tapped by Brunei, it is not surprising that achieving

[37] Even though only the higher quality timber was being exported, once the slump hit, the f.o.b. unit value of sawlogs dropped to an all-time low. By February 1972 almost all hill forest operators in Sarawak were reported to have ceased operations. Only those with swamp area concessions were still operating. *Sarawak Tribune,* 4 and 9 February 1972.

final agreement on the sharing of royalties was such a tortuous process.[38] In the interim all royalties were placed in a frozen account.

It has been relatively simpler to ameliorate the situation of the coastal dwellers than it has been to help those dwelling in the ulu (up-river). The former have been assisted markedly by the provision of simple drainage schemes that have then permitted large new tracts of land to be planted with wet padi and coconuts. Padi earns at least the government guaranteed price and copra has been yielding a reasonable return on the capital and labour invested to grow it.

The situation of those reliant upon rubber and hill padi is much more parlous. Following two successive years of bad crops many Dayaks have not produced enough rice for subsistence and have been heavily reliant upon cash income from rubber, irregular fruiting of illipe nuts, wages from timber companies and sale of occasional logs of valuable timber species. The imposition of curfews in some localities has further restricted economic activity. Actual starvation looms in the absence of each of these sources of cash income.[39]

Chinese rubber planters in the lower Rejang, especially those holding land that is too swampy for pepper, have also been very hard hit by low rubber prices and incessant curfews. A serious social problem has emerged as a result of the migration to the towns of nearly all young women from affected areas. A great many families have also moved— seeking security and subsistence employment.

Internal Security

The security situation has been exacerbated by this worsening economic situation and by the rising expectations of material improvement. The situation of the Iban has led to adoption of various local strategies. In some districts they co-operate with the Sarawak Communist Organization, in others SNAP is the channel of political dissension and in other areas government parties can readily gain support with almost any material inducements. This is a situation of communal fragmentation rather than unity.

For many Chinese the increasing pace of Malaysianization, the dire economic plight of a great many farmers, and the lack of employment for youth, serve to promote recourse to the communist organization as the only possible salvation. Compared with the situation that existed in 1969-70, the communists are much more daring, much better funded[40] and in receipt of a great deal more co-operation from the Dayaks than ever before.

The worsening of the security situation dates also from the formation of the Sarawak Coalition Government. The significance of the timing

[38] See p. 133 for a brief account of the dispute between Penghulu Tawi Sli and Kuala Lumpur concerning royalties from oil on the continental shelf.
[39] For instance, see 'Hunger is rife up the Baram', *Borneo Bulletin*, 29 January 1972.
[40] They reportedly have received protection money from certain large timbermen whose jungle operations are obviously vulnerable.

appears to be that the communist organization can no longer pursue its open front strategy through SUPP and communist supporters no longer see SUPP as a credible vehicle. When SUPP leaders first entered the government they faced a machinery that had become accustomed to regarding their whole party as crypto-communist. Now the situation has altered to the point where Stephen Yong is even a member of the State Security Committee.[41] Permission to hold the seventh annual SUPP Delegates Conference was withheld for nearly a year, much to the relief of party leaders who were subject to mounting rank-and-file criticism for their lack of progress on such sensitive issues as the release of political detainees.[42] When the Conference was finally held (4-5 September 1971) the top leadership was duly re-elected. A few SUPP members had been detained just prior to the meeting. The actual focus of hostility during the conference was Ong Kee Hui's acceptance of a Federal Ministership, rather than SUPP's implementation of its policies through the coalition government. SUPP Ministers appear to have reneged on their promises to secure the release or trial of detainees. This was partly because they were unable to negotiate any deals with the federal government on behalf of the detainees, who do not trust SUPP Ministers and are unwilling to accept any but unconditional releases. On the other hand, Malaysia has a mandatory death sentence for those convicted of illegal possession of any weapon—even a bullet. Thus many detainees are said to be better off not being formally charged before a court of law.

The communists' use of selective terror has been particularly effective in the third division, the government acknowledging that they were involved in the murder of thirty-eight civilians there during 1971.[43] Communist efforts reached a crescendo in and around Sibu during May, June and July 1971. In each case the alleged government informers were confronted publicly by a group of terrorists, who first checked their name and identity card numbers. The the communists purportedly stated exactly what information was supplied to the government, the reward paid in return (including the cheque number), and what had then happened to the communist cadre who had been betrayed. This was followed by an explanation that a blood debt must be paid, an opportunity for recantation, and then the execution. The communists have been most effective in creating the impression that no-one can inform and be secure, that they have knowledge from the highest echelons of the government security apparatus.

The youth are of particular importance to the communists and during those three months almost all Sibu schools were visited by cadres, who proceeded to lecture the students. In one school across river from Sibu

---

[41] The membership was announced on 28 April 1971. The only politicians included are the Chief Minister, the two Deputy Chief Ministers and the Minister for Sarawak Affairs.

[42] Such a dissident membership can be an asset to the leadership in their intra-government negotiations, as it provides the party leaders with strong arguments in favour of concessions to hold their restive members in check.

[43] *Borneo Bulletin*, 29 January 1972. The comparable number killed in 1970 was 23 and 3 in 1969.

a teacher was executed for acting as an informer.[44] Teachers also received a long duplicated letter which they were instructed to read to their assembled classes. The open letter, entitled 'Smash resolutely the spiritual lock that is being put on us—filthy culture',[45] was a highly moralistic call to youth to abhor the corrosive poisons spread by 'self-seeking fellows'. To 'win the victory' students were told to 'oppose and stop to wear Mini-skirt and funny dresses' and were warned against teachers: 'some of them even teach the students how to twist, and thus really lead the students into darkness'. A letter was also addressed to the patriarchs and another one was later sent to class monitors. In addition school buildings were regularly daubed with slogans.[46]

By the end of July the town of Sibu was extremely tense. Almost all government officers had received threatening letters from the communist organization. Security forces discovered a large field hospital just across the river from Sibu and documents indicating an impending attempt to 'liberate' the town. A twenty-four-hour curfew was imposed to forestall such an eventuality. The total curfew area covered much of the lower Rejang, including the towns of Sibu, Binatang and Sarikei, and was not relaxed for three days. The government simultaneously launched Operation Ngayau (total war or head-hunt in Iban) hoping to enlist maximum Iban co-operation, and extended the round-the-clock curfew into the Kanowit and Kapit districts in order to facilitate freedom of action by the security forces.

Since 1970 there have been certain predominantly Iban areas in the Kanowit district that no government officer will visit, so badly has security deteriorated. Some of the local Iban population have been rendered destitute as curfews prevented both harvesting and planting of padi. Yet any government relief assistance soon finds its way to the sco. The Communist Organization has won local Iban support by a mixture of beneficial agricultural extension work and intimidation of those who are known to be pro-government.[47] One indication of the tense security situation is that the new Council Negri member for Machan (Kanowit) had not felt it safe to visit his constituency in the two years since he was elected. In March 1972 communists ambushed a troop convoy killing fifteen security forces and capturing their weapons. That attack took place near Lundu in the first division.[48]

The Communist Organization has successfully undermined government authority throughout considerable areas of the third and first divisions of the state and in pockets of the second and fourth divisions.

[44] *Sarawak Tribune*, 11 May 1971.
[45] The letter was addressed to 'our schoolmates', mimeographed and dated 4 May 1971.
[46] Two cadres were shot dead whilst painting slogans on the wall of St Elizabeth's School, Sibu. As a result of retribution threats all the nuns forthwith left the country.
[47] On 23 December 1971 a group of sco surrounded the longhouse of Tadoh, at Ng. Jek. Tadoh was accused of killing Tay, the supp Parliamentary candidate for Kanowit, and summarily executed. (For the earlier reference to the death of Tay see p. 133.
[48] *Sarawak Tribune*, 28 and 30 March 1972.

However, there are serious limits on their possible achievements beyond this stage. Neither the Malaysian nor the Indonesian governments are likely to tolerate the existence of 'liberated areas' which they would clearly perceive as an extension of Chinese-led communist influence. Across the border in Kalimantan the Indonesian army has unequivocally demonstrated its ability and willingness to wreak havoc upon local Chinese as a group in retaliation for the support given by some of them to the communists. All Chinese have been totally cleared from the interior (southwest of Sarawak) and re-settled along the coast, thus uprooting settlements dating back more than a century. Indonesian officers have been known to chide their Malaysian counterparts for failing to adopt such a 'simple' solution.

The Malaysian government has responded to the security situation by launching a series of operations designed to contain communist recruitment of Ibans[49] and to weed out active pro-communists within the Chinese community. For instance, some 124 people, mostly students, were arrested and detained in a week-long sweep of the third division during March 1972. A few days later the communists responded by ambushing a troop convoy, killing fifteen troops.[50]

The government has also instituted a scheme of registering all tenants in the Sibu district. When introducing the white paper on the threat of armed communism in Sarawak the Deputy Prime Minister canvassed the possibility of other measures such as food denial and re-settlement.[51] Re-settlement would be prohibitively expensive if it followed the pattern of the controlled villages (Siburan, Tapah and Beratok). However, the government is considering regroupment of the scattered Chinese population (without barbwire fences, guards, etc.), offering them as inducement clinics, piped water and general amenities that can only be provided to concentrations of population.

Early in 1972 control over schools was taken from the hands of local authorities and vested in the state government, a measure designed to aid the process of countering subversion. In addition the Prime Minister declared the troubled third division a special security area, thereby vesting all governmental functions under the direct control of the Rejang Security Command (RASCOM). Finally, armed vigilante corps were formed under government sponsorship and some Iban living in remote areas were also armed by the government.[52] Such a policy of trust in the Iban is fraught with considerable danger as the communists are desperately short of modern weapons and will do all they can to induce the Iban to hand over their newly-acquired guns.

---

[49] Following Operation Ngayau (headhunt) came Operation Sarak (meaning 'divorce' in Iban) launched early in February 1972. See *Straits Times*, 14 February 1972.
[50] *Vanguard*, 28 March 1972.
[51] Press statement by Tun Dr Ismail, 11 February 1972, p. 2.
[52] *Sarawak Tribune*, 6 May 1972. More than 200 shotguns (and ammunition) were passed out in May as the initial phase of an experiment to distribute up to 5,000 such guns. A small number of guns were also supplied to Chinese and Malays.

Since the 1970 election Sarawak has politically entered Malaysia. The politics of the state are beginning to conform much more closely to the West Malaysian pattern, with the primacy of a predominantly Islamic party and a secondary (accommodating) Chinese coalition partner. In the very act of joining with BUMIPUTERA to protect Chinese interests SUPP forfeited much of its claim to include important Dayak representation, and to develop its multi-racial support. The lines of ethnic cleavage could well have been sharpened by this arrangement of a coalition government, for the Dayak peoples are poorly represented with their most popular leaders again in the opposition, within the ranks of SNAP.

The quest for a unity based upon race and religion, successfully achieved by BUMIPUTERA for the Islamic community, may set in motion a process that will lead to a sharpening of the cleavages between ethnic groups. For it was the divisions within each ethnic group that facilitated ready compromise and the maintenance of pan-ethnic coalitions, both within and without the government. Formerly, the only group that was inadequately represented within government were the Chinese, but they of all groups were best equipped to utilize economic power to redress their lack of political representation. But now it is the Dayaks who suffer inadequate political representation and there is even more reason for them to seek unity for political purposes. The Dayaks have few economic resources that are immediately realizable and must rely upon their numbers for political potency. One reason why timber licences became a source of political patronage and power was that they did provide a quick cash flow that could be used by Dayak leaders for political purposes.

In the absence of such funding communal unity will be perceived as of paramount importance to the Dayaks and one might expect SNAP to gain in response a stronger ethnic cohesiveness.

Thus the politics of Sarawak are on the verge of conforming to the Malaysian pattern, as each ethnic group becomes identified with a communal party, and the lines of cleavage deepen. Much will depend upon the degree to which SNAP can maintain its cohesion as the nationalist party of Sarawak. Its wide base of support in the last election gives some reason to believe that it will have the resilience to attract all the Dayak groups and the Chinese.

CONCLUSION

The creation of Sarawak's political parties each based upon a segment of one major ethnic group, set in motion a process that threatened to displace the established leadership in each ethnic community. For each of the three major ethnic groups one party (namely PANAS, PESAKA and SCA) claimed official support. The other three parties (BARJASA, SNAP and SUPP) sought to usurp power from the influential leadership, as represented by the former three parties. Campaigning energies and bitterness were principally directed inward, within each ethnic group. The very cleavages that militated against communal unity created a multiplicity of disagreements which have in fact promoted conflict resolution through a process of flexible realignments. Rather than making racial blocks more rigid, this political division *within* ethnic groups provided a ready basis for compromise, forcing the factions to seek allies outside their group in the quest for political power.

External impingement upon Sarawak politics since independence has been characterized by:

(a) the simple transfer of the instruments of control from the British to the Malaysian government.

(b) the development of those instruments in an effort to mobilize the support of the populace behind the central government, but not so as to heighten their participation in unofficial movements of a political character.

(c) the growing limitation of popular participation in politics in the name of security and stability. The aura of emergency that prevailed from the time of the Brunei revolt (1962) to the ending of confrontation (1966) and was reimposed with greater severity following the communal bloodshed in West Malaysia (1969) provided the legitimization of this trend.

In an effort to subsume the geographic entity Sarawak within Malaysia the Alliance government has relied upon an organizational mode of political control that has exacerbated relations between ethnic groups within Sarawak. The Centre has supported efforts to assert the primacy of racial politics over those based upon shared interest, so that Sarawak will accord with the national pattern. Federal links have been critical to the establishment and continuance of the Alliance pattern in Sarawak, that is, the larger system has sought to determine the direction of the development of the sub-system. However, the resilience and vitality of multi-ethnic parties has enabled them to resist total regression to a situation where race would subsume all other issues and become the one all-pervasive cleavage. The phenomenon of Sarawak nationalism has

161

cut across ethnic lines and has been successfully exploited by both SNAP and SUPP. The peculiar ethnic complex, with three major groups, not one of which approaches a majority of the population, has facilitated accommodation within Sarawak: the tripartite division being understood in contrast to the predominance of a racial Malay versus non-Malay dichotomy in West Malaysia.

Were the present flexible arrangement of competing factions to have its freedom of competition severely curtailed, the latent potentialities of the simple racial category Native versus non-Native could be realized and race would become the real and all-pervasive political cleavage. On the other hand, the more that the factional divisions in the polity are allowed to express themselves, the more likely the whole society will come to resemble politically any other society that is not racially divided and the sooner racial distinctions will decline in political importance. The key is the continued presence of a high frequency of disagreement resting upon a multiplicity of frameworks and social differentiations and the continued failure of efforts to unite politically each racial group, in spite of encouragement by the central government in order to reduce 'Bornean parochialism' or Sarawak nationalism.

If those linked to the central Malaysian leadership can successfully pattern Sarawak politics along exclusively communal lines, they will have extended Alliance control at the expense of worsening communal relations. The Alliance goal of centralizing the polity is at variance with the persistence of harmonious ethnic relations within the state of Sarawak.

APPENDIX I

THE ELECTED LEADERSHIP OF SARAWAK

A detailed knowledge of the types of councillors elected over time provides us with an important indicator of the direction of politican change, as the criteria employed in the selection of leaders reflect prime values and the distribution of power in a society. As change occurs, its direction can be indicated by observing the characteristics of the newly recruited leadership and observing which economic, cultural or geographic groups are gaining or losing representation amongst the elected leadership. Whereas knowledge of the formal governmental structures would convey a deceptive image of stability, close scrutiny of the leadership permits a more precise distinction between continuities and changes.

We shall be using extensive biographical data concerning the local leadership, data obtained almost entirely through interviews. A picture can be drawn of the types of leaders selected and elected over time and one can begin to determine accurately the character of the various parties. Ten parameters are employed to delineate the basic cleavages so as to depict the lines of conflict between parties as well as the changes over time.

Parameters

Personal characteristics:
    Age
    Ethnic group
    Religion

Acquired experience:
    Size of present locality
    Spatial mobility
    Occupation
    Officially-sponsored leadership
    Education—level attained
    Education—medium of instruction
    Education—type of school attended

This is hardly 'elite' data as such, for the group under consideration numbers over 1,500 persons, most of them 'leaders' (elected or appointed) of not more than a few hundred persons. With care they can therefore be seen as reflections of societal political development. In the absence of other data commonly accessible to analysts of Western polities, this relatively hard data acquires considerable importance.

The character of each political party and its impact upon the political system can also be understood by a close examination of the councillors which it successfully nominated for elective office. This is based upon the understanding that all Sarawak's parties found their *raison d'être* in the nomination of candidates for political office in accordance with established constitutional procedures. From information concerning each of the 429 councillors elected in 1963, the 304 candidates nominated in 1970 and the 72 actually elected in 1970 a profile is drawn which can serve to explicate the policies formulated and implemented by particular parties. The formative experiences and life styles of the leadership of each party will be examined in order to expand knowledge of the underlying motivations that create party policy. This approach also enables us to advance a good distance beyond a simple communal analysis, for though the pre-eminent cleavage throughout Malaysia may well be that of race, due consideration must be accorded to other significant variables. In the following pages the biographical character-istics of the following groups have been identified and tabulated.

A. District Councillors who held office during four periods.

(1) 1950-4. This was the introductory phase, during which 157 different local persons were nominated to serve on district councils. As only ten such men had been nominated to councils before 1950 they may be safely passed over in this statistical analysis. The only councillors deliberately excluded from our consideration here, are the nominated European members. Their distinct characteristics would skew our results in an artificial direction, and mask local political change.

(2) 1955-9. This was the phase during which the elective concept was introduced, though only a few councils were fully-elected during these years. There was a large turnover of councillors, some 618 individuals serving during this period during which councils were introduced to every district of Sarawak.

(3) 1960-2. District council elections were held throughout the state at the end of 1959. All councils except Miri were fully elected by the beginning of the new decade. Though one political party (SUPP) had been formed before 1960 its electoral impact prior to the 1959-60 polling was confined largely to the Kuching district. Party membership *per se* was not a key criterion for success in that election, though since then some 41 per cent of all councillors elected during this phase did join one or other of the parties. Some 480 councillors served during this elective but pre-political party phase.

(4) 1963. This was the political party phase. General elections for all members of every council took place from April to June 1963, and political parties dominated this election in most districts of the first, second and third divisions of Sarawak. Independent members predominated in the interior of the fourth and fifth divisions but most of those independents in due course aligned themselves with one of the various parties. Some 429 councillors were elected in 1963 and they are analysed here as a total group, and then broken down according to the parties that nominated them, or to which they chose to adhere. The latter distinction is particularly important as most of the independent councillors (87 of 117) did align themselves with one party or another after the election. The characteristics of the parties' councillors after the re-alignment of independents are given in parentheses.

B. Members of Council Negri and the Dewan Ra'ayat (the lower house of the Federal Parliament) who were selected through the three-tier system. In essence the district councillors elected divisional advisory councillors, who in turn elected the members of the Council Negri, who then selected Sarawak's representatives in the Dewan Ra'ayat.[1] In these tables the members of the Council Negri and of the Dewan Ra'ayat are analysed separately, then grouped together in order to aggregate a sufficient number to be broken down and analysed by party.

[1] See Chapter 2, Figure 1 for a diagrammatic representation of the tier structure.

C. The members of the Council Negri and Dewan Ra'ayat were all directly elected to their respective legislatures in the 1970 election, following abandonment of the earlier three-tier system. These legislators have also been grouped together here and then all 72 analysed according to the political party that nominated them for office. The characteristics of all the 304 different candidates for the state and federal legislatures have been appended in parentheses for an extra dimension is added to our understanding when the type of candidate each party sought to nominate for office is considered.

The '% data' column is included with each table in order to indicate that proportion of councillors, candidates or members for whom the pertinent data are known. All percentages within the tables are calculated on the basis of known information.[2]

Table 35

Median Year of Birth of District Councillors by Year of Election, Political Party Allegiance and New Recruitment to Elective Office[a]

	Councillors median year of birth	% data[b]	Total number
District Councillors			
1950-4	1908	92	157
1955-9	1913	96	618
1960-2	1920	99	480
District Councillors			
1963	1922	98	429
BARJASA	1926 (1924)	100 (100)	44 (73)
PESAKA	1923 (1923)	100 (100)	43 (61)
SNAP	1923 (1923)	100 (100)	48 (73)
SCA	(1919)	(100)	(5)
Alliance	1923	100	138
PANAS	1920 (1920)	100 (100)	58 (63)
SUPP	1920 (1921)	93 (93)	115 (123)
Independents	1923 (1925)	100 (100)	117 (30)
Newly recruited	1924	97	235

a. The figures in paretheses refer to the councillors adhering to each party in July 1963, after the re-alignment of the independent councillors.
b. The '% data' column indicates that proportion of councillors for whom pertinent data are known. For instance, the median year of birth of the 429 councillors elected in 1963 is calculated on the basis of the 98% whose birthdate is known. In this case it can be assumed that the unknown 2% will not materially alter the result.

[2] Most of this biographical data was obtained through interviews in each of the twenty districts of Sarawak. The author is deeply indebted to all who so patiently gave of their time and expertise.

Characteristics of the Elected Leadership

Age

Upon analysis of the average (median) age of district councillors elected during each of the four periods we arrive at the somewhat surprising conclusion that there has been virtually no change at all. The average age at time of election throughout the 1950s stood at 42 years, it dropped to 40 years in 1960-2 and rose marginally to 41 years following the 1963 election. Those councillors who were members of the two oldest established parties, PANAS and SUPP, were themselves somewhat older than average whilst the BARJASA councillors were distinctly younger—as were those of SNAP and PESAKA to a lesser degree.

The age difference was accentuated amongst the 1963 members of the Council Negri and the Dewan Ra'ayat, with the PANAS members being much older, the SUPP above average and BARJASA and SNAP well below average. At district council and higher levels the SCA representatives were also older.

In 1970 the age at election of Council Negri members held steady, but that of members of Parliament rose seven years compared with 1963. The PESAKA members were now the oldest and those of SNAP the youngest, a difference of fourteen years reflecting the high proportion of new recruits introduced by SNAP.

Table 36

Median Year of Birth of Sarawak Dewan Ra'ayat and Council Negri Members Selected in 1960 and 1963 by Political Party Allegiance

	Members median year of birth	% data	Total number
Council Negri			
1960-2	1920	97	33
1963	1919	100	39
Members of			
Parliament 1963	1921	100	24
Members of			
Council Negri &			
Parliament 1963[a]	1920	100	52
PANAS	1912	100	6
BARJASA	1923	100	11
PESAKA	1921	100	13
SNAP	1923	100	9
SCA	1917	100	5
SUPP	1919	100	6

a. Eleven persons belonged concurrently to both the Dewan Ra'ayat and the Council Negri.

Table 37

Median Year of Birth of Sarawak Dewan Ra'ayat and Council Negri Members Elected in 1970 (and Candidates) by Political Party Allegiance and New Recruitment to Elective Office

	Members median year of birth	(Candidates year of birth)	% data		Total number	
Members of Parliament 1970	1921	(1924)	100	(95)	24	(93)
Council Negri members 1970	1926	(1925)	100	(93)	48	(220)
Members of Council Negri & Parliament 1970	1924	(1925)	100	(94)	72	(304)
BUMIPUTERA	1923	(1923)	100	(94)	17	(32)
PESAKA	1921	(1923)	100	(96)	10	(50)
SNAP	1935	(1927)	100	(94)	21	(69)
SCA	1923	(1927)	100	(100)	5	(13)
SUPP	1923	(1924)	100	(94)	17	(56)
Independent	1929	(1926)	100	(89)	2	(84)
Newly recruited	1933	(1928)	100	(88)	33	(162)

Note: The figures in parentheses to the candidates who stood for election in 1970

Ethnicity

Throughout each phase Malay and Melanau district councillors have continued to be slightly over-represented in relation to their share of the total population. Dramatic changes have taken place amongst the other major communities. In the first phase (1950-4) Chinese were 13 per cent over-represented in relation to their proportion of the population, whilst the Iban and Land Dayak together were 17 per cent under-represented. As local government spread through the rural districts this discrepancy was corrected so that by the second phase (1955-9) Chinese over-representation was reduced to 3 per cent and Iban-Land Dayak under-representation to 6 per cent. A contributing demographic change was a 4 per cent increase of the proportion of Chinese in the population between 1947 and 1960, and a 3 per cent decrease in the proportion of the population who were Iban. The 1960-2 proportions saw a 1 per cent increase in each of those disproportions (i.e., Iban and Land Dayak under-representation $=$ 7 per cent, Chinese over-representation $=$ 4 per cent) but by 1963 there were no variations exceeding 2 per cent. The elected councillors en toto fairly accurately reflected the ethnic composition of the total population. By 1963 political activity had spread throughout rural Sarawak. The predominantly Chinese and Malay areas no longer were the focal points of all politics.

Table 38

Ethnic Group of District Councillors by Year of Election, Political Party Allegiance and New Recruitment to Elective Office

	Percentage of Councillors by ethnic group							
	Malay	Melanau	Iban	Land Dayak	Other	Chinese	% data	Total number
Total 1947 population	18	6	35	8	6	27	100	
District Councillors								
1950-4	19	6	24	2	9	40	100	157
1955-9	18	7	28	6	7	34	100	618
1960-2	18	7	28	5	7	35	100	480
Total 1960 population	17	6	32	8	6	31	100	
District Councillors								
1963	19	6	32	6	7	30	100	429
BARJASA	34 (33)	18 (30)	23 (18)	16 (11)	9 (8)	— (—)	100	44 (73)
PESAKA	— (—)	5 (3)	91 (80)	— (—)	5 (16)	— (—)	100	46 (61)
SNAP	— (—)	— (1)	85 (82)	15 (10)	— (4)	— (3)	100	48 (73)
SCA	— (—)	— (—)	— (—)	— (—)	— (—)	— (100)	100	— (5)
Alliance	11	7	65	10	4	2	100	138
PANAS	84 (79)	2 (2)	2 (2)	9 (13)	— (—)	3 (5)	100	58 (63)
SUPP	1 (1)	— (—)	7 (7)	3 (3)	1 (1)	89 (88)	100	115 (123)
Independent	13 (20)	14 (3)	31 (13)	4 (—)	20 (33)	19 (30)	100	117 (30)
Newly recruited	20	5	29	5	7	34	100	235

Notes: The figures in parentheses refer to the councillors adhering to each party in July 1963, after the re-alignment of the independent councillors.
All percentages in each table are rounded to nearest whole number.

Table 39

Ethnic Group of Sarawak Dewan Ra'ayat and Council Negri Members Selected in 1960 and 1963 by Political Party Allegiance

| | Percentage of members by ethnic group | | | | | | | Total |
	Malay	Melanau	Iban	Land Dayak	Other	Chinese	% data	number
Council Negri								
1960-2	21	—	27	6	12	34	100	33
1963	8	10	38	3	12	28	100	39
Members of Parliament 1963	25	4	38	4	—	29	100	24
Member of Council Negri & Parliament 1963	15	10	37	2	9	27	100	52
PANAS	66	—	—	17	—	17	100	6
BARJASA	36	46	9	—	9	—	100	11
PESAKA	—	—	77	—	23	—	100	13
SNAP	—	—	78	—	—	22	100	9
SCA	—	—	—	—	—	100	100	5
SUPP	—	—	17	—	—	83	100	6

Viewed by political party, BARJASA elected a significant proportion of councillors from all major native ethnic groups. No other single party could boast such a broad base of support. SNAP drew its support from the Iban and some Land Dayak, and PESAKA from the Iban, the Kayan and Kenyah and a few Melanau. SUPP was heavily Chinese and PANAS predominantly Malay, with some Land Dayak adherents. The subsequent realignment of independents served to decease the numerical dominance of the strongest ethnic group within each party.

At the higher levels of the Council Negri and Dewan Ra'ayat Ibans were somewhat better represented (at Chinese expense) but the Land Dayaks had only one representative—a fact that caused them a good deal of resentment, often expressed through letters to the editor in the *Sarawak Tribune* and *Vanguard*. The party breakdown in 1963 showed:

(a) PANAS with four Malays, one Land Dayak and one Chinese;
(b) BARJASA with five Melanau, four Malay, one Kedayan and one Iban;
(c) PESAKA with ten Iban and three Kayan and Kenyah;
(d) SNAP with seven Iban and two Chinese;
(e) SUPP with five Chinese and one Iban.

Between the levels of district councillor and the Council Negri BARJASA and SNAP had abandoned their Land Dayaks in favour of Melanau and Chinese respectively.

The overall ethnic composition of those elected to Parliament and the Council Negri (taken together) in 1970 remained remarkably similar to those of 1963. The ethnic composition of all parties (except SCA) had however undergone significant changes. Party BUMIPUTERA provided most Malay and Melanau representatives but, despite its having fielded a higher proportion of Land Dayak candidates than any other party, it completely forfeited the claim of its predecessors (PANAS and BARJASA) to represent the Land Dayaks. PESAKA became exclusively Iban and Malay, losing its prior role as representative of the Kayan and Kenyah. SNAP diluted its exclusively Iban posture becoming, together with SUPP, the representative of the Land Dayak, Kayan and Kenyah. SUPP's representation was also less Chinese than hitherto, though it failed in its effort to elect more than one Iban representative.

Religion

Throughout the full length of the period analyzed, Christians have been markedly over-represented in relation to their proportion of the population. Their abnormally high representation is derived from the pivotal significance of mission schools for all segments of the population. There is one distinct and systematic error in this first table, for between 12 per cent and 20 per cent of councillors interviewed did not respond to questions concerning their religious affiliation. We would suspect that those for whom we have no data would not be evenly distributed but would be aligned more with the categories animism or Chinese religion. Assuming that this is true then Muslims may well be represented according to their proportion of the population, for adherents to that religion are readily identifiable and few would thus appear in the unassigned category. The overall pattern of Christian over-representation at the particular expense of animists remains the case. As most educated Dayak councillors attended Mission schools their educational level is quite closely correlated with adherence to the Christian religion. Thus as education has gained in significance as a criterion for election, so has the proportion of Dayak councillors who are Christian.

'Chinese religion' includes Buddhists, freethinkers and ancestor worshippers. The category is crude but does move one step from the census practice of

Table 40

Ethnic Group of Sarawak Dewan Ra'ayat and Council Negri Members Elected in 1970 (and Candidates) by Political Party Allegiance and New Recruitment to Elective Office

	Percentage of members by ethnic group							Total number
	Malay	Melanau	Iban	Land Dayak	Other	Chinese	% data	
Members of Parliament 1970	13 (12)	13 (4)	37 (44)	8 (9)	4 (8)	25 (23)	100 (100)	24 (93)
Council Negri Members 1970	17 (16)	8 (5)	33 (35)	6 (6)	4 (7)	31 (31)	100 (100)	48 (220)
Members of Council Negri & Parliament 1970	15 (15)	10 (5)	35 (39)	7 (7)	4 (7)	29 (27)	100 (100)	72 (304)
BUMIPUTERA	53 (60)	41 (22)		(12)	(3)	6 (3)	100 (100)	17 (32)
PESAKA	10 (10)	(8)	90 (62)	(8)	(10)	(2)	100 (100)	10 (50)
SNAP	5 (12)		62 (48)	14 (7)	10 (7)	9 (26)	100 (100)	21 (69)
SCA						100 (100)	100 (100)	5 (13)
SUPP	(6)		6 (27)	12 (9)	6 (9)	76 (50)	100 (100)	17 (56)
Independent	(13)	(6)	100 (45)	(4)	(6)	(26)	100 (100)	2 (84)
Newly recruited	15 (12)	15 (8)	38 (35)	9 (9)	9 (7)	15 (28)	100 (100)	34 (162)
Total 1970 Population	19	5	31	9	6	30	100	

Note: The figures in parentheses refer to the candidates who stood for election in 1970.

Table 41

Religion of District Councillors by Year of Election, Political Party Allegiance and New Recruitment to Elective Office

	Percentage of councillors by religion				% data	Total number
	Islam	Christian	Animism	'Chinese religion'		
District Councillors						
1950-4	31	25	27	17	82	157
1955-9	31	26	30	13	80	618
1960-2	31	32	26	11	81	480
District Councillors 1963	30	32	22	17	88	429
BARJASA	58 (65)	14 (11)	28 (24)	— —	98 (99)	44 (61)
PESAKA	3 (2)	61 (65)	36 (33)	— —	91 (93)	43 (61)
SNAP	— —	67 (49)	33 (50)	— (1)	88 (90)	48 (73)
SCA	— —	— (50)	— —	— (50)	(80)	5
Alliance	21	47	32	1	91	138
PANAS	89 (84)	9 (11)	— (2)	2 (3)	97 (97)	58 (63)
SUPP	2 (2)	30 (30)	9 (9)	59 (58)	70 (70)	115 (123)
Independents	29 (38)	27 (24)	31 (14)	12 (24)	97 (97)	117 (30)
newly recruited	31	31	18	20	97	235
Total 1960 population	23	16	61			

Note: The figures in parentheses refer to the councillors adhering to each party in July 1963, after the realignment of the independent councillors.

Table 42

Religion of Sarawak Dewan Ra'ayat and Council Negri Members Selected in 1960 and 1963 by Political Party Allegiance

| | Percentage of members by religion | | | | | |
	Islam	Christian	Animism	'Chinese religion'	% data	Total number
Council Negri						
1960-2	26	65	3	6	94	33
1963	22	56	8	14	92	39
Members of Parliament 1963	29	54	4	13	100	24
Member of Council Negri & Parliament 1963	29	55	6	10	94	52
PANAS	80	20	—	—	83	6
BARJASA	91	—	9	—	100	11
PESAKA	—	85	15	—	100	13
SNAP	—	89	—	11	100	9
SCA	—	60	—	40	100	5
SUPP	—	75	—	25	67	6

Note: It should be noted that the number of causes for each individual party varies considerably, and that therefore the percentages should be treated with care.

assigning animists, Buddhists and freethinkers into the omnibus category of 'other religion'. There is one other interesting change that warrants mention. Though the proportion or Chinese elected as councillors dropped some 5 per cent in 1963, the proportion of councillors adhering to Chinese religion rose appreciably. The proportion of Christians dropped fractionally that year for the first time. This change was a reflection of SUPP success in recruiting a rather different type of Chinese to political office. Whereas Christian mission-educated Chinese had hitherto exercised a leadership role disproportionate to their numbers, now those educated in Chinese private schools and without mission training were brought to the fore.

The Christian category was composed of three major parts:
(1) Roman Catholic: the proportion of councillors of that demonination rising from 5 per cent (1950-4), through 8 per cent (1955-9) to 12 per cent (1960-2) and 11 per cent (1963).
(2) Anglican (SPG): their share of all councillors also rising steadily from 3 per cent to 6 per cent to 7 per cent to 10 per cent over the same four periods.
(3) Methodist: dropping fairly consistently from 13 per cent to 8 per cent, then up to 9 per cent in 1960-2 and finally down to 6 per cent in 1963.

When subdivided by political parties it is apparent that PANAS and BARJASA councillors are predominantly Islamic, PESAKA and SNAP two-thirds Christian and one-third animist, and within SUPP and SCA those who adhere to Chinese religion form a majority.

In 1963 Muslims were accorded representation at the higher levels of government similar to that they received in the district councils. But those of Christian persuasion gained dramatically at the expense of those of Chinese religion and especially of animists, whose share was reduced by almost three-quarters. At the higher levels BARJASA excluded Christians and all but one animist, and its representation became nearly exclusively Islamic. SNAP, PESAKA, SUPP and SCA tended to choose Christian members to represent their respective parties at high levels of government.

In 1970 the proportions of Muslims and Christians elected to the Council Negri and Dewan Ra'ayat was reduced somewhat, the categories of animist and Chinese religion each demonstrating a 5 per cent gain. BUMIPUTERA was overwhelmingly Islamic, SNAP, PESAKA and SCA strongly Christian, and SUPP had a majority who believed in Chinese religion. PESAKA and SUPP also each elected two animists. As far as religion is concerned the characteristics of those newly recruited to political office did not differ appreciably from those who had hitherto held elective office.

Size of present locality
An examination of the residence pattern of all councillors as a group reveals that consistently about half have resided in small units with populations of less than five hundred persons. The numerical significance of those councillors residing in towns of over a thousand persons has steadily fallen over time. There appears to have been no propensity to elect town dwellers. This fact is accounted for in large part by the residential requirements that had to be met by aspirants to elective office. They must have actually resided in the area of the district council for which they decided to stand, thus preventing urban nominees from standing as councillors in other districts.

Most of the PESAKA and SNAP councillors were found to reside in the smaller units of population, characteristically longhouses. By contrast, half the SUPP and PANAS councillors resided in towns of a thousand persons or more. The BARJASA councillors lived in a wide range of localities.

Table 43

Religion of Sarawak Dewan Ra'ayat and Council Negri Members Elected in 1970 (and Candidates) by Political Party Allegiance and New Recruitment to Elective Office

	Percentage of members by religion					
	Islam	Christian	Animism	'Chinese religion'	% data	Total number
Members of Parliament 1970	25 (19)	54 (53)	8 (22)	13 (6)	100 (89)	24 (93)
Council Negri Members 1970	25 (24)	43 (45)	11 (15)	21 (16)	100 (91)	48 (220)
Members of Council Negri & Parliament 1970	25 (23)	47 (47)	10 (17)	18 (13)	100 (91)	72 (304)
BUMIPUTERA	88 (84)	6 (13)		6 (3)	100 (97)	17 (32)
PESAKA	10 (13)	70 (57)	20 (30)		100 (94)	10 (50)
SNAP	5 (13)	84 (65)	11 (13)	— (8)	91 (87)	21 (69)
SCA		60 (69)		40 (31)	100 (100)	5 (13)
SUPP	(15)	27 (35)	13 (15)	60 (35)	88 (86)	17 (56)
Independent	(21)	50 (43)	50 (25)	(12)	100 (92)	2 (84)
Newly recruited	28 (23)	44 (50)	12 (13)	16 (13)	94 (85)	34 (162)
Total 1960 population	23	16	61			

Note: The figures in parentheses refer to the candidates who stood for election in 1970.

Table 44

Size of Present Locality of District Councillors by Year of Election, Political Party Allegiance and New Recruitment to Elective Office

| | Percentage of Councillors from localities with a population of: | | | | | | Total |
	0-249	250-499	500-999	1000-4999	5000+	% data	number
District Councillors							
1950-4	35	10	9	11	35	93	157
1955-9	38	12	12	17	21	94	618
1960-2	38	13	14	16	20	93	480
District Councillors 1963	38	14	15	15	18	94	429
BARJASA	37 (35)	21 (20)	19 (17)	14 (22)	9 (6)	98 (97)	44 (73)
PESAKA	78 (71)	12 (19)	2 (5)	—	7 (5)	95 (95)	43 (61)
SNAP	77 (76)	9 (12)	5 (6)	4 (3)	5 (3)	92 (93)	48 (73)
SCA	(—)	(20)	(40)	(20)	(—)	(100)	(5)
Alliance	63	14	9	7	7	95	138
PANAS	18 (18)	16 (18)	18 (18)	35 (32)	14 (14)	98 (98)	58 (63)
SUPP	13 (13)	9 (9)	21 (21)	11 (13)	46 (44)	95 (94)	115 (123)
Independent	44 (38)	19 (5)	13 (19)	19 (29)	5 (9)	89 (70)	117 (30)
Newly recruited	34	12	19	15	20	92	235

Note: The figures in parentheses refer to the councillors adhering to each party in July 1963, after the re-alignment of the independent councillors.

Table 45

Size of Present Locality of Sarawak Dewan Ra'ayat and Council Negri Members Selected in 1960 and 1963 by Political Party Allegiance

	Percentage of members from localities with a population of:						
	1-249	250-499	500-999	1000-4999	5000+	% data	Total number
Council Negri							
1960-2	22	9	9	16	44	97	33
1963	33	17	11	6	33	92	39
Members of Parliament 1963	30	—	13	9	48	96	24
Members of Council Negri & Parliament 1963	31	12	10	4	43	94	52
PANAS	—	—	17	17	67	100	6
BARJASA	30	10	20	—	40	91	11
PESAKA	36	27	9	—	27	85	13
SNAP	67	11	11	—	11	100	9
SCA	—	—	—	20	80	100	5
SUPP	—	17	—	—	83	100	6

Table 46

Size of Present Locality of Sarawak Dewan Ra'ayat and Council Negri Members Elected in 1970 (and Candidates) by Political Party Allegiance and New Recruitment to Elective Office

	Percentage of members from localities with a population of:					% data	Total number
	0-249	250-499	500-999	1000-4999	5000+		
Members of Parliament 1970	33 (41)	12 (6)	8 (7)	21 (18)	25 (28)	100 (91)	24 (93)
Council Negri Members 1970	18 (26)	16 (11)	11 (11)	13 (17)	42 (36)	94 (91)	48 (220)
Members of Council Negri & Parliament 1970	23 (31)	14 (9)	10 (10)	16 (17)	36 (33)	96 (91)	72 (304)
BUMIPUTERA	12 (16)	6 (10)	12 (13)	29 (23)	41 (39)	100 (97)	17 (32)
PESAKA	33 (44)	— (4)	22 (13)	11 (9)	33 (29)	90 (90)	10 (50)
SNAP	35 (34)	30 (11)	10 (11)	10 (13)	15 (31)	95 (90)	21 (69)
SCA	—	—	20 (8)	20 (15)	60 (77)	100 (100)	5 (13)
SUPP	13 (23)	19 (14)	— (10)	13 (19)	56 (35)	94 (93)	17 (56)
Independent	100 (38)	— (10)	— (6)	— (20)	— (26)	100 (87)	2 (84)
Newly recruited	19 (25)	13 (8)	16 (10)	16 (19)	36 (38)	91 (90)	34 (162)

Note: The figures in parentheses refer to the candidates who stood for election in 1970.

Table 47

Spatial Mobility of District Councillors by Year of Election, Political Party Allegiance and New Recruitment to Elective Office

	Percentage of councillors spatially mobile				Total number
	Never moved	Moved within district of birth	Moved outside district of birth	% data	
District Councillors					
1950-4	62	5	33	85	157
1955-9	69	6	25	85	618
1960-2	69	8	23	85	480
District Councillors 1963	69	9	22	89	429
BARJASA	74 (78)	9 (10)	16 (12)	98 (95)	44 (73)
PESAKA	80 (82)	14 (15)	5 (3)	98 (98)	43 (61)
SNAP	72 (69)	12 (13)	16 (18)	90 (92)	48 (73)
SCA	(50)	(25)	(25)	(80)	(5)
Alliance	75	12	13	94	138
PANAS	84 (84)	8 (9)	8 (7)	88 (91)	58 (63)
SUPP	48 (47)	4 (4)	48 (49)	79 (80)	115 (123)
Independents	72 (70)	12 (4)	16 (26)	94 (90)	117 (30)
Newly recruited	68	8	24	84	235

Note: The figures in Parentheses refer to the councillors adhering to each party in July 1963, after the re-alignment of the independent councillors.

Table 48

Spatial Mobility of Sarawak Dewan Ra'ayat and Council Negri Members Selected in 1960 and 1963 by Political Party Allegiance

	Percentage of members spatially mobile			% data	Total number
	Never moved	Moved within district of birth	Moved outside district of birth		
Council Negri					
1960-2	55	23	23	94	33
1963	52	24	24	97	39
Members of Parliament 1963	58	17	25	100	24
Members of Council Negri & Parliament 1963	53	22	25	98	52
PANAS	67	17	17	100	6
BARJASA	55	9	36	100	11
PESAKA	54	31	15	100	13
SNAP	36	33	11	100	9
SCA	60	20	20	100	5
SUPP	40	20	40	83	6

Table 49

Spatial Mobility of Sarawak Dewan Ra'ayat and Council Negri Members Elected in 1970 (and Candidates) by Political Party Allegiance and New Recruitment to Elective Office

| | Percentage of members spatially mobile | | | | Total |
	Never moved	Moved within district of birth	Moved outside district of birth	% data	number
Members of Parliament 1970	61 (66)	17 (12)	22 (22)	96 (89)	24 (93)
Council Negri Members 1970	45 (60)	19 (14)	36 (26)	98 (96)	48 (220)
Members of Council Negri & Parliament 1970	50 (62)	19 (14)	31 (25)	97 (94)	72 (304)
BUMIPUTERA	69 (62)	6 (16)	25 (23)	94 (97)	17 (32)
PESAKA	30 (59)	30 (20)	40 (20)	100 (98)	10 (50)
SNAP	50 (56)	25 (15)	25 (29)	95 (90)	21 (69)
SCA	40 (61)	20 (8)	40 (31)	100 (100)	5 (13)
SUPP	47 (61)	18 (14)	35 (25)	100 (91)	17 (56)
Independent	50 (68)	— (9)	50 (23)	100 (94)	2 (84)
Newly recruited	44 (56)	16 (13)	41 (30)	94 (91)	34 (162)

Note: The figures in parentheses refer to the candidates who stood for election in 1970.

Members of Parliament and Council Negri selected in 1963 were drawn disproportionately from the largest towns. The discrepancy was particularly striking for PANAS, BARJASA and SUPP whose representation from those towns was more than 30 per cent greater than at the district council level.

Compared with those of 1963 somewhat fewer 1970 state and federal legislators reside in the smaller localities and fewer in the larger towns too. The areas that have gained most are the population centres of between 500 and 5,000 persons. Over a third of the Parti BUMIPUTERA and PESAKA legislators reside in these smaller towns. By contrast SNAP draws most heavily from small settlements with less than 500 population. SCA and SUPP legislators came from the largest towns, though one must add that nearly a third of SUPP representatives came from the small localities.

Spatial mobility

In excess of two-thirds of all elected councillors had not changed their residence from their place of birth. This compares with a figure of 83 per cent for the total population, as recorded in the 1960 census of population. The proportion of councillors who had actually moved outside the district in which they were born steadily dropped over time, but the proportion spatially mobile within the confines of their respective districts did rise appreciably, a rise closely linked to the increasing proportion of Dayaks amongst the councillors. The Iban practice of shifting cultivation necessitates such migration in the never-ending quest for fertile land. The search for virgin land is a time-honoured custom for those whose existence is basically dependent upon slash-and-burn hill rice cultivation, as is the case for almost all Iban farmers. (Note the high proportion of those who had moved within district of birth in PESAKA, SNAP and Independents—the three groups with the greatest Dayak representation.) Some 40 per cent of all SUPP councillors elected in 1963 were born in China, and this alone accounted for the high proportion of their councillors who had moved outside the district of birth.

The members of Council Negri and the Dewan Ra'ayat were considerably more mobile (both within and without their districts of birth) than were those at the district council level. The members of Council Negri and Dewan Ra'ayat elected in 1970 were spatially more mobile than those of 1963. There was a distinct difference between the members and candidates of Council Negri and those of Parliament—those associated with the Council Negri being much more spatially mobile outside their district of birth than were the members (and candidates) of the Dewan Ra'ayat. By 1970 only one SUPP Council Negri member was actually born in China and SUPP figures for spatial mobility were close to the average of all members. PESAKA and SNAP members still continued to exhibit the greatest mobility within district of birth, and BUMIPUTERA members (and candidates) were the least mobile group of all.

Occupation

Occupation has been classified broadly and individuals have not exclusively been placed in one category or another. For instance, one whose income is derived from pepper planting and trading has been classified in the category 'agriculture' and in the category 'commerce'. As occupation also covers a time span an individual who was formerly a government employee and is now a padi planter would be included both in the category 'government' and in the category 'agriculture'. (Due to this practice the percentage will add up to more than 100.)

There appears to have been relatively little change over time in the proportions of councillors in each of these broad occupational classifications since

Table 50

Occupation of District Councillors by Year of Election, Political Party Allegiance and New Recruitment to Elective Office

	Percentage of councillors by occupation					Total number
	Agriculture	Commerce	Profession	Government	% data	
District Councillors						
1950-4	49	44	9	15	96	157
1955-9	55	39	8	10	98	618
1960-2	53	44	8	13	97	480
District Councillors 1963	58	41	8	11	98	429
BARJASA	65 (63)	34 (33)	9 (10)	22 (18)	98 (99)	44 (73)
PESAKA	79 (82)	23 (26)	12 (10)	21 (15)	100 (100)	43 (61)
SNAP	83 (82)	23 (19)	8 (6)	8 (5)	100 (100)	48 (73)
SCA	(—)	(80)	(—)	(20)	(80)	(5)
Alliance	75	24	9	16	99	138
PANAS	46 (47)	38 (35)	5 (8)	20 (20)	98 (98)	58 (63)
SUPP	36 (35)	60 (62)	7 (6)	7 (7)	97 (97)	115 (123)
Independents	64 (59)	43 (60)	9 (10)	5 (3)	99 (97)	117 (30)
Newly recruited	66	40	9	7	97	235

Note: The figures in parentheses refer to the councillors adhering to each party in July 1963, after the re-alignment of the independent councillors.

Table 51

Occupation of Sarawak Dewan Ra'ayat and Council Negri Members Selected in 1960 and 1963 by Political Party Allegiance

	Percentage of members by occupation				% data	Total number
	Agriculture	Commerce	Profession	Government		
Council Negri						
1960-2	19	51	24	45	97	33
1963	28	51	26	38	100	39
Members of Parliament 1963	17	58	37	50	100	24
Members of Council Negri & Parliament 1963	23	56	31	42	100	52
PANAS	—	33	17	67	100	6
BARJASA	27	54	36	82	100	11
PESAKA	46	46	46	31	100	13
SNAP	33	33	33	33	100	9
SCA	—	100	—	—	100	5
SUPP	—	83	17	33	100	6

Table 52

Occupation of Sarawak Dewan Ra'ayat and Council Negri Members Elected in 1970 (and Candidates) by Political Party Allegiance and New Recruitment to Elective Office

| | Percentage of members by occupation | | | | | Total |
	Agriculture	Commerce	Profession	Government	% data	number
Members of Parliament 1970	29 (39)	37 (39)	25 (18)	42 (31)	100 (94)	24 (93)
Council Negri Members 1970	19 (32)	54 (47)	29 (19)	37 (28)	100 (96)	48 (220)
Members of Council Negri & Parliament 1970	22 (35)	49 (43)	28 (19)	39 (28)	100 (96)	72 (304)
BUMIPUTERA	18 (23)	35 (44)	29 (37)	71 (47)	100 (97)	17 (32)
PESAKA	30 (42)	30 (36)	40 (28)	70 (31)	100 (96)	10 (50)
SNAP	24 (28)	33 (32)	38 (32)	29 (30)	100 (97)	21 (69)
SCA	—	100 (92)	20 (23)	20 (23)	100 (100)	5 (13)
SUPP	23 (44)	76 (57)	12 (7)	6 (11)	100 (96)	17 (56)
Independent	50 (40)	— (39)	— (4)	50 (29)	100 (93)	2 (84)
Newly recruited	15 (25)	35 (34)	41 (21)	56 (34)	100 (93)	34 (162)

Note: The figures in parentheses refer to the candidates who stood for election in 1970.

introduction of elective mechanisms. Between parties however, there were great differences. The members of SNAP and PESAKA were the most agricultural and least commercial. Government employees (not including incumbents of such offices as Penghulu and Tua Kampong) were best represented in BARJASA, PESAKA and PANAS. SUPP included the greatest share of commercial bent, and a third of the PANAS and BARJASA councillors were also at one time engaged in commerce.

Those in agriculture were poorly represented at the higher levels of government whereas the professional, governmental and commercial were heavily over-represented in relation both to the district councillors elected in 1963 and to the total population of the state. The over-representation of councillors who were government employees in PANAS and BARJASA, and those councillors in commerce in SUPP and SCA, was further accentuated at the higher levels of government. The professionals made up a third of PESAKA's, BARJASA's and SNAP's representatives were eight teachers, three medical dressers and two lawyers.

The overall occupational breakdown of the 1970 Council Negri and Dewan Ra'ayat members was quite similar to that of 1963. However, the 1970 members of Federal Parliament were distinctly more agricultural and less commercial than were the elected members of the Council Negri. This was true also for the candidates aspiring to enter each chamber. SNAP and PESAKA professionals were mostly school teachers; BUMIPUTERA and SUPP commercial men were mainly small businessmen, and the former government employees of BUMIPUTERA were all regular civil servants. Numbered among PESAKA's government employees were two who had formerly worked for the police and military. The Alliance component parties drew very heavily upon those who had acquired experience working for the government in a permanent capacity. Some two-thirds of all elected Alliance Council Negri and Dewan Ra'ayat members could be numbered in this category. If one also adds to these permanent civil servants the four paid Tua Kampongs and Penghulus, plus school teachers, then the close relationship between government and elected members of the Alliance party becomes even more strikingly apparent. By contrast SUPP numbered only one civil servant among its members elected in 1970 but relied heavily upon those engaged in commerce. SNAP members were found in a very broad spectrum of occupations, the highest number in any single occupation being five teachers and four lower ranking civil servants.

The occupational groups newly recruited to politics were principally drawn from the spheres of government and the professions. Agriculture and commerce were still represented, but in much lower proportions than in earlier years. In this respect the elected members of the Council Negri and Dewan Ra'ayat were becoming occupationally less representative of the state's population and closer to the urban civil service and professions.

Officially-sponsored leadership

Occupants of the offices of Kapitan, Tua Kampong (paid) and Pengarah, Penghulu and Orang Kaya Pemancha became progressively less represented with the passage of time. By 1963 the Kapitans comprised an insignificant share of all councillors. At higher levels of government the Tua Kampong were also not significant from that year onward. Only PANAS, which drew heavily from the government-supported Malay leaders of the first division, introduced a group of councillors who concurrently held the office of Tua Kampong.

PESAKA earned and maintained its reputation as the 'penghulu's party', between 40 per cent and 50 per cent of its elected members at all levels of

Table 53

Officially-Sponsored Leaders Among District Councillors by Year of Election, Political Party Allegiance and New Recruitment to Elective Office

	Percentage of councillors who are:				Total number
	Penghulu[a] + Pengarah	Paid Tua Kampong	Kapitan China	% data	
District Councillors					
1950-4	17	11	6	100	157
1955-9	18	11	8	100	618
1960-2	10	9	4	100	480
District Councillors 1963	11	8	2	100	429
BARJASA	9 (7)	11 (18)	— —	100 (100)	44 (73)
PESAKA	40 (36)	2 (2)	— —	100 (100)	43 (61)
SNAP	23 (23)	2 (4)	— (1)	100 (100)	48 (73)
SCA	—	—	— (40)	(100)	(5)
Alliance	23	5	1		138
PANAS	2 (3)	28 (25)	—	100 (100)	58 (63)
SUPP	—	— (1)	3 (3)	100 (100)	115 (123)
Independents	13 (7)	11 (7)	1 —	100 (100)	117 (30)
Newly recruited	6	4	—	100	235

Note: The figures in parentheses refer to the councillors adhering to each party in July 1963, after the re-alignment of the independent councillors.

a. Included with the Penghulu are their Land Dayak equivalent, the Orang Kaya Pemancha.

Table 54

Officially-Sponsored Leaders Among Sarawak Dewan Ra'ayat and Council Negri Members Selected in 1960 and 1963 by Political Party Allegiance

	Percentage of members who are:				
	Penghulu + Pengarah	Paid Tua Kampong	Kapitan China	% Data	Total number
Council Negri					
1960-2	12	6	3	100	33
1963	20	3	5	100	39
Members of Parliament 1963	8	—	4	100	24
Members of Council Negri & Parliament 1963	15	2	4	100	52
PANAS	—	—	—	100	6
BARJASA	—	9	—	100	11
PESAKA	46	—	—	100	13
SNAP	22	—	11	100	9
SCA	—	—	—	100	5
SUPP	—	—	17	100	6

Table 55

Officially-Sponsored Leaders Among Sarawak Dewan Ra'ayat and Council Negri Members Elected in 1970 (and Candidates) by Political Party Allegiance and New Recruitment to Elective Office

	Percentage of members who are:				
	Penghulu Pengarah Temenggong	Paid Tua Kampong	Kapitan China	% data	Total number
Members of Parliament 1970	17 (15)	4 (2)	4 (1)	100 (100)	24 (93)
Council Negri Members 1970	8 (8)	— (2)	2 (2)	100 (100)	48 (220)
Members of Council Negri & Parliament 1970	11 (10)	1 (2)	3 (2)	100 (100)	72 (304)
BUMIPUTERA	—	6 (9)	—	100 (100)	17 (32)
PESAKA	50 (26)	—	—	100 (100)	10 (50)
SNAP	10 (4)	—	(3)	100 (100)	21 (69)
SCA	—	—	20 (8)	100 (100)	5 (13)
SUPP	(2)	(2)	6 (2)	100 (100)	17 (56)
Independent	50 (17)	(2)	(1)	100 (100)	2 (84)
Newly recruited	6 (2)	— (1)	—	—	34 (162)

Note: The figures in parentheses refer to the candidates who stood for election in 1970.

government occupying that office—in 1963 as well as in 1970. Though nearly a quarter of SNAP's 1963 representatives were Penghulus, Pengarah or Orang Kaya Pemancha, by 1970 only two elected members held such an office. Of the members newly recruited in 1970 to the Council Negri and Dewan Ra'ayat just two were penghulus, less than half the proportion of penghulus amongst those who had formerly held elective office. Thus by 1970, except for PESAKA, the holding of an officially-sponsored leadership position seemed all but irrelevant to the election to a legislative body.

Level of attained education

Acquired educational qualifications have shown a dramatic change over time and at different levels of elective government. The standard of education of elected councillors has risen consistently with the passage of time. By 1960 councillors were disproportionately well educated by comparison with the general population, some 73 per cent of whom (aged ten years or over) had received no education whatsoever. The councillors selected during the first phase (1950-4) were distinct from those of the succeeding period, for they included a relatively high proportion who had achieved senior secondary or tertiary educational qualifications. Apart from this exception, attributable to the selection process exercised by European District Officers, there has been a steady growth in the proportion of councillors who have acquired primary and junior-secondary levels of education.

PESAKA, SNAP and BARJASA members were the least educated councillors, though a third of the SNAP councillors had been educated to the junior secondary level. By contrast most of the SUPP and PANAS representatives had received an education, the majority of PANAS councillors at the primary level and the majority of the SUPP councillors at the secondary level. Those newly recruited to politics at the district council level were no better educated than those formerly elected.

Each party chose better educated members to represent them in the Council Negri and the Dewan Ra'ayat. All the representatives of PANAS, SNAP and SUPP had received some secondary education.

The 1970 legislators are somewhat less educated than those of 1963, though the new recruits among them are better educated. Again there is an interesting difference between those elected (and nominated) to the Council Negri and to the Dewan Ra'ayat. The latter are significantly less well educated. Members of Parti BUMIPUTERA (like PANAS in 1963) and SNAP members have attained a relatively high level of education, with the latter peaking at the junior secondary level. The educational level of SUPP members elected in 1970 has dropped well below that of the 1963 representatives but that of PESAKA has risen slightly.

Medium of instruction of those who have received a formal education

Before the war the medium of instruction in the Rajah's government schools was Malay, the mission schools used English as well as some Iban vernacular at the lowest levels, and the Chinese community supported their own Chinese language schools. Since the war the Colonial government has stressed the English medium in all its new government and local authority schools and used government aid as a means of inducing the Chinese secondary schools to convert to English medium. The Colonial government has viewed English as the language of Sarawakian unity. In the negotiations prior to Malaysia the central government guaranteed not to alter the medium to Malay before 1973 and then not without the concurrence of the Council Negri. Changing the medium of instruction remains an unresolved contentious political issue and

Table 56

Level of Education Attained by District Councillors by Year of Election, Political Party Allegiance and New Recruitment to Elective Office

	Percentage of councillors by attained educational level						
	No education	Primary	Junior secondary	Senior secondary	Tertiary	% data	Total number
District Councillors							
1950-4	52	23	15	6	4	75	157
1955-9	54	26	13	5	3	77	618
1960-2	39	32	21	5	3	78	480
District Councillors 1963	35	34	23	5	2	85	429
BARJASA	39 (48)	42 (38)	18 (24)	—	—	86 (89)	44 (73)
PESAKA	49 (53)	44 (41)	2 (2)	—	5 (5)	95 (97)	43 (61)
SNAP	46 (56)	22 (20)	33 (23)	— (1)	—	96 (96)	48 (73)
SCA	—	(40)	(40)	(20)		(100)	(5)
Alliance	44	35	19	—	2	93	138
PANAS	15 (16)	63 (61)	17 (18)	4 (4)	— (2)	79 (71)	58 (63)
SUPP	12 (13)	22 (23)	48 (47)	13 (13)	5 (5)	78 (71)	115 (123)
Independent	53 (37)	30 (33)	12 (26)	4 (4)	—	92 (90)	117 (30)
Newly recruited	37	33	23	4	2	82	235

Note: The figures in parentheses refer to the councillors adhering to each party in July 1963, after the re-alignment of the independent councillors.

Table 57

Level of Education Attained by Sarawak Dewan Ra'ayat and Council Negri Members Selected in 1960 and 1963 by Political Party Allegiance

	No education	Primary	Junior secondary	Senior secondary	Tertiary	% data	Total number
	Percentage of members by attained educational level						
Council Negri							
1960-2	10	23	43	7	17	91	33
1963	11	32	37	5	16	97	39
Members of Parliament 1963	5	24	33	19	19	88	24
Members of Council Negri & Parliament 1963	8	27	40	10	15	92	52
PANAS	—	—	50	33	17	100	6
BARJASA	12	50	13	—	25	73	11
PESAKA	23	46	15	—	15	100	13
SNAP	—	—	89	11	—	100	9
SCA	—	60	20	20	—	100	5
SUPP	—	—	50	17	33	100	6

Table 58

Level of Education Attained by Sarawak Dewan Ra'ayat and Council Negri Members Elected in 1970 (and Candidates) by Political Party Allegiance and New Recruitment to Elective Office

	Percentage of members by attained educational level						
	No education	Primary	Junior secondary	Senior secondary	Tertiary	% data	Total number
Members of Parliament 1970	13 (25)	39 (36)	26 (29)	4 (4)	17 (6)	96 (86)	24 (93)
Council Negri Members 1970	9 (18)	26 (27)	44 (37)	12 (11)	9 (6)	90 (85)	48 (220)
Members of Council Negri & Parliament 1970	11 (21)	30 (30)	38 (34)	9 (8)	12 (6)	92 (86)	72 (304)
BUMIPUTERA	8 (4)	38 (52)	23 (24)	8 (4)	23 (16)	77 (78)	17 (32)
PESAKA	20 (22)	30 (40)	30 (20)	10 (4)	10 (13)	100 (90)	10 (50)
SNAP	5 (12)	28 (23)	62 (53)	5 (10)	— (2)	100 (87)	21 (69)
SCA	—	40 (15)	20 (46)	20 (23)	20 (15)	100 (100)	5 (13)
SUPP	20 (30)	13 (21)	33 (34)	13 (9)	20 (6)	88 (84)	17 (56)
Independent	— (31)	100 (31)	— (29)	— (9)	—	100 (83)	2 (84)
Newly recruited	7 (14)	32 (28)	35 (40)	10 (11)	16 (7)	91 (81)	34 (162)

Note: The figures in parentheses refer to the candidates who stood for election in 1970.

it is most interesting to scrutinize the background of those who will vote on this issue. The medium of instruction of those educated can also be employed as a useful indicator of the exclusiveness of the milieu from which councillors emerge.

There has been a steady accretion in the proportion educated in the Malay and Malay/English mediums, with those educated in the vernacular (usually Iban) representing a small but static share of all councillors.[3] From a predominant position throughout the 1950s, by 1960 the Chinese medium was relegated to second place after English, as a result of the dramatic educational expansion in the English language rather than of a reduction in the total number of students graduated from the Chinese stream.

Most of the educated councillors of the Alliance component parties SNAP, PESAKA and BARJASA were English educated. However, BARJASA did attract a good number of Malay educated independents so that, after they were taken into account, BARJASA had a higher proportion of members educated in Malay than in English. A majority of PANAS councillors were Malay educated and a majority of SUPP councillors were Chinese educated. SUPP in fact had the lowest proportion of English educated of all parties.

Each of the parties in 1963 tended to choose as higher level representatives persons who had received a full English medium education, or who had at least a partial English language education. The only exceptions were three BARJASA members and one PESAKA member who had received an exclusively Malay education, one SCA member who had been educated exclusively in the Chinese medium and one member of PESAKA who had been educated only in the Iban vernacular. Two-thirds of the SUPP members were fully English educated and the others partly so. All PANAS members had at least part of their education in English. Thus acquaintance with the English language was a prime shared characteristic of those selected to the Council Negri and the Dewan Ra'ayat in 1963, over 80 per cent having received some education in the English medium.

This was less true for the total group elected in 1970, though still two-thirds of the members had received some English medium education. The proportion who had received an education exclusively in Malay, Chinese or Iban doubled to 24 per cent. Most of the BUMIPUTERA members were educated in Malay or Malay and English. Practically all the SNAP members were exclusively English-educated. These two parties represent opposite poles on the national language question, particularly on the problem of subsituting Malay for English as the medium of instruction in government schools. Of those Council Negri members who have been educated nearly half were exclusively English-educated, a quarter Chinese or Chinese/English and a quarter Malay or Malay/English. On the basis of the educational experience of the members of the Council Negri it is difficult to see how that body would vote for a change from English to Malay. But such a tally takes no account of the inducements and/or deprivations that could be brought to bear on those who will make this decision.

[3] One should note that the percentages here and in the subsequent set of tables are the percentages of all councillors, not just of those educated. Hence they will not total as high as 100%, for the percentage who have not received an education must first be included, and account taken of the small proportion for which there is no available data.

Table 59

Medium of Instruction of Educated District Councillors by Year of Election, Political Party Allegiance and New Recruitment to Elective Office

	Percentage of educated councillors by medium of instruction							Total number
	Malay	Malay/English	Chinese	Chinese/English	Vernacular	English	% data	
District Councillors								
1950-4	6	3	22	8	2	13	85	157
1955-9	10	3	18	8	2	13	91	618
1960-2	12	4	16	13	2	20	92	480
District Councillors 1963	13	5	17	8	2	23	9	429
BARJASA	21 (24)	8 (10)	—	— (—)	—	32 (19)	86 (92)	43 (61)
PESAKA	3 (3)	3 (2)	—	— (—)	10 (7)	33 (33)	91 (93)	48 (73)
SNAP	2 (1)	—	—	— (1)	4 (4)	48 (38)	96 (97)	
SCA	—	—	(60)	(40)	—	—	(100)	(5)
Alliance	8	3	2	1	5	37	91	138
PANAS	50 (47)	12 (12)	2 (3)	2 (2)	— (—)	21 (22)	90 (92)	58 (63)
SUPP	2 (2)	1 (1)	54 (53)	20 (22)	— (—)	14 (13)	93 (93)	115 (123)
Independent	11 (14)	7 (11)	8 (11)	8 (11)	1 (—)	16 (18)	99 (93)	
Newly recruited	12	5	23	7	1	20	93	235

Note: The figures in parentheses refer to the councillors adhering to each party in July 1963, after the re-alignment of the independent councillors.

Table 60

Medium of Instruction of Educated Sarawak Dewan Ra'ayat and Council Negri Members Selected in 1960 and 1963 by Political Party Allegiance

	Percentage of educated members by medium of instruction							
	Malay	Malay/ English	Chinese	Chinese/ English	Vernacular	English	% data	Total number
Council Negri								
1960-2	6	9	—	19	3	53	97	33
1963	5	16	3	13	3	50	97	39
Members of Parliament 1963	8	13	—	21	4	50	100	**24**
Members of Council Negri & Parliament 1963	8	16	2	14	2	51	98	**52**
PANAS	—	50	—	17	—	33	100	6
BARJASA	30	30	—	—	—	30	91	11
PESAKA	8	8	—	11	8	54	100	13
SNAP	—	—	—	11	—	89	100	9
SCA	—	—	20	60	—	20	100	5
SUPP	—	—	—	33	—	67	100	6

Table 61

Medium of Instruction of Educated Sarawak Dewan Ra'ayat and Council Negri Members Elected in 1970 (and Candidates) by Political Party Allegiance and New Recruitment to Elective Office

	Percentage of educated members by medium of instruction							Total number
	Malay	Malay/ English	Chinese	Chinese/ English	Vernacular	English	% data	
Members of Parliament 1970	14 (13)	— (2)	5 (2)	10 (12)	10 (5)	48 (43)	96 (93)	24 (93)
Council Negri Members 1970	9 (10)	13 (10)	7 (7)	15 (12)	4 (3)	44 (42)	96 (91)	48 (220)
Members of Council Negri & Parliament 1970	12 (10)	9 (8)	6 (5)	13 (11)	6 (3)	45 (43)	96 (92)	72 (304)
BUMIPUTERA	35 (40)	29 (27)	6 (3)	—	—	23 (27)	100 (94)	17 (32)
PESAKA	— (4)	11 (9)	—	11 (2)	11 (4)	44 (58)	90 (90)	10 (50)
SNAP	5 (3)	— (3)	— (2)	— (11)	9 (5)	81 (66)	100 (93)	21 (69)
SCA	—	—	40 (15)	60 (54)	—	— (31)	100 (100)	5 (13)
SUPP	6 (12)	— (4)	6 (13)	31 (19)	— (2)	37 (23)	94 (93)	17 (56)
Independent	— (9)	— (8)	— (5)	— (8)	100 (4)	— (36)	50 (89)	2 (84)
Newly recruited	18 (9)	— (6)	6 (6)	6 (10)	6 (3)	58 (54)	97 (88)	34 (162)

Note: The figures in parentheses refer to the candidates who stood for election in 1970.

Type of school attended by those who have received a formal education

There is a consistent growth in the proportion of councillors educated in government and local authority schools and in mission schools, though a small drop in the significance of mission schools can be perceived after the 1963 elections. This is attributable to the widespread expansion of the government educational system since the war. Most of the councillors have been educated in mission schools, whereas the smallest number of councillors have attended private schools. The number of councillors educated in China has dropped from an early position of prominence equal to that of mission schools, to one of less importance than those who attended government and local authority schools. The downward drift in the significance of those educated in China will likely continue in the future, because in 1950 all immigration from China was terminated. Those who still wish to study in China have since been supplied with one-way exit visas from Sarawak.

SNAP councillors were educated exclusively in mission schools, as were most of PESAKA's councillors. A majority of PANAS councillors went through government schools, as did a quarter of those who chose to adhere to BARJASA. SUPP councillors were split, with a third educated in mission schools, a third in China and a sixth went through private Chinese schools. Thus for SNAP and PESAKA's councillors the mission schools were all-important and they were also quite significant for SUPP, BARJASA and PANAS councillors.

At the higher levels of elective government those educated in mission school were predominant, a full 100 per cent of Council Negri and Dewan Ra'ayat members who belonged to SNAP, PANAS and SUPP came from those schools. All the SNAP members were educated in Anglican (SPG) mission schools and all the SUPP members had attended St Thomas's school (SPG), Kuching.

In 1970 the proportion elected who had attended mission schools was reduced by 7 per cent, but still exceeded two-thirds of all members. SNAP and PESAKA had high shares, but more than half of BUMIPUTERA and SUPP members had also gone through the Christian mission schools. One interesting aside is that all those BUMIPUTERA members educated in mission schools had attended the schools run by the Catholic mission.

Summary

The introduction and utilization of the elective process to select district councillors (from 1950 to 1963) thus brought to the fore particular types of councillors. Certain groups of people gained representation at the expense of others—on the level of councillor and above as members of the Council Negri and thee Dewan Ra'ayat.

(1) The average age of councillors when elected remained quite constant over time, but at the higher levels of government rose from forty years in 1960, through to forty-six years in 1970. A good many of those who were elected at the time of independence zealously retained their elective office and thus forced up the average age.

(2) The Iban and Land Dayak have progressively gained prominence, steadily reducing Chinese numerical over-representation, in relation to their proportion of the general population.

(3) Christians gained representation at the expense of animists. At the level of the Council Negri and Dewan Ra'ayat half those elected were Christians.

(4) The councillors residing in small towns (with a population of less than 1,000) gained representation, whereas the dwellers of the larger towns lost. By contrast, the members of Parliament and Council Negri have been drawn disproportionately from the largest towns—though population centres of between 1,000 and 5,000 persons gained extra representation in 1970.

Table 62

Type of School Attended by Educated District Councillors by Year of Election, Political Party Allegiance and New Recruitment to Elective Office

	Percentage of councillors who attended each type of school					
	Christian Mission	Government/ Local authority	Private School	School in China	% data	Total number
District Councillors						
1950-4	18	5	5	18	73	157
1955-9	21	7	5	12	74	618
1960-2	31	13	5	9	72	480
District Councillors 1963	30	15	6	9	75	429
BARJASA	29 (17)	23 (29)	—	—	71 (80)	44 (73)
PESAKA	36 (29)	8 (12)	—	—	84 (85)	43 (61)
SNAP	49 (39)	—	—	—	85 (88)	48 (73)
SCA	(50)	—	(25)	(25)	(80)	(5)
Alliance	40	9	—	1	80	138
PANAS	24 (27)	49 (46)	6 (5)	—	57 (59)	58 (63)
SUPP	38 (36)	1 (1)	16 (16)	33 (33)	67 (66)	115 (123)
Independents	16 (25)	18 (21)	4 (8)	4 (4)	84 (80)	117 (30)
Newly recruited	24	12	6	13	69	235

Note: The figures in parentheses refer to the councillors adhering to each party in July 1963, after the re-alignment of the independent councillors.

Table 63

Type of School Attended by Educated Sarawak Dewan Ra'ayat and Council Negri Members Selected in 1960 and 1963 by Political Party Allegiance

	Percentage of members who attended each type of school					
	Christian Mission	Government/ Local authority	Private school	School in China	% data	Total number
Council Negri						
1960-2	75	14	—	—	85	33
1963	81	8	—	—	95	39
Members of Parliament 1963	83	9	—	4	96	24
Members of Council Negri & Parliament 1963	80	10	—	2	94	52
PANAS	100	—	—	—	100	6
BARJASA	60	30	—	—	91	11
PESAKA	69	8	—	—	100	13
SNAP	100	—	—	—	100	9
SCA	67	—	—	33	60	5
SUPP	100	—	—	—	100	6

Table 64

Type of School Attended by Educated Sarawak Dewan Ra'ayat and Council Negri Members Elected in 1970 (and Candidates) by Political Party Allegiance and New Recruitment to Elective Office

	Percentage of members who attended each type of school				% data	Total number
	Christian Mission	Government/ Local authority	Private school	School in China		
Members of Parliament 1970	67 (52)	17 (13)	— (3)	—	75 (66)	24 (93)
Council Negri Members 1970	76 (58)	7 (13)	7 (9)	— (1)	88 (80)	48 (220)
Members of Council Negri & Parliament 1970	73 (55)	10 (13)	5 (7)	— (1)	83 (76)	72 (304)
BUMIPUTERA	60 (50)	27 (42)	7 (4)		88 (75)	17 (32)
PESAKA	78 (65)	— (10)	—		90 (80)	10 (50)
SNAP	81 (65)	13 (12)	— (10)		76 (74)	21 (69)
SCA	100 (100)	—	—		40 (77)	5 (13)
SUPP	69 (44)	— (7)	13 (13)	— (4)	94 (80)	17 (56)
Independent	100 (44)	— (13)	— (7)		100 (73)	2 (84)
Newly recruited	64 (58)	20 (15)	8 (9)	— (2)	74 (68)	34 (162)

Note: The figures in parentheses refer to the candidates who stood for election in 1970.

(5) With the passage of time councillors came to be rather less spatially mobile outside their district of birth, but more so within the confines of that district. The members of higher legislative bodies were considerably more spatially mobile than councillors, and further increased that mobility in 1970.

(6) With the spread of district councils those engaged in agricultural pursuits came to be better represented than hitherto, and there was a drop in the proportion who had formerly worked for the government. Quite the reverse was true at the higher levels of government on which those in agriculture were poorly represented whereas the professional, governmental and commercial were heavily over-represented. This discrepancy was further exaggerated in 1970 with those newly recruited to politics being principally drawn from government and the professions, the members of Parliament and the Council Negri thus becoming occupationally less representative of the state's population and closer to the urban civil service and the professions.

(7) From a position of prominence in the early years of district councils, by 1963 the only officially-sponsored leaders of any particular importance within the elective structures were the Dayak penghulus, and by 1970 the fact of being a penghulu no longer appeared to be a determinative considera-tion at election time.

(8) Since 1955 educated councillors have consistently gained representation at the expense of those who have received no formal education. The members of Parliament and the Council Negri were even better educated than the councillors, disproportionately so in comparison with the general population.

(9) Whereas the most prominent medium of education for councillors elected during the 1950s had been Chinese, this was no longer the case after 1960, when English assumed that role. Throughout the whole period those councillors educated in the Malay medium remained third in prominence, increasing their proportion but at the expense of the uneducated rather than of those educated in the other language streams. Most of those elected to the Council Negri and the Dewan Ra'ayat had received an education in the English medium.

(10) Those councillors who had been educated in mission schools remained numerically most important, but the group educated in government schools steadily gained significance.

The mission-school educated predominated at the higher levels of government, comprising more than two-thirds of all members in 1963 and 1970.

The Contrast Between the Members of the Council Negri and the Dewan Ra'ayat

The members (and candidates) of the Dewan Ra'ayat from Sarawak elected in 1970 were distinctly different from the elected members (and candidates) of the Council Negri. They were older, less urbanized, less well educated, more agricultural, less commercial and less spatially mobile, though there were more Christians amongst them. Nomination for a vacancy in the Federal Parliament appears to serve as an important mechanism 'for the release of political personnel who are no longer abreast of their times or whose presence blocks the admission of pressing new elements'.[4] For Sarawakians the Dewan Ra'ayat has played a distant and remote role, in contrast to their Council Negri which has been the locus of meaningful political activity, that which was amenable to locally influenced change, and that which could dispense timber contracts—the source of many Bornean fortunes.

[4] Frederick W. Frey, *The Turkish Political Elite,* Institute of Technology Press, Cambridge, Mass. 1965, p. 392.

The Members Who were Newly Recruited to the Elective Office

Some 39 of the Council Negri and Dewan Ra'ayat members elected in 1970 had formerly held elective office and the remaining 33 were new recruits. When contrasting the characteristics of the 33 who are completely new to elective office with the 39 who have hitherto held such a position it becomes evident that those who are newly recruited to the political system exhibit quite distinct characteristics, differences that cannot adequately be explained by ethnicity. Those newly recruited to elective office, by almost every important criteria were very significantly different from those who had formerly held elective office. The newly recruited were an average ten years younger than those formerly elected. All major Dayak groups and the Melanau were more adequately represented amongst the new recruits, whereas the Malays and particularly the Chinese predominate amongst those who had formerly held elective office. Many more of the newly recruited members were born in larger centres of population, and continue to reside in towns having a population of over 500 persons. The newly recruited were also spatially much more mobile moving outside the district of their birth. Agricultural and commercial pursuits were much less significant amongst the newly recruited, but the proportion who had formerly worked in the professions and for the government rose appreciably; most of the latter had been regular civil servants. Only two of the new recruits had ever held an officially-sponsored leadership position. The new recruits enjoyed distinctly better educational qualifications, and those educated exclusively in the English medium of instruction nearly doubled their representation relative to those who had formerly held elective office—to the extent that almost 60 per cent of all new recruits had been educated only in the English medium.

The two parties with the highest share of new recruits were PESAKA (with 6 out of 10) and SNAP (12/21), each with approximately 60 per cent of new members. Only 40 per cent or less of the members of the other three parties were newly recruited in 1970: BUMIPUTERA (7/17), SCA (2/5) and SUPP (5/17).

Members of the Council Negri and Dewan Ra'ayat (1970) by their Party Allegiance

It has been conventional to regard each of the Sarawak political parties as representing a particular racial group:

> BUMIPUTERA, the Malay-Islamic
> SCA and SUPP, the Chinese
> PESAKA and SNAP, the Dayak.

But this communal caricature of political recruitment is very far from watertight and is quite inadequate as an explanation of political behaviour. To underline this contention we shall discuss in turn the types of elected members nominated by each individual political party. The two parties that best fit this caricature are BUMIPUTERA and SCA, PESAKA fits it somewhat less so, and SUPP and SNAP considerably less so.

Parti BUMIPUTERA is a Malay and Melanau, Islamic party in terms of ethnic group and religion. However, its ethnic and religious identification does not take into account the close ties that BUMIPUTERA members have with the government. Almost three-quarters of the elected members of BUMIPUTERA have been employed in government service. Conversely relatively few have been engaged in agriculture. Their medium of education tended to be solely Malay, or Malay and English. BUMIPUTERA had the smallest share of the mission school educated (though still over 50 per cent) and nearly a third of its members had received their education in government and local authority schools. This reflects the fact that government schools under the

Rajah were Malay-medium schools and many BUMIPUTERA members would have received their education before Sarawak formally became a British colony. BUMIPUTERA members were the least spatially mobile group of all parties. But a high proportion of them have travelled a long distance overseas, half to Mecca and beyond.

The SCA members are exclusively Chinese and they are all engaged in commerce—as large-scale businessmen in their own right and as directors of timber companies. Not one SCA elected has been an agricultural worker. They are the *nouveaux riches* 'Lion's club' Chinese who want an expanding share of the economy and would like a relationship with those in political power such as that enjoyed by the leadership of MCA in West Malaysia prior to the riots of 13 May 1969. Their dialect composition is quite different from that of the Chinese members of other parties. More than half the SCA candidates and two out of five of its successful (1970) members are Foochow and no Hokkien were elected by the party. By contrast Hokkien and Hakka are the most numerous Chinese elected by SUPP. The Foochow are now basic business rivals to the Hokkien and this dialect-based rivalry is clearly articulated in the political arena. The SCA members were born and continue to reside in the large towns. Most come from the third division of Sarawak and all were born in the state. All are educated, most in both the Chinese and English mediums. All have travelled outside Malaysia and most have even gone as far as Europe and America.

PESAKA nominated members (and candidates) were appreciably older than average and had a great deal more experience as officially-sponsored leaders than had the nominees of any other party. One Temenggong, one Pengarah and three Penghulus are numbered amongst the ten successful PESAKA candidates. All ten of the PESAKA members had worked for the government as such leaders, as regular civil servants or in the police and military. The party elected nine Iban and one Malay. Seven PESAKA members were Christians, two adhered to animism and one was Islam. Half were born in small settlements, generally longhouses. The overall level of education attained is lower than for any other party. Half the members attended Christian mission schools and received their education in the English medium.

SNAP members were drawn less exclusively from any one ethnic group than were the representatives of the other parties. In addition to 13 Iban, SNAP successfully nominated three Land Dayak, two Chinese, one Malay, one Kayan and one Kenyah. Nearly all the SNAP members were Christians (half of those being Anglican-SPG). SNAP drew more heavily from the small settlements with less than 500 population than did any other party. Officially-sponsored leaders have never played an important role in the party, in stark contrast to PESAKA. PESAKA reliance upon penghulus is largely attributable to the relative absence of educated alternative leadership in the third division, in contrast to the abundance of educated Dayaks in the second division, SNAP's original heartland. SNAP members were spread throughout the major occupational categories, again more evenly than were the elected members of any other political party. SNAP numbered five teachers and four lower level civil servants, those two groups being quite important within its elected ranks. The SNAP members were exceptionally well educated, nearly three-quarters having completed a junior secondary level but none higher. Nearly all were educated in the English medium and most attended mission schools.

SUPP was the first party formed in Sarawak and prior to the Brunei revolt (December 1962) enjoyed widespread support throughout the state, drawing from most ethnic groups. Since that revolt, and the ensuing Indonesian armed incursions which appeared to legitimize widespread arrests of SUPP cadres, the breadth of appeal of the party has substantially been reduced to a

Chinese core. This core was principally Hakka and Hokkien, but for the younger Chinese SUPP's appeal has cut across dialect barriers. The party did elect thirteen Chinese, two Land Dayaks, one Iban and one Kayan. SUPP shared with BUMIPUTERA the distinction of electing relatively few Christians, but the majority of SUPP's members were Buddhists or freethinkers. The occupational pattern of SUPP members is quite distinct. Of the seventeen elected only two are professionals and only one has ever worked as a government employee, and then as a low ranking civil servant. One other is an elected Kapitan China. The low incidence of government employees and professionals is in dramatic contrast to the representation of all other parties. Three-quarters were engaged in commerce: two as employees, five as small 'towkays' and six in charge of large businesses. Equally striking is the fact that SUPP has a higher than average proportion of its members engaged in agriculture. SUPP nominated a number of native farmers, and farming is also the principal occupation of Sarawak Chinese—a fact often overlooked by those who see no further than the bazaar economy.

To focus our analysis upon the sole criteria of race is to simplify needlessly at the risk of forfeiting a realistic understanding of politics. There is no single all-pervasive cleavage between all of the parties under consideration, though many commentators persist in labelling all the parties as if such a racial difference did in fact exist.

What is particularly interesting about the three Alliance parties—BUMI-PUTERA, SCA and PESAKA—is that they are each led by those who have histori-cally held a privileged position within their own communities, either as government employees or as 'officially-sponsored' leaders. The two opposition parties—SNAP and SUPP—have instead created their own political organization at the branch level and their elected members reflect more closely the populace they represent. Thus the most vital parties are the ones which cannot rely upon official backing and feel compelled to develop the broadest possible local base. The tide of events is not necessarily flowing in the direction of the parties with the most communal appeal. The two parties that have the broadest appeal (not limited by race) are also the ones that gained the strongest electoral support in the voting of 1970. SNAP and SUPP also had the least in common with the political pattern favoured by Kuala Lumpur.

If the flexible arrangement of small competing factions has its freedom of competition severely circumscribed then the latent potentialities of racial categories could be realized and race would then become *the* real and all-pervasive political cleavage. The quest for political unity of the ethnic group is fraught with just such a danger, for if successful then the factions within each ethnic group will be subsumed and race will become the one meaningful political cleavage. However, the more the many and varied factional divisions in the polity, the more likely the whole society will come to politically resemble any other society that is not racially divided, and the sooner racial distinctions will decline in political importance. The key is the continued presence of a high frequency of disagreement resting upon a multiplicity of frameworks and social differentiations and the continued failure of efforts to unite politically each racial group.

APPENDIX II

The Results of the 1970 Sarawak Election

STATE CONSTITUENCIES

S.1   Lundu   (90.9% voted)

Chong Kim Mook	SUPP	1,496
Sidi Munan	PESAKA	1,275
TK Suud bin Udin	BUMI	1,198
Charles Linang	SNAP	1,105
Jimmy Sim Moh Huat	INDEP	82
Peter Chung	INDEP	67
Rejected ballot papers		222

S.2   Bau   (89.4% voted)

Ong Ah Kim	SUPP	2,902
Michael Sadin	SNAP	2,225
Aloysius Dom Nagok	BUMI	1,257
Gabriel Dan anak Nganjau	PESAKA	818
Ong Guan Cheng	INDEP	539
Rejected ballot papers		641

S.3   Kuching Barat   (86% voted)

Cheng Yew Kiew	SCA	5,410
Ong Kee Hui	SUPP	4,103
Hj. Mohd. Ali bin Ahmad	SNAP	1,076
King Shih Fan	INDEP	192
Rejected ballot papers		317

S.4   Kuching Timor   (81% voted)

Stephen K. T. Yong	SUPP	7,560
Lo Yik Fong	SCA	989
Thomas Lim Thian Huat	SNAP	641
Teo Sing Chiu	INDEP	124
Kenneth Lau Ah Lah	INDEP	81
Rejected ballot papers		291

S.5   Semariang   (84.83% voted)

Ajibah Abol	BUMI	3,233
Abdul Kadir Merican	SUPP	971
Chegu Shukri	INDEP	954
Abang Bueng Abg. Amin	SNAP	526
Haji Ben bin Jomel	INDEP	250
Rejected ballot papers		401

S.6   Sekama   (78.1% voted)

Sim Kheng Hong	SUPP	4,435
Clarence Tan	SCA	2,236
Paul F. Kueh Jee It	SNAP	738
Chai Kuet Sung	INDEP	180
Rejected ballot papers		416

S.7   Sebandi   (83.7% voted)

Ikhwan Abang Hj. Zainie	BUMI	3,775
Tua Kampong Suaidi	SUPP	1,530
Abg. Hj. Adenan Hj. Azahari	PESAKA	1,069
Rejected ballot papers		331

S.8   Muara Tuang   (89% voted)

Mohamad Musa	BUMI	1,934
Chung Kok Chiong	SUPP	1,232
Dato Abang Othman	SNAP	717
Arthur Ernest Muda	INDEP	294
Rejected ballot papers		175

S.9   Batu Kawah   (83.5% voted)

Chong Kiun Kong	SUPP	3,748
Mrs Kong Yu Siung	SNAP	1,650
Shii Dai Seng	SCA	1,534
Rejected ballot papers		512

S.10   Bengoh   (88.11% voted)
By-election declared on 30 July 1970

Segus Ak. Ginyai	SUPP	1,796
Akui Ak. Asu	SNAP	1,532
George Si Ricord	PESAKA	498
Hj. Mohd. Hj. Bakeri	BUMI	231
William Nais	INDEP	230
Rejected ballot papers		116

S.11   Tarat   (89.50% voted)

Nelson Kundai Ngareng	SNAP	3,160
Datu Teo Kui Seng	SCA	2,091
Nyadang ak. Nador	SUPP	2,062
Rejected ballot papers		392

S.12   Tebakang   (88.6% voted)

Michael Ben	SNAP	2,869
Richard Dampeng	SUPP	1,920
Justin Ahan ak. Engkoyong	BUMI	1,606
Rejected ballot papers		473

S.13   Semera   (88% voted)

Lee Thiam Kee (Puteh)	BUMI	3,092
Wan Alkap	SNAP	1,240
Salleh bin Zen	SUPP	497
Rejected ballot papers		385

S.14   Gedong   (86% voted)

Abang Hj. Abdulrahim	BUMI	1,757
Liew Ming Chung	SNAP	1,647
Andrew Jika Landau	PESAKA	600
Entri ak. Tusan	SUPP	522
Rejected ballot papers		313

S.15   Lingga-Sebuyau   (77.5% voted)

Dato Penghulu Tawi Sli	PESAKA	2,134
Augustine Mercer Jangga	SNAP	1,915
Barbara Bay	SUPP	1,160
Awg. Morni Awg. Jaya	BUMI	698
Sydney Sentu	INDEP	98
Rejected ballot papers		479

S.16   Simanggang   (80.1% voted)

Nelson Liap Kudu	SNAP	2,513
Hollis ak. Tini	SUPP	1,879
Rabaie Ahmad (Wang)	BUMI	1,048
Jimbai ak. Maja	PESAKA	718
Awg. Johari Pengiran Azid	INDEP	279
Joshua Jangga	INDEP	192
Goh Teo Chun	INDEP	143
Anthony Jiram	INDEP	73
Rejected ballot papers		445

S.17   Engkilili-Skrang   (78% voted)

Simon Dembab Maja	PESAKA	1,101
Chang Shui Foh	SUPP	976
Pengeran ak. Bliang	SNAP	946
Legan Penghulu Narok	INDEP	225
Rejected ballot papers		391

S.18   Ulu Ai   (75.6% voted)

David ak. Jemut	SNAP	934
Tutong ak. Ningkan	PESAKA	889
Rabit ak. Nanang	SUPP	531
Penghulu Manau	INDEP	351
Ebai ak. Inyang	INDEP	86
Ahmad Ibrahim alias Ieck	BUMI	80
Rejected ballot papers		365

S.19   Saribas   (70.56% voted)

Kihok b. Amat	BUMI	1,849
Jocelyn Beduru Makap	SNAP	1,312
Hj. Hamsawi Hj. Omar	PESAKA	747
Denis Luat	INDEP	252
Cr. Laili	INDEP	181
Rejected ballot papers		266

S.20   Layar   (78.11% voted)

Dato Stephen K. Ningkan	SNAP	2,546
Charles H. Ingka	INDEP	1,157
Edmun Derom	PESAKA	713
Juing Insoll	INDEP	209
Rejected ballot papers		381

S.21   Kalaka   (87.36% voted)

Wan Alwi Tuanku Ibrahim	PESAKA	1,963
Al-Ustaz Kadir Hassan	BUMI	1,407
William ak. Lampas	SNAP	1,164
Haji Jais bin Sejin	INDEP	83
Rejected ballot papers		263

S.22   Krian   (79.72% voted)

Dunstan Endawi Enchana	SNAP	2,933
Meling ak. Jan	PESAKA	872
Robinson Jelemin	SUPP	824
Rejected ballot papers		404

S.23   Kuala-Rejang   (88.8% voted)

Dato Hj. Abdul R. Ya'kub	BUMI	2,161
Drahman bin Karia	SUPP	831
Ainnie bin Dhoby	SNAP	743
Then Kwan Long (Mok)	INDEP	656

Biliang ak. Tinggi	PESAKA	371
Majidi bin Suhaili	INDEP	103
Rejected ballot papers		222

S.24   Repok   (85.8% voted)

Khoo Peng Loong	SUPP	2,399
Chen Ko Ming	SCA	1,787
Ngo King Huong	SNAP	844
Ching Ting Chiok	INDEP	58
Rejected ballot papers		255

S.25   Matu-Daro   (86.4% voted)

Awg. Hipni Pengiran Anu	BUMI	3,360
Awg. Mashor Awg. Laga	PESAKA	565
George Haji Drahman	SUPP	506
Waini bin Haji Sahari	INDEP	429
Sia Siong Yung	INDEP	136
Abg. Hj. Abdul Razak	SNAP	124
Hj. Rosli bin Kiok	INDEP	46
Rejected ballot papers		286

S.26   Binatang   (82.62% voted)

Anthony Teo Tiao Gin	SUPP	3,048
Luk Tai Lik	SCA	2,130
Sandom ak. Nyuak	PESAKA	1,077
Teng Tun Hsin	SNAP	849
Rejected ballot papers		300

S.27   Sibu Tengah   (74.9% voted)

Chew Kim Poon	SUPP	4,470
Chieng Hie Kwong	SCA	2,098
Yap Siew Hoe	SNAP	493
Lim Ung Chiew	INDEP	380
Rejected ballot papers		363

S.28   Sibu Luar   (76.9% voted)

Wong Kah Sing	SUPP	2,969
Tai Sing Chii	SCA	2,261
Joseph C. C. Tang	SNAP	562
Peter Hwang	INDEP	135
Jamal bin Hj. Dris	INDEP	92
Ngu Teck Sing	INDEP	75
Rejected ballot papers		324

S.29   Igan   (89.1% voted)

Ling Beng Siong	SCA	3,264
Wong Tuong Kwang	SUPP	2,495
Gelanggang ak. Mujan	SNAP	213
Ampi ak. Matari	INDEP	75
Jawi ak. Sureng	INDEP	46
Penghulu Pengabang Impak	INDEP	35
Rejected ballot papers		288

S.30   Dudong   (78.8% voted)

Kong Chung Siew	SUPP	1,675
Jonathan Bangau	PESAKA	1,434
Sandah Penghulu Jarrow	SNAP	1,138
Galau ak. Kumbang	INDEP	195
Langgai ak. Abol	INDEP	119
Rejected ballot papers		280

S.31   Balingian   (63.4% voted)

Mohd. Fauzi Hamdani	BUMI	1,555
Ho Thian Ting	SUPP	856
Jang ak. Kandawang	SNAP	827
Mohd. Noh bin Hamdan	INDEP	606
Sipuk bin Ani	PESAKA	523
Tampang ak. Basek	PESAKA	267
Tan Yong Bee	INDEP	231
Rejected ballot papers		362

S.32   Oya   (75.25% voted)

Vincent Ferrer Suyong	BUMI	1,510
Sim Boon Liang	SNAP	1,339
Aleh ak. Jueng	PESAKA	702
Augustine Druce Dawan	PESAKA	618
Ting Ung Pang	SUPP	468
Ibrahim bin Takong	INDEP	396
Song Ing Huo	INDEP	200
Rejected ballot papers		436

S.33   Pakan   (70% voted)

Mandi ak. Sanar	PESAKA	748
Lau Mee Ee	INDEP	677
Dundang ak. Ibi	SNAP	667
Laiyau ak. Boleng	INDEP	305
Rejected ballot papers		327

S.34   Meluan   (70.1% voted)

Gramong ak. Jelian	SNAP	880
Philip Nyadang Janting	PESAKA	810
Empaling	INDEP	381
Tedong ak. Entalai	INDEP	234
Rejected ballot papers		347

S.35   Machan   (80.9% voted)

Thomas Kana	PESAKA	2,459
Kong Foh Kim	SUPP	1,589
Stephen Mapang Sanggau	SNAP	327
Rejected ballot papers		71

S.36   Ngemah   (71.3% voted)

Lias ak. Kana	INDEP	796
Penghulu F. Umpau Empam	PESAKA	660
Jarrau ak. Serit	SNAP	603
Guntol ak. Bana	INDEP	539
Ansi ak. Anyau	SUPP	428
Ungai ak. Sumpon	INDEP	47
Penghulu Ujok ak. Andeng	INDEP	33
Rejected ballot papers		267

S.37   Song   (76.89% voted)

Ngelambong Bangau	SNAP	1,614
Mangai ak. Lajang	PESAKA	1,294
Dingai ak. Ujom	SUPP	1,204
Rejected ballot papers		395

S.38   Pelagus   (74.71% voted)

Bennett Jarrow	PESAKA	1,389
Jugah ak. Lasah	SUPP	1,069

Francis ak. Nyuak	SNAP	716
Rejected ballot papers		241

S.39 Baleh (80.32% voted)

Kanyan Temenggong Koh	PESAKA	1,953
Wesley Ajan Nabau	SNAP	1,528
Kulleh ak. Semada	SUPP	806
Pengarah Sibat Semada	INDEP	492
Rejected ballot papers		371

S.40 Belaga (74.96% voted)

Nyipa Kilah	SUPP	772
Tajang Laing	PESAKA	688
Penghulu Matu Puso	INDEP	606
Lisut Tinggang	SNAP	67
Rejected ballot papers		136

S.41 Tatau (73.2% voted)

Awg. Ismail Pg. Zainuddin	BUMI	1,340
Nanang ak. Entigai	SNAP	1,191
Goh Ngiap Joon	SUPP	827
Julaihi Hanaffie	INDEP	571
Pg. Angkalom Latib	PESAKA	415
Meng Cheng	INDEP	125
Rejected ballot papers		253

S.42 Kemena (71.2% voted)

Abok ak. Jalin	PESAKA	1,366
Asghar Khan	BUMI	1,155
Ting Lian Tung	SNAP	884
Png Tai Yok	SUPP	733
Medan ak. Suhang	INDEP	212
Rejected ballot papers		349

S.43 Subis (75.2% voted)

Francis Loke	SNAP	1,728
Lee Fuong Chew	SUPP	1,420
Hashim Hj. Ladid	INDEP	1,387
Jackie Yong	PESAKA	832
Rejected ballot papers		583

S.44 Miri (72% voted)

Chia Chin Shin	SCA	2,876
Yang Siew Siang	SUPP	2,511
John Leong Chee Yun	SNAP	1,256
Kepol Samat	INDEP	166
Lau Siu Wai	INDEP	142
Rejected ballot papers		277

S.45 Marudi (73.88% voted)

Edward Jeli Blayong	SNAP	3,134
Tama Weng Tinggang Wan	SUPP	958
Baya Malang	PESAKA	910
Penghulu Arin	INDEP	110
Rejected ballot papers		275

S.46 Telang Usan (68.1% voted)

Balan Seling	SNAP	1,718
Lee Kee Bian	INDEP	868
Nawan Lawai	PESAKA	750

Penghulu Balan Lejau	INDEP	226
Rejected ballot papers		363

S.47 Limbang (79.09% voted)

James Wong Kim Min	SNAP	2,935
Haji Bakar bin Abdullah	BUMI	1,068
Pugi ak. Yabai	INDEP	385
Tahir bin Hassan	INDEP	220
Rejected ballot papers		330

S.48 Lawas (80.7% voted)

Awg. Daud Awg. Metusin	BUMI	1,698
Chegu Pudun Rangat	SNAP	1,472
Racha Umong	PESAKA	1,053
Ling Tung Kiet	INDEP	82
Mah Chuan Sin	INDEP	48
Rejected ballot papers		190

Parliamentary Constituencies

P.121 Bau-Lundu (89.7% voted)

Siyium ak. Mutit	SUPP	4,539
Lee Nyan Choi	SNAP	3,733
John Loyar	BUMI	2,655
Kureng anak Lasif	PESAKA	2,164
Rejected ballot papers		753

P.122 Bandar Kuching (83.5% voted)

Ong Kee Hui	SUPP	13,410
Kenneth Lau Ah Lah	INDEP	1,284
Kai Yan	INDEP	972
Rejected ballot papers		5,113

P.123 Santubong (80.9% voted)

Hj. Awg. Awal Awg. Abu	BUMI	6,404
Ho Ho Lim	SUPP	5,744
Major Ngu Kuang Kee	SNAP	1,421
Rejected ballot papers		769

P.124 Samarahan (89% voted)

Abdul Taib bin Mahmud	BUMI	5,842
W. M. Khan	SUPP	2,852
Abang Anwar	SNAP	1,837
Rejected ballot papers		525

P.125 Padawan (85.13% voted)

Stephen K. T. Yong	SUPP	5,583
Cyril Nichols	SNAP	3,136
Minah ak. Ranggok	PESAKA	1,203
John Turing	INDEP	1,145
Rejected ballot papers		806

P.126 Serian (89.04% voted)

Pengarah Rahun Dabak	SNAP	6,001
Peter Ng Eng Lim	SUPP	3,993
Dago anak Randan	BUMI	3,737
Rejected ballot papers		835

P.127 Simunjan (87.21% voted)

Bojeng bin Andot	BUMI	4,920
Jubang anak Tawi	SNAP	3,076

| T. K. Bujang Hj. Amin | INDEP | 1,142 |
| Rejected ballot papers | | 921 |

P.128 Batang Lupar (78.8% voted)

Edwen ak. Tangkon	SNAP	4,751
Hollis ak. Tini	SUPP	3,247
Yaman bin Mohd. Tahir	PESAKA	3,142
Abg. Hj. Hamid Salam	BUMI	1,800
Rejected ballot papers		836

P.129 Lubok Antu (77.1% voted)

Jonathan Narwin Jinggong	SNAP	1,867
Unah ak. Dudong	PESAKA	1,577
Bauk ak. Lang	SUPP	1,480
Buda ak. Ulan	INDEP	620
Belon ak. Ubak	INDEP	585
Rejected ballot papers		744

P.130 Betong (74.3% voted)

Mara ak. Walter Unjah	SNAP	3,816
Abg. Hj. Hood Suhaimi	BUMI	2,441
Langgi ak. Jilap	PESAKA	1,611
Umpang ak. Pelima	INDEP	1,007
Rejected ballot papers		741

P.131 Saratok (83.34% voted)

Edmund Langgu ak. Saga	SNAP	3,968
Nibong ak. Linggang	PESAKA	2,536
Hj. M. Su'ut Tahir	BUMI	1,792
Bauk ak. Buma	SUPP	1,132
Rejected ballot papers		483

P.132 Sarikei (87.2% voted)

Chen Ko Ming	SCA	4,041
Lo Pek Ung	SUPP	3,337
Wong Yuk Feng	SNAP	1,389
Then Kwan Long (Mok)	INDEP	960
Ching Ting Chiok	INDEP	114
Rejected ballot papers		571

P.133 Payang (83.5% voted)

Hj. Abdul-Rahman Ya'kub	BUMI	5,839
Nyandang ak. Linang	SUPP	4,025
Abuseman bin Merais	PESAKA	1,394
Charlie Yu Chee Chiong	SNAP	884
Rejected ballot papers		598

P.134 Bandar Sibu (75.73% voted)

Khoo Peng Loong	SUPP	7,655
Ting Tieng Tong	SCA	3,560
Joseph C. C. Tang	SNAP	1,212
Lim Ung Chiew	INDEP	519
Peter Hwang	INDEP	398
Rejected ballot papers		877

P.135 Rajang (83.8% voted)

Tribuoh ak. Rantai	SUPP	4,217
Penghulu Poh	PESAKA	2,596
Alexander ak. Seli	SNAP	1,540
Anyau ak. Bakit	INDEP	1,423

Salleh ak. Garasi	INDEP	573
Rejected ballot papers		909

P.136   Mukah   (69% voted)

Latip bin Hj. Dris	BUMI	3,632
Ugil ak. Unchong	SNAP	2,300
Stephen Kule	PESAKA	1,892
Richard Hanya	SUPP	1,368
Jawan ak. Kapong	INDEP	896
Rejected ballot papers		819

P.137   Julau   (80.5% voted)

Pengarah Banyang	PESAKA	2,330
Salang ak. P. Siden	SNAP	2,267
Rejected ballot papers		689

P.138   Kanowit   (66.5% voted)

By-election declared on 29 July 1970

Unting Ak. Umang	INDEP	2,020
Chua Kai Siong	SUPP	1,532
Bujang Ak. Manja	PESAKA	949
Penghulu Masam	INDEP	787
Blaja Ak. Angkin	SNAP	686
Jarit Anak Meluda	INDEP	463
Lee Ghin Ching	INDEP	257
Rejected ballot papers		102

P.139   Kapit   (75.28% voted)

Penghulu Abit ak. Angkin	SNAP	3,008
Penghulu Jinggot Atan	PESAKA	2,598
Penghulu Kuleh	INDEP	1,609
Rejected ballot papers		706

P.140   Ulu Rajang   (78.28% voted)

Jugah ak. Bareng	PESAKA	2,795
Sibat ak. Tagong	SNAP	1,428
Rabong ak. Langgot	SUPP	1,424
Kupa ak. Kanyan	INDEP	1,107
Rejected ballot papers		643

P.141   Bintulu   (72.171% voted)

Ting Ming Kiong	SCA	2,919
Jilan ak. Nyeggang	PESAKA	2,183
Ismail bin Hj. Sebli	SNAP	2,038
Tedong ak. Taboh	INDEP	1,461
Jubin ak. Magah	INDEP	96
Rejected ballot papers		728

P.142   Miri-Subis   (74% voted)

James Wong Kim Min	SNAP	4,391
Ekoon bin Bantar	SUPP	3,892
Penghulu Guyang	INDEP	1,189
Rejected ballot papers		3,684

P.143   Baram   (71.35% voted)

Luhat Wan	SNAP	5,100
Tama Weng Tinggan Wan	SUPP	1,863
Penghulu Gau Jau	PESAKA	1,795
Rejected ballot papers		550

P.144 Limbang-Lawas (89.5% voted)

Chegu Bungsu Abdullah	SNAP	4,744
Awg. Baja Awg. Besar	BUMI	2,773
Pengarah Ngang Bundan	INDEP	1,348
Rejected ballot papers		630

BIBLIOGRAPHY

GOVERNMENT PUBLICATIONS

Bain, L. *Report of the Commission on the Public Services of the Government of Sarawak, North Borneo and Brunei.* Government Printing Office, Kuching 1956.

Bedale, Harold. *Local Government in Sarawak; a Guide for Use of Members and Officers of Local Authorities.* Government Printing Office, Kuching 1959.

Clarke, Sir Charles Noble Arden. 'Note on Development of Local Government in Sarawak'. 1947. Never printed or published; photocopy of the original typewritten text in the Library, Colonial Office, London.

Federation of Malaya, Department of Education. *Federation of Malaya Annual Report on Education for 1949 by M. R. Holgate.* Government Printing Office, Kuala Lumpur 1950.

Fisher, J. C. B. *Report on the Kuching Municipal Council Elections, Held on 4.11.56.* Government Printing Office, Kuching 1957.

Great Britain. *Malaysia, Agreement Concluded Between the United Kingdom of Great Britain and Northern Ireland, the Federation of Malaya, North Borneo, Sarawak and Singapore.* Command Paper #2094. HMSO, London 1963.

Great Britain, Colonial Office. *Sarawak Report.* Kuching, 1947-1962 (annual).

Le Gros Clark, C. D. *1935 Blue Report.* Part I. Government Printing Office, Kuching 1935.

McFazdean, I. 'Memorandum on Development in Sarawak'. Kuching, 19 March 1947 (mimeographed).

Malaysia. *The Communist Threat to Sarawak.* Government Printer, Kuala Lumpur 1966.

Malaysia. *Indonesian Intentions Towards Malaysia.* Government Printing Office, Kuala Lumpur 1964.

Malaysia. *Official Year Book,* Volume Four, 1964. Government Press, Kuala Lumpur 1966.

Malaysia. *Organisation of the Government of Malaysia, 1967.* Government Printer, Kuala Lumpur 1967.

Malaysia. *Report of the Election Commission on the Delimitation of Parliamentary and State Constituencies in the State of Sarawak.* Government Printing Office, Kuala Lumpur 1968.

Malaysia. *The Threat of Armed Communism in Sarawak.* Government Printer, Kuala Lumpur 1972.

Malaysia, Department of Information. *Indonesian Involvement in Eastern Malaysia.* Public Printers, Kuala Lumpur 1964.

Malaysia, Information Department, Sarawak. 'Lists of Sarawak Councillors (January 1964) and Report on the General Elections 1963'. Kuching 1964 (mimeographed).

218 THE RISING MOON

Porter, A. F. *Land Administration in Sarawak: An Account of the Development of Land Administration in Sarawak from the Rule of Rajah James Brooke to the Present Time (1841-1967).* Government Printing Office, Kuching 1968.

Report of the Commission of Enquiry, North Borneo and Sarawak. Government Printer, Kuala Lumpur 1962.

Richards, A. J. N. *Dayak Adat Law in the First Division and Adat Bidayuh.* Government Printing Office, Kuching 1964.

——. *Dayak Adat Law in the Second Division.* Government Printing Office, Kuching 1963.

——. *Sarawak. Land Law and Adat.* Government Printing Office, Kuching 1961.

Sarawak. *Communism and the Farmers.* Government Printing Office, Kuching 1961.

Sarawak. *The Constitution of the State of Sarawak.* Government Printing Office, Kuching 1963.

Sarawak. *The Countryman's Guide to Politics.* Government Printing Office, Kuching 1962.

Sarawak. *Government Staff List.* Government Printing Office, Kuching 1959-71.

Sarawak. *Report on the Census of Population Taken on June 15, 1960 by L. W. Jones.* Government Printing Office, Kuching 1962.

Sarawak. *Report on Secondary Education.* Government Printing Office, Kuching 1960.

Sarawak. *What You Must Know about the General Elections.* Government Printing Office, Kuching 1963.

Sarawak, Central Statistics Bureau. *Report on Gross Domestic Product and Gross Capital Formation for the Year 1961.* Government Printing Office, Kuching 1963.

Sarawak, Council Negri. *Official Report.* Government Printing Office, Kuching 1945-66.

Sarawak, Council Negri. *Malaysia, Report of the Inter-Governmental Committee, 1962.* Sessional Paper No. 1 of 1963. Government Printing Office, Kuching 1963.

Sarawak, Council Negri. *Report of the Public Accounts Committee.* Government Printing Office, Kuching 1965-1967.

Sarawak, Council Negri. *Sessional Papers,* Kuching, No. 1, 1959; Nos. 1-3, 1960; Nos. 1-4, 1961; Nos. 1-7, 1963.

Sarawak Information Service. *The Danger Within: A History of the Clandestine Communist Organisation in Sarawak.* Government Printing Office, Kuching 1963.

Sarawak Information Service. *A Guide to Education in Sarawak.* Brunei Press, Kuala Belai 1961.

Sarawak Information Service. *Sarawak by the Week.* Published weekly from 1956.

Sarawak Information Service. 'Sarawak Who's Who'. 1964 (mimeographed).

Sarawak, Land Committee. *Report 1962.* Government Printing Office, Kuching 1963.

Sarawak Electricity Supply Corporation. *Report.* Kuching 1956-70.

Silcock, T. H. *Fiscal Survey Report of Sarawak.* Government Printing Office, Kuching 1956.

United Nations. *Malaysia Mission Report.* Government Printer, Kuala Lumpur 1964.

Woodhead, E. W., *Report upon Financing of Education and Conditions of Service in the Teaching Profession in Sarawak.* Government Printing Office, Kuching 1955.

BOOKS, ARTICLES, AND THESES

Basry, H. Hassan. *Kisah Gerila Kalimantan (Dalam Revolusi Indonesia) 1945-1949.* Lambung Mangkurat, Bandjarmasin 1961.

Brackman, Arnold C. *Southeast Asia—Second Front: The Power Struggle in the Malay Archipelago.* Praeger, New York 1965.

Brown, Donald E. 'Socio-Political History of Brunei, a Bornean Malay Sultanate'. Unpublished PhD dissertation, Cornell University, 1969.

Doering, Otto Charles III. 'The Institutionalization of Personal Rule in Sarawak'. Unpublished MA thesis, Cornell University, 1965.

Duverger, Maurice. *Political Parties: Their Organization and Activity in the Modern State.* Wiley, New York 1963.

The Facts About Sarawak. Balding and Mansell, London 1947.

Freeman, J. D. *Iban Agriculture: A Report on the Shifting Cultivation of Hill Rice by the Iban in Sarawak.* Colonial Research Studies No. 18. HMSO, London 1955.

——. *Report on the Iban of Sarawak.* Vol. 1: *Iban Social Organization.* Vol. 2: *Agriculture, Land Usage and Land Tenure Among the Iban.* Government Printing Office, Kuching 1955.

Frey, Frederick W. *The Turkish Political Elite.* MIT Press, Cambridge, Mass. 1965.

Geddes, W. R. *The Land Dayaks of Sarawak: A Report on a Social Economic Survey of the Land Dayaks of Sarawak Presented to the Colonial Social Science Research Council.* Colonial Research Studies No. 14. HMSO for Colonial Office, London 1954.

Glick, H. R. 'Political Recruitment in Sarawak: A Case Study of Leadership in a New State', *Journal of Politics,* 28, February 1966, pp. 81-99.

Grossholtz, Jean. 'An Exploration of Malaysian Meanings', *Asian Survey,* VI, No. 4, April 1966, pp. 227-40.

Harrison, Tom. *Background to a Revolt, Brunei and the Surrounding Territory.* Light Press, Brunei 1963.

Harrison, T. H. *The Borneans.* Straits Times Press, Singapore 1963.

——. 'The Malays of South-west Sarawak before Malaysia', *Sarawak Museum Journal,* XI, No. 23-24, 1964, pp. 341-511.

Harrison, Thomas Harnett (ed.). *The Peoples of Sarawak.* Government Printing Office, Kuching 1959.

Harrison, Tom. *World Within, A Borneo Story.* The Crescent Press, London 1959.

Hyde, Douglas. *Roots of Guerilla Warfare.* Bodley Head, London 1967.

Jones, L. W. *The Population of Borneo, a Study of the Peoples of Sarawak, Sabah and Brunei.* University of London, The Athlone Press, London 1966.

Leach, Edmund Ronald. *Social Science Research in Sarawak: A Report on the Possibilities of a Social Economic Survey of Sarawak.* Colonial Research Studies No. 1. HMSO, London 1950.

Lee, Y. L. 'The Chinese in Sarawak (and Brunei'), *Sarawak Museum Journal*, No. 23-24, 1964, pp. 516-31.

——. 'The Development of Resources in British Borneo and Its Impact on Settlement', *Sarawak Museum Journal*, 10, No. 19/20, December 1962, pp. 563-89.

Liang Kim Bang. *Sarawak, 1941-1957*. Department of History, University of Singapore, 1964.

Lockard, Craig. 'Chinese Immigration into Sarawak, 1868-1917'. *Unpublished* MA thesis, University of Hawaii, 1967.

Means, Gordon P. 'Eastern Malaysia: The Politics of Federalism', *Asian Survey*, 4, 1968, pp. 289-308.

Milbrath, Lester W. *Political Participation*. Rand McNally, Chicago 1965.

Milne, R. S. *Government and Politics in Malaysia*. Houghton Mifflin, Boston 1967.

Morris, H. S. *Report on a Melanau Sago Producing Community in Sarawak*. Colonial Research Studies No. 9. HMSO for the Colonial Office, London 1953.

Ongkili, J. P. *The Borneo Response to Malaysia 1961-1963*. Donald Moore Press, Singapore 1967.

Payne, Pierre S. R. *The White Rajahs of Sarawak*. Funk and Wagnalls, New York 1960.

Pringle, Robert Maxwell. *Rajahs and Rebels: The Ibans of Sarawak under Brooke rule 1841-1941*. Cornell University Press, Ithaca 1970.

Purcell, Victor. *The Chinese in Southeast Asia*. 2nd ed. Oxford University Press, London 1965.

Rawlins, Joan. *Sarawak—1839 to 1963*. Macmillan, London 1966.

Royal Institute of International Affairs, Information Department. *Sarawak: Political and Economic Background*. Oxford University Press, London 1957.

Runciman, Steven. *The White Rajahs: A History of Sarawak from 1841 to 1946*. Cambridge University Press, Cambridge 1960.

Sandin, Benedict. *The Sea Dayaks of Borneo before White Rajah Rule*. Macmillan, London 1967.

Seymour, James Madison. 'Education in Sarawak under Brooke Rule, 1841-1941'. Unpublished MA thesis, University of Hawaii, 1967.

Starner, Frances L. 'Malaylsia and the North Borneo Territories', *Asian Survey*, III, No. 11, November 1963, pp. 519-34.

T'ien, Ju-k'ang. *The Chinese of Sarawak: A Study of Social Structure*. Monographs on Social Anthropology No. 12. London School of Economics and Political Science, London 1953.

Tilman, Robert O. 'The Alliance Pattern in Malaysian Politics: Bornean Variations on a Theme', *South Atlantic Quarterly*, LXIII, Winter 1964.

——. 'The Sarawak Political Scene', *Pacific Affairs*, XXXVII, No. 4, Winter 1964-5, pp. 412-25.

——. 'Elections in Sarawak', *Asian Survey*, III, No. 10, October 1963.

Tiong Teck Hie and Lee Ting Sing. *The Sarawak Commercial Directory*. Kai Ming Press, Sibu 1965.

Van der Kroef, Justus M. 'Chinese Minority Aspirations and Problems in Sarawak', *Pacific Affairs*, XXXIX, Nos. 1 and 2, Spring-Summer 1966, pp. 64-82.

Van der Kroef, J. M. 'Communism and Chinese Communalism in Sarawak', *China Quarterly* (London), October-December 1964.

———. 'Communism and the Guerilla War in Sarawak', *World Today*, February 1964.

———. 'The Sarawak-Indonesian Border Insurgency', *Modern Asian Studies*, 2, Part 3, July 1968, pp. 245-65.

Ward, A. B. *Rajah's Servant*. With a preface by Robert M. Pringle and Otto C. Doering III. Cornell Southeast Asia Program, Data Paper No. 61, Ithaca 1966.

Yusuf bin Abang Puteh, Abang. *Some Aspects of the Marriage Customs Among the Sarawak Malays, with Special Reference to Kuching*. Dewan Bahasa dan Pustaka, Kuala Lumpur 1966.

NEWSPAPERS AND JOURNALS

The Age, Melbourne.
Borneo Bulletin, Brunei.
Daily Citizen, Kuala Lumpur.
Eastern Sun, Singapore.
Far Eastern Economic Review, Hong Kong.
The Mirror, Singapore.
Sarawak Gazette, Kuching.
Sarawak Government Gazette, Kuching.

Sarawak Museum Journal, Kuching.
Sarawak Tribune, Kuching.
See Hua Daily News, Sibu.
Straits Budget, Kuala Lumpur.
Straits Times, Kuala Lumpur.
Suara Malaysia, Kuala Lumpur.
The Times, London.
Utusan Melayu, Kuala Lumpur.
Utusan Sarawak, Kuching.
The Vangard, Kuching.

INDEX

Abdul Ghani bin Ishak, 53n
Abdul Kadir bin Hassan, Ustaz, 31
Abdulrahim, Abang Haji, 106, 116, 207
Abdul Rahman, Al-Ustadz Anis, Dato, 129
Abdul Rahman, Tunku, 40, 87-8, 98, 98n, 100, 100n, 101, 101n, 102-3, 104n, 105, 110-11, 129-31, 147
  National language, 88, 90-1
Abdul Rahman bin Talib
  education system, 93, 93n
Abdul Rahman bin Ya'kub, Datuk Haji, 31, 56n, 78-9, 83, 84n, 97-8, 106n, 107, 107n, 115, 129, 132, 142-4, 146n, 147, 149n, 152n, 153, 154n, 208, 213
  biographical details, 31
  support of Malayan Alliance, 82-3
  Chief Minister, 147-8
  extends his power, 148, 151
  advisers, 148-9
  policies, 151
Abdul Taib bin Mahmud, 31, 82-3, 86, 87, 87n, 97, 105-7, 114, 115, 115n, 116, 127n, 129, 140n, 212
Abell, Sir Anthony, 13, 13n, 40
Abit anak Angkin, Penghulu, 148n, 214
Abok anak Jalin, Penghulu, 146-7, 148n, 211
Agriculture
  developments, 154-5
  occupation of politicians, 182-6, 202
Ahmad Zaidie bin Adruce, 28-30
Ainnie bin Dhobi, 31, 208
Ajan anak Nabau, Wesley, 153, 153n, 211
Ajibah binte Abol, 31, 206
Alliance, Malayan
  characteristics, 53-4
  fragility of, 54
  1963 election, 55-6
Alliance, National Council, 104-5
Alliance Sarawak
  inauguration, 53
  composition, 53n, 115
  cf. Malayan Alliance, 54
  difficulties, 54
  withdrawal of PANAS, 55
  1963 election results, 57, 64-5

Dayak voters, 61
  support of Independents, 72-3
  Council Negri members, 77
  dependence on expatriates, 81
  BARJASA, expulsion and readmission, 87
  background 1966 Crisis, 94-9
  1966 Crisis, 102-11
  restructured, 106-8
  Malays, 108
  government agencies, 123
  1970 party representation, 142
Alwi, Wan, 31-2, 127, 143, 208
Angkatan Nahdatul Islam Bersatu (BINA), 129
Anglican, 37, 174, 198
Arrests
  after May 1969 riots, 131
Azahari, A.M., 29, 45
Azahari, Taib, 53n
Azarias Malong, 35

Bangau, Jonathan, 37, 93n, 113, 209
Bank, Bian Chian, see Bian Chian Bank
Banyang, Pengarah, 36, 36n, 214
Barisan Pemuda Sarawak, (BPS), 24, 28-30
Barisan Ra'ayat Jati Sarawak, see BARJASA
BARJASA, 28-9
  registered, 30
  attitude to Chinese, 31
  members and elected candidates cf. PANAS, 32
  appeal of, 32
  merger with PANAS, 32
  urbanized Malays, 62
  1963 election, 64, 70, 72
  ministers conflict with SCA ministers, 79-80
  link with Malayan Alliance, 83
  Sarawak Alliance, 87
  PESAKA, 94
  Elected members and candidates
    age, 165, 166; ethnic group, 168-70; religion, 172-4; residence, 174, 176-7, 182; spatial mobility, 179-80; occupation, 183-4, 186; education, 190-2; medium of instruction, 194-6; schools, 198-200

223

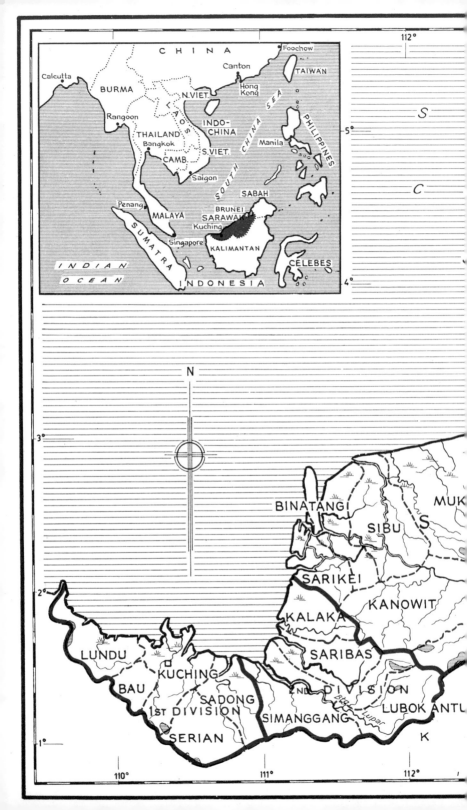